IMAGES
of America

LAWRENCE AND THE 1912 BREAD AND ROSES STRIKE

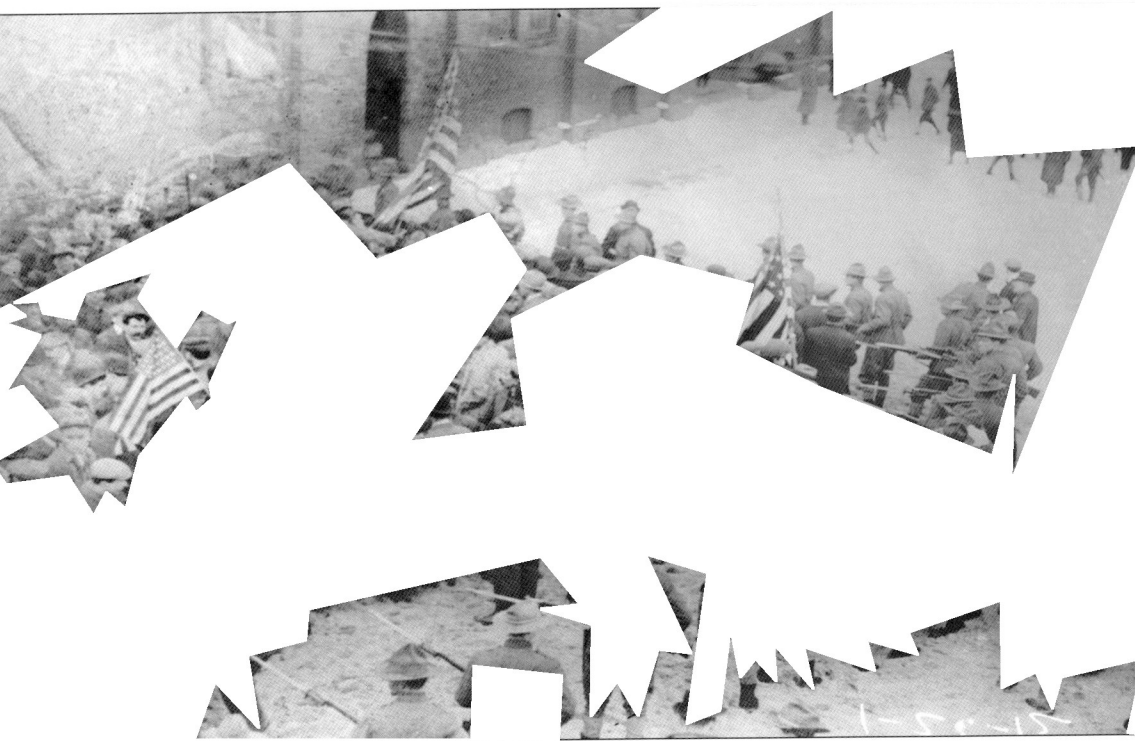

This image shows one of many dramatic confrontations between strikers and the militia. Some of the media and most mill owners made numerous efforts to blame the strike on a handful of "radical immigrants" in hopes of dividing the strikers, which failed. It is interesting to note that in almost every street scene, the strikers bore large American flags. (Courtesy of the Library of Congress.)

ON THE COVER: This photographs shows the final mass meeting of strikers on the Lawrence Common on March 14, 1912. (Courtesy of University of New Hampshire Special Collection's Roland D. Sawyer Papers.)

IMAGES
of America

LAWRENCE AND THE 1912 BREAD AND ROSES STRIKE

Dr. Robert Forrant and Susan Grabski

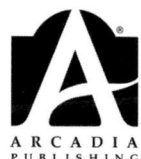

ARCADIA
PUBLISHING

Copyright © 2013 by Dr. Robert Forrant and Susan Grabski
ISBN 978-0-7385-9939-7

Published by Arcadia Publishing
Charleston, South Carolina

Printed in the United States of America

Library of Congress Control Number: 2012955776

For all general information, please contact Arcadia Publishing:
Telephone 843-853-2070
Fax 843-853-0044
E-mail sales@arcadiapublishing.com
For customer service and orders:
Toll-Free 1-888-313-2665

Visit us on the Internet at www.arcadiapublishing.com

To the women, men, and children of Lawrence, Massachusetts, who braved a cold New England winter in an inspiring fight for a better life

Contents

Acknowledgments		6
Introduction		7
1.	A City Is Born	11
2.	A Place to Live and Work	21
3.	The 1912 Strike	35
4.	Children Are Sent Away	75
5.	Congressional Hearings Begin	85
6.	Victory	93
7.	In Defense of Caruso, Ettor, and Giovannitti	101
8.	"God & Country"	111
9.	How Do We Remember?	117
Strike Time Line		125
Bibliography		126
About the Lawrence History Center		127

Acknowledgments

Through lessons learned from the strikers of the 1912 Bread and Roses Strike, creating this book has truly been a *collective effort*. Numerous individuals helped us gather images, edit, and get the story right. They are: Dexter Arnold, Jim Beauchesne, Joe Buschini, Elizabeth Clemens, Kathleen Flynn, Bob Frishman, Liz Grube, Abby Henry, Amita Kiley, Daniel Solomon Koff, Jack Lahey, Karen Lane, Emily Levine, Lisa Lyons, Joe Manning, David Meehan, Marianne Paley Nadel, Clarrise Poirier, Marjorie Power, William Ross, Louise Sandberg, Jurg Siegenthaler, Linda Siegenthaler, Jonas Stundzia, Ethan Snow, Gabriella Thurman, Jane Ward, and Jennifer Williams.

Organizations that provided images and played an important role in helping us preserve the history of Lawrence and the 1912 strike are as follows: the Lawrence History Center and its board of directors; the Aldrich Public Library in Barre, Vermont; the American Textile History Museum; the Barre Historical Society; the Bread and Roses Heritage Committee; Everett Mills Real Estate; the Lawrence Public Library; Lawrence Heritage State Park; the Library of Congress; Small Planet Communications; University of New Hampshire Special Collections; University of Massachusetts-Lowell; the University of Massachusetts president's office; and the Walter P. Reuther Library at Wayne State University in Detroit.

Special thanks to the students in my fall 2011 Lawrence History Seminar; their inquisitiveness made me a far better student of the strike. —Dr. Robert Forrant

Special thanks go to my husband, Robert, and my daughters, Ula and Halina, for their patience and understanding as this book evolved. —Susan Grabski

Unless otherwise noted, all images and documents appear courtesy of the Lawrence History Center. Other images appear courtesy of the American Textile History Museum in Lowell, Massachusetts (ATHM); the Lawrence Public Library (LPL); the Library of Congress (LOC); the University of New Hampshire Special Collections' Roland D. Sawyer Papers (UNH); and the Walter P. Reuther Library, Wayne State University (WSU).

INTRODUCTION

"In Lawrence, Massachusetts, fully one-half of the population 14 years of age or over is employed in the woolen and worsted mills and cotton mills, and approximately 60,000 of the 85,982 people living in Lawrence are directly dependent upon earnings in these textile mills." Thus begins the federal government's *Report on Strike of Textile Workers in Lawrence, Massachusetts in 1912*. Completed at the end of June 1912 under the direction of the commissioner of labor, Charles Neill, the report offers readers an extraordinary look at the strike that unfolded between January 11 and March 14, 1912. Neill noted, "Although dissatisfaction over the possibility of a reduction in earnings on account of the shortened hours had really begun before the 1st of January, it is evident that the mill officials did not appreciate the extent of their dissatisfaction or the possibilities latent in it." The city's mill agents believed that the worst reaction "would probably be confined to a strike in a single mill." Mill overseers went to their beds on the evening of January 10, 1912, oblivious to the commitment workers had made to each other to stand firm and fight for a better life for themselves and their children.

In 1912, Lawrence, Massachusetts, a planned New England industrial city, erupted into a dramatic struggle between mill owners and workers from several countries, including Ireland, Italy, Lithuania, Poland, Russia, Syria, Lebanon, and Turkey. When it commenced, a call went to workers across Lawrence and beyond from the Committee of Ten, the group bargaining directly with William Wood and the American Woolen Company. It read, in part, as follows:

> Now that the combination of capitalists have shown the unity of all our adversaries, we call on you as brothers and sisters to join hands with us in this great movement. Our cause is just . . . Workers quit your hammers, thrown down your files, let the dynamos stop, the power cease to turn the wheels and the looms, leave the machinery, bank the fires, tie up the plants, tie up the town.

Sparked by a wage cut when the legal workweek in Massachusetts went from 56 hours to 54 hours for women and children, simmering resentments over nearly every aspect of mill workers' lives came to a boil. In 1910, Lawrence had the eighth-highest death rate per 1,000 people in the country, and the seventh-highest death rate for infants. The Massachusetts Labor Commission found that "the lowest total wages for human living conditions for an individual was $8.28 a week," and one-third of families in Lawrence earned less than $7 a week. The United States Bureau of Labor's *Report on the Strike* (1912) noted that weekly rents varied from $1 to $6, but the amount commonly paid in Lawrence was $2 to $3 for a four-room apartment and $3 to $3.50 for a five-room apartment. Thus, wages could not cover food and family necessities. Life was desperately short for mill workers. Lawyers and clergy had the longest life expectancy in the area, at 65.4 years; manufacturers were next, at 58.5 years; for mill operatives, it was 39.6 years.

Shortly after the walkout began, strikers also circulated an "open letter" explaining what they hoped to gain:

> In our fight we have suffered and borne patiently the abuse and calumnies of the mill owners, the city government, police, militia, state government, legislature, and the local police court judge. We feel that in justice to our fellow workers we should at this time make known the causes which compelled us to strike against the mill owners of Lawrence. We hold that as useful members of society and as wealth producers we have the right to lead decent and honorable lives; that we ought to have homes and not shacks; that we ought to have clean food and not adulterated food at high prices; that we ought to have clothes suited to the weather and not shoddy garments. That to secure sufficient food, clothing and shelter in a society made up of a robber class on the one hand and a working class on the other hand, it is absolutely necessary for the toilers to band themselves together and form a union, organizing its powers in such form as to them seem most likely to affect their safety and happiness.

The strike spread, defying the popular assumption that immigrant, largely female, and linguistically and ethnically distinct workers could not or would not organize. Polish women weavers at the Everett Cotton Mills were the first to shut off their machines when they realized that their wages had been cut approximately 30¢ to reflect the shorter workweek. The next day, 25,000 more workers joined the fray. Blocked by the militia from standing in front of mills and canal bridges, strikers perfected the loud, moving picket line. Upwards of 5,000 singing, chanting strikers regularly marched across the city's commercial district, challenging the militia and the police to stop them. They maintained soup kitchens and nurseries for children. Meetings were simultaneously translated into nearly 30 languages. And, to keep workers unified, representatives from every nationality formed a 50-person strike leadership group. On February 10, a reporter for the *Outlook* wrote the following:

> The impression of Lawrence which I gained during my first evening was that of a besieged city. The militia, armed with guns and bayonets, guarded the streets and bridges in the mill district and challenged all comers. The hulking factories, with their massive gates and iron doors, appeared in the semi-darkness like fortresses, and along the face of these mills there played a strange, trembling light from the search lanterns opposite.

Mill owners wrongly predicted a quick end to the strike. They were shocked when they learned that enraged Italian women who had happened upon a lone police officer on an icy bridge stripped him of his gun, club, and badge, sliced the officer's suspenders, took off his pants, and dangled the officer over the freezing river. Lawrence's district attorney lamented, "One policeman can handle 10 men, while it takes 10 policemen to handle one woman." A horrified boss described female activists as full of "lots of cunning and also lots of bad temper. They're everywhere, and it's getting worse all the time."

Lawrence mayor Michael Scanlon wasted little time calling in the militia. On January 29, the militia cornered a large group of marchers at the corner of Union and Garden Streets. After some pushing and shoving, a shot rang out, and Annie LoPizzo, a 34-year-old striker, lay dead in the street. Witnesses charged that the bullet was fired by police officer Oscar Benoit, but he and others insisted someone specifically targeting LoPizzo fired the shot from behind the police. Two important strike leaders, Arturo Giovannitti and Joseph Ettor, were arrested for murder conspiracy in her death. Striker Joseph Caruso was arrested in April and charged with murder. The three remained in jail without bail until the end of November 1912.

Though the initial arrests were made, in part, to break the strike, that did not happen. On the contrary, the week following the arrests saw the largest turnout of the entire strike. Other dramatic events marked the strike, including a dynamite plot to discredit the strikers, the death of striker John Ramey, a "children's exodus" from the city, a train station riot in which several mothers with children in hand were arrested, and stunning congressional testimony by several young workers. In October, a third striker, Jonas Smolskas, lost his life when some city residents turned against the Industrial Workers of the World and the memory of the walkout.

As the strike dragged on, scores of children were sent from Lawrence to live with supporters in several cities. When police and the militia tried to block children from boarding a train to Philadelphia, the ensuing melee led to injuries and arrests and the sort of negative publicity that the mill owners did not want. Congress held hearings on the strike in which child workers and others described the horrors of life and work in Lawrence. The publicity forced mill owners to the settlement table. An agreement was finally reached and then voted on by strikers in an open-air meeting on the Lawrence Common on March 14. The workers had won.

By spring, attention turned to the fates of Caruso, Ettor, and Giovannitti. The *Outlook*'s reporters returned to Lawrence, and a June 1 article on the pending trial explained why the three were arrested and remained in jail: "The strike was then at its height and the situation was so dangerously tense that the authorities took advantage of the homicide to arrest Ettor and Giovannitti, two leaders of the working men. No one claims that they were anywhere in the vicinity of the killing. No one supposes that they desired the death of the victim, who, indeed, was one of the strikers. They are to be put on trial for life, however, charged, as leaders of the strike, with using language which incited riot, the incidental result of which was the homicide."

In *Radicals of the Worst Sort*, historian Ardis Cameron noted:

> In Lawrence, fears over the rise of a separate and permanent class of immigrant workers took on new immediacy as the fight for bread and roses brought into focus the widespread poverty and ill health of the nation's industrial workers. As the melting pot boiled over, a startled nation evaluated the peasant masses of unskilled workers with new intensity, leading many who were once indifferent to conclude now that the 'new' immigrants were dangerously alienated from American life.

Here, the last word goes to a jubilant mill worker quoted in a Lawrence newspaper at the conclusion of the March 14 meeting that ended the strike: "We are a new people," he said. "We have hope. We will never stand again what we stood before."

"Bread and Roses"
by James Oppenheim

As we come marching, marching in the beauty of the day,
A million darkened kitchens, a thousand mill lofts gray,
Are touched with all the radiance that a sudden sun discloses,
For the people hear us singing: "Bread and roses! Bread and roses!"

As we come marching, marching, we battle too for men,
For they are women's children, and we mother them again.
Our lives shall not be sweated from birth until life closes;
Hearts starve as well as bodies; give us bread, but give us roses!

As we come marching, marching, unnumbered women dead
Go crying through our singing their ancient cry for bread.
Small art and love and beauty their drudging spirits knew.
Yes, it is bread we fight for—but we fight for roses, too!

As we come marching, marching, we bring the greater days.
The rising of the women means the rising of the race.
No more the drudge and idler—ten that toil where one reposes,
But a sharing of life's glories: Bread and roses! Bread and roses!

One
A City Is Born

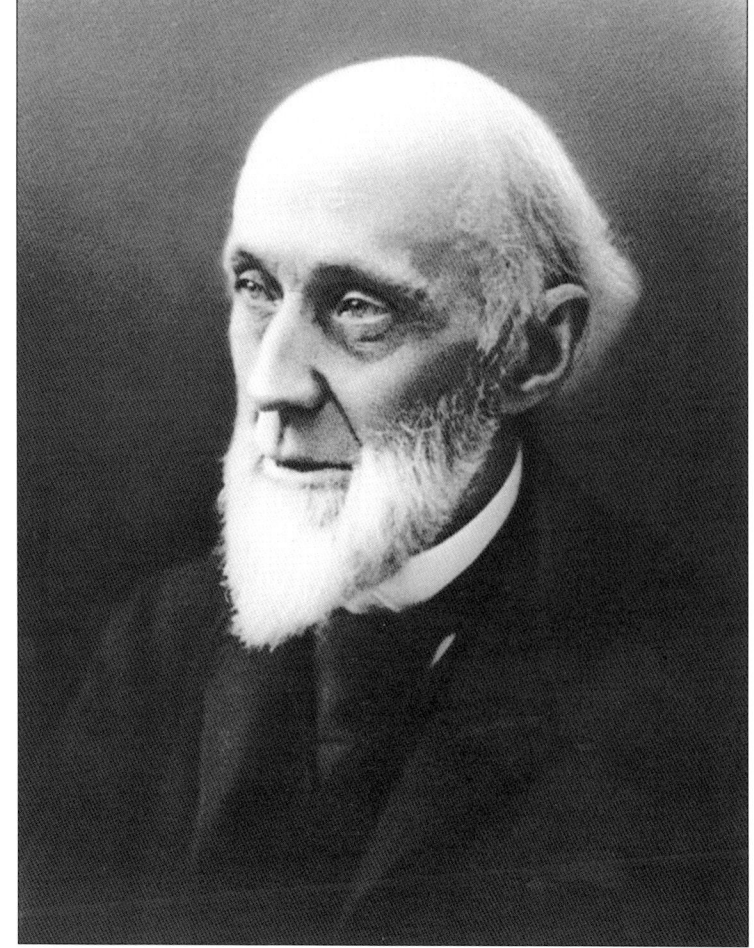

In the 1830s, Daniel Saunders, known as the founder of Lawrence, purchased strips of land on either side of the Merrimack River to gain control of waterpower rights. In 1843, he, along with other visionaries, formed the Merrimack Water Power Association and accelerated land purchases along the Merrimack, including a total of 7.5 square miles from Methuen to Andover, which would eventually become the city of Lawrence.

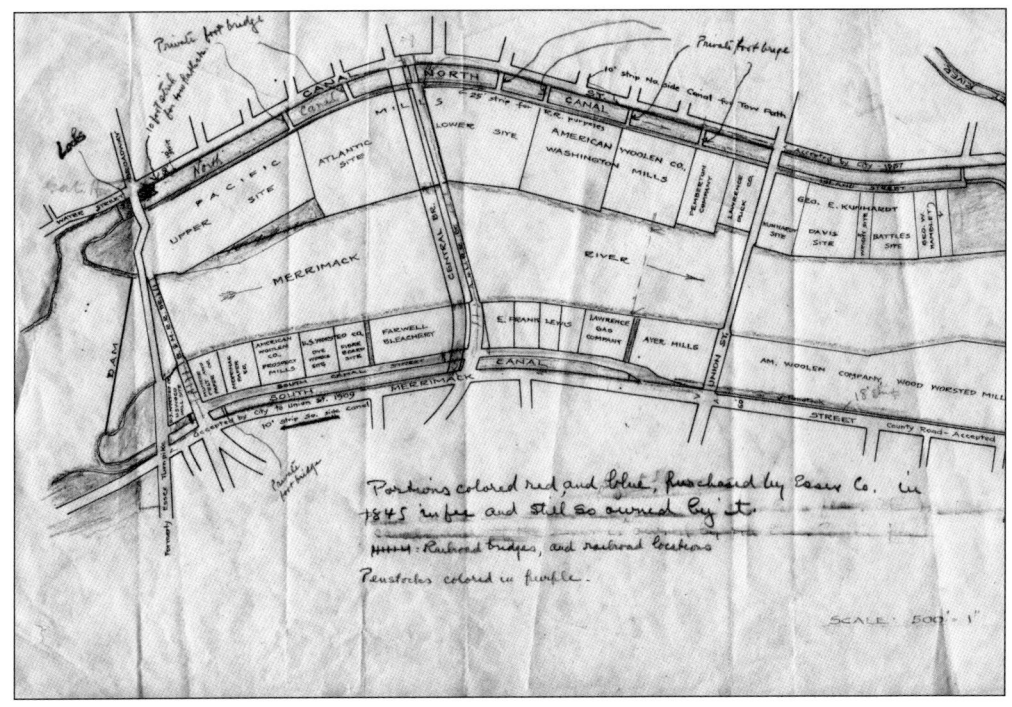

Boston-based investors, the Boston Associates, had already developed nearby Lowell as one of the first planned industrial cities. They sought to replicate their success 10 miles downriver in Lawrence, at the confluence of the Merrimack, Shawsheen, and Spicket Rivers. In so doing, key players, including Daniel Saunders Sr., John Nesmith, Edmund Bartlett, and Samuel Lawrence, took steps to secure ample capital and petitioned the state to build a dam and to create and sell waterpower between Lowell and Lawrence. In 1930, historian Orra Stone, in *History of Massachusetts Industries: Their Inception, Growth, and Success*, said this about the city: "The influx of Boston capital created a mill city almost overnight and for nearly a mile on both banks of the stately Merrimack there tower the red brick walls of manufacturing establishment."

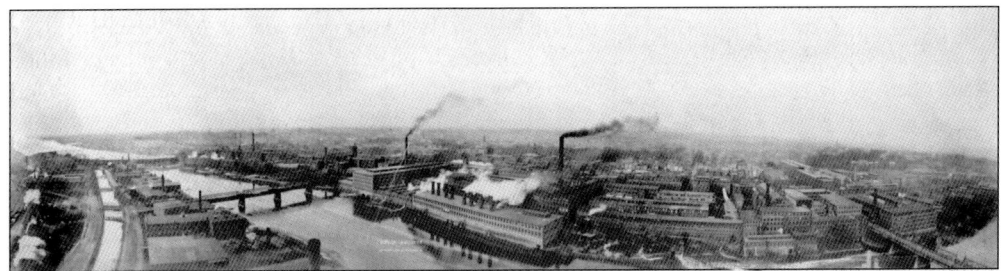

The Essex Company was chartered in March 1845, explicitly to build a dam and canals on the Merrimack River for the purpose of providing waterpower for textile mills. The charter above, held in the collection of the Lawrence History Center, reads: "A purchase having been made of about two thousand acres on the Merrimac River, in the towns of Andover and Methuen, and a charter obtained for a Corporation, called 'The Essex Company' with the capital of One Million of Dollars for the purpose of creating Waterpower to be used and sold by said company." Abbott Lawrence pledged $100,000 to purchase stock in the Essex Company, and 82 others put up $900,000, for a total of $1 million. The directors of the Essex Company included the interlocked families—the Lawrences, Lowells, Appletons, Jacksons, and many others—who controlled most of the New England textile industry, were influential in the early development of the railroad in New England, and were largely responsible for the growth of the major institutions and cityscape of Boston.

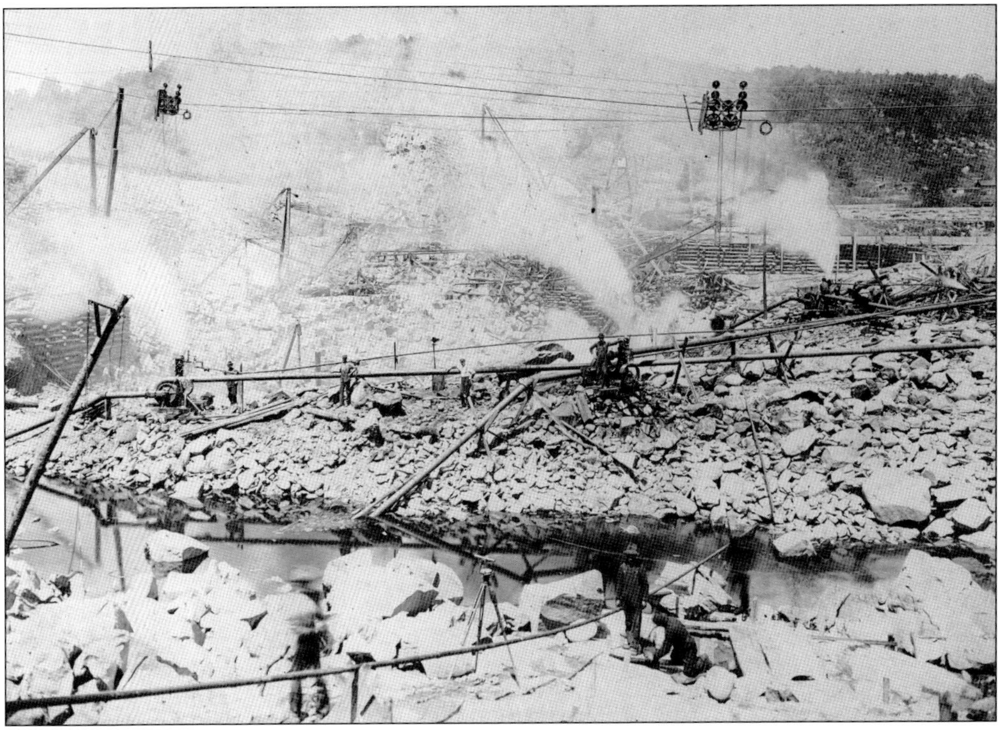

Engineer Charles Storrow worked for the Boston & Lowell Railroad when he was approached by Daniel Saunders in 1845 to join the Essex Company. First and foremost, Storrow was trained in hydraulics, and the prospect of working with waterpower appealed to him greatly. He agreed, knowing that the construction of the dam would be critical to the success of the new industrial city. Storrow, as chief engineer, determined that Bodwell's Falls was the best location for the dam over the Merrimack River. At the time the Great Stone Dam was completed in 1848, it was the largest in the world at nearly 1,000 feet wide. It remains in excellent condition today because of innovative engineering.

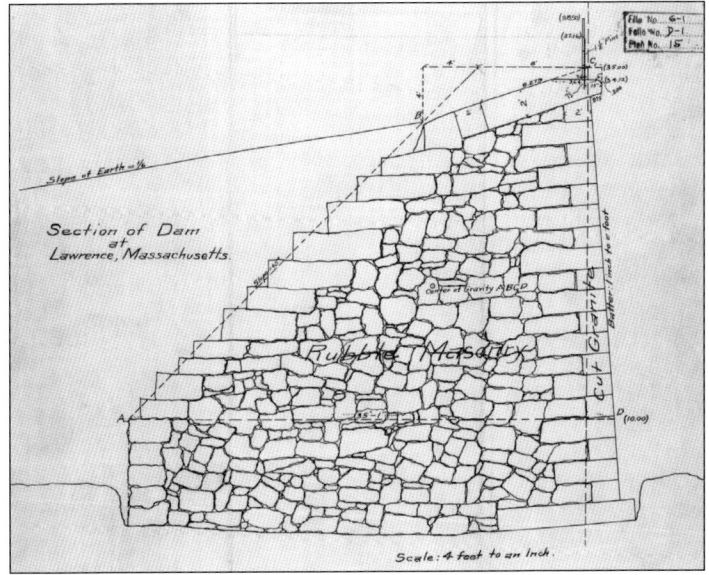

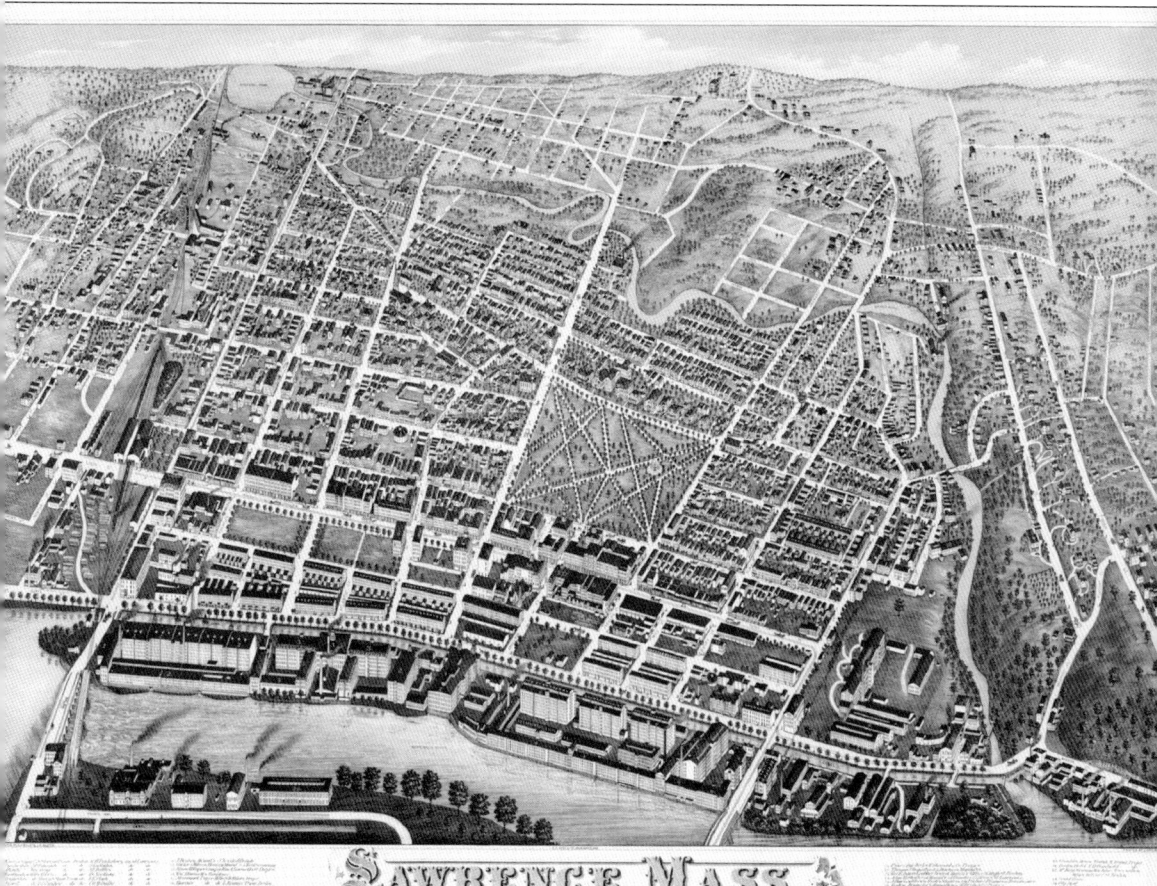

This 1876 map shows how the Essex Company laid out the city, which by 1848 had grown from a small number of farmers to nearly 6,000 people, more than one-third of whom were Irish. Blocks of residential neighborhoods, vast expanses of industrial space, long commercial boulevards such as Essex Street, and a meticulously planned park are all visible. All roadways out of the neighborhoods led workers over north canal bridges and into the mills. These bridges became highly contested spaces during the strike. The Great Stone Dam (lower left) created the foundation for the city's growth. From the Great Stone Dam, a canal was constructed to the north of the Merrimack River to carry water to the mills. The nearly mile-long north canal provided greater space for manufacturers to position their mills parallel to the river on what appears to be an island across the lower portion of the map. In *Bread and Roses: Mills, Migrants, and the Struggle for the American Dream*, Bruce Watson sums up the area in the early days, writing, "And all along the river's banks, merchants, peddlers, blacksmiths, and machinists set up shop."

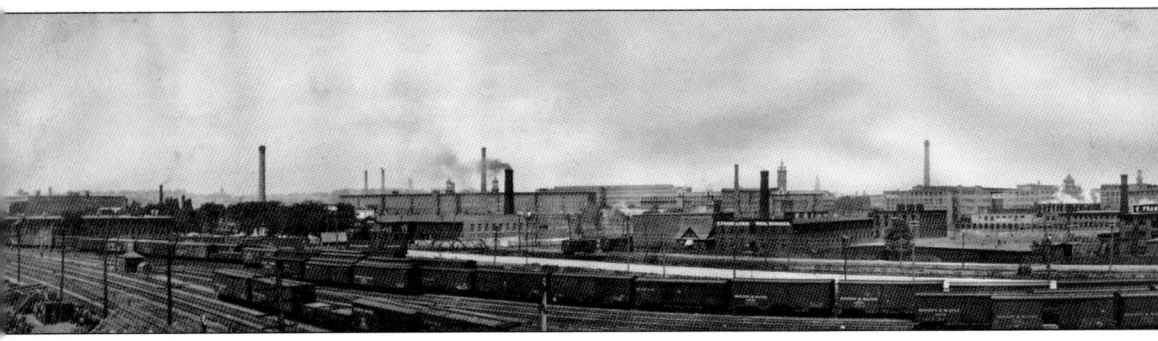

The panoramic photograph above reveals train yards in the foreground and the Ayer Mill, with its stately mill clock, to the right. In a March 16, 1912, article in *Harper's Weekly* entitled "The Trouble at Lawrence," Mary Heaton Vorse wrote, "The mills are Lawrence; you cannot escape them; the smoke of them fills the sky. The great mills of Lawrence make the Lawrence sky-line; they dominate and dwarf the churches. From Union Street to Broadway along the canal the mills stretch, a solid wall of brick and wide-paned glass, imposing by their vastness and almost beautiful, as is everything

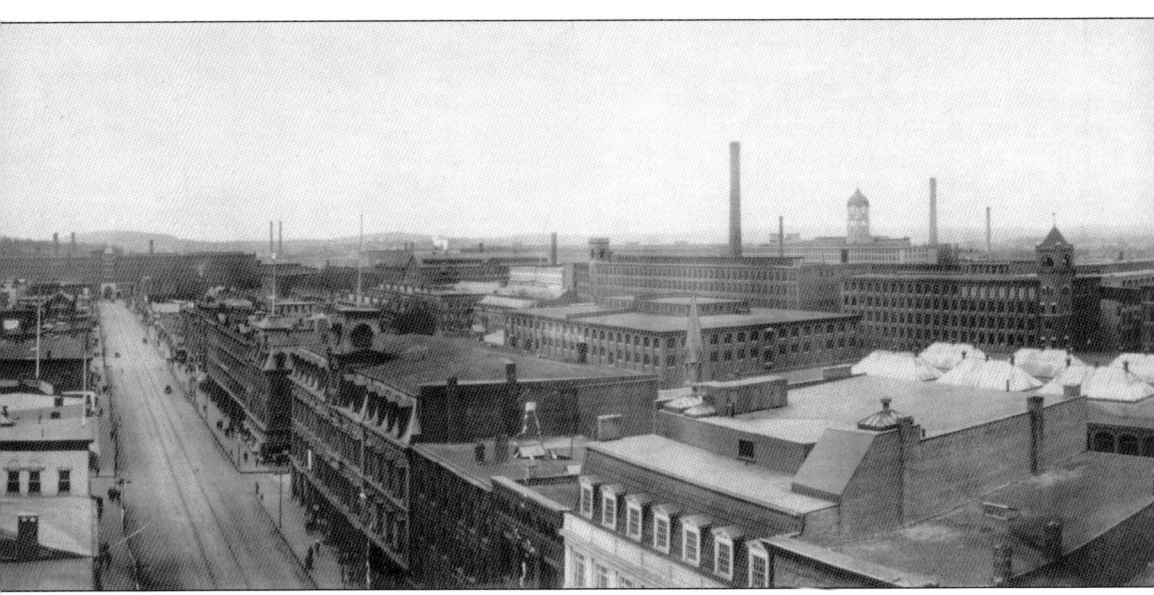

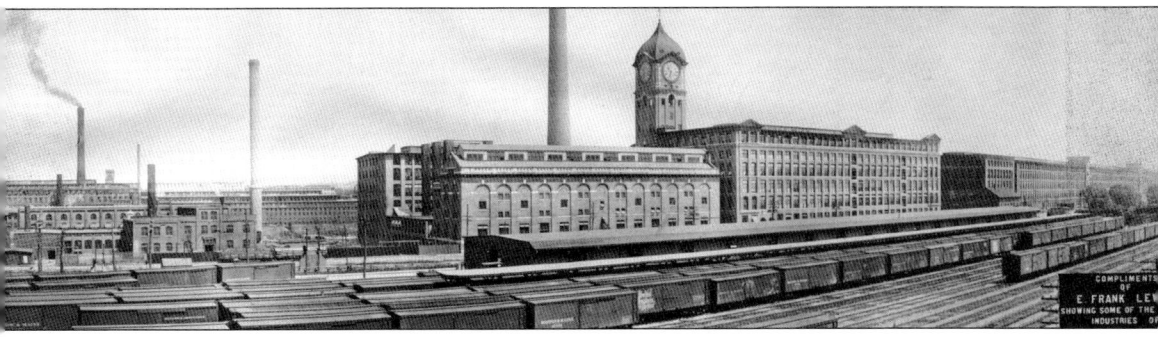

that without pretense is adapted absolutely to its own end." On the left side of the panorama below, the Everett Mill at 15 Union Street and the Essex Company headquarters at 6 Essex Street (now home to the Lawrence History Center) anchor Essex Street. Panning to the right, the skyline of mills, towers, and smokestacks along the North Canal and the Merrimack River that Mary Heaton Vorse describes in her quote is clearly shown—from the Ayer to the Washington to the Pacific Mills.

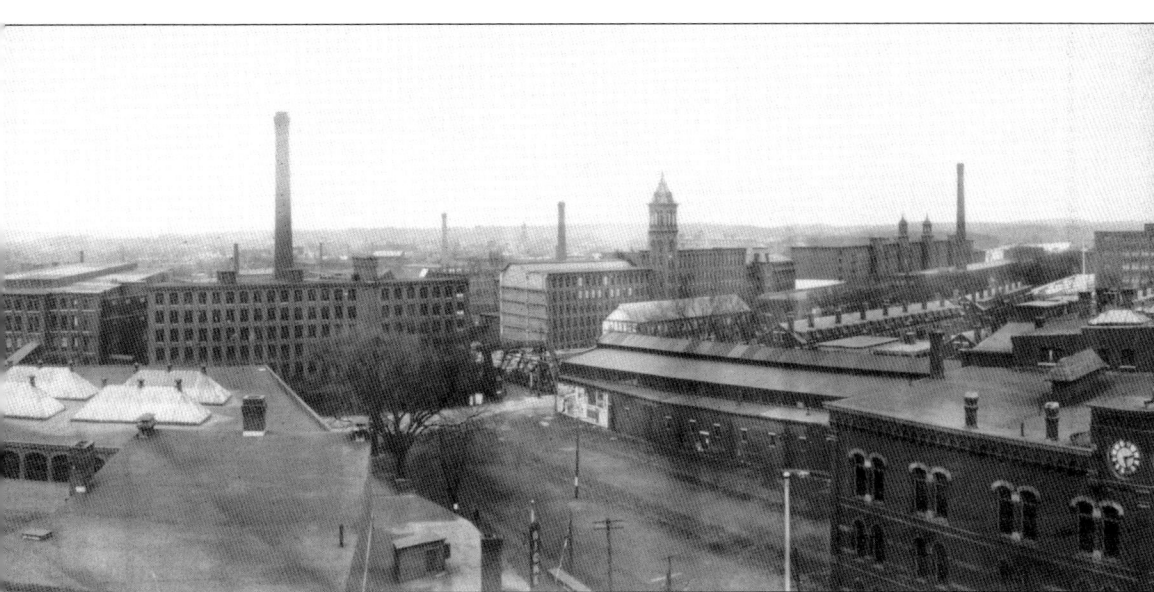

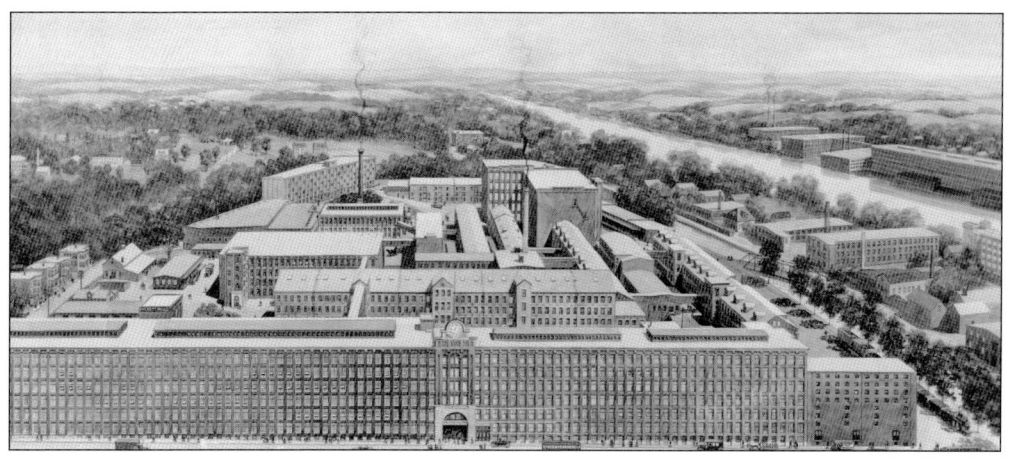

Less than 40 years after the Essex Company's incorporation, 338,100 spindles, 9,057 looms, and 10,200 employees wove two million yards of worsted a week. In the above rendering of the Everett Mills complex, the 525,000 square foot red brick Everett Cotton Mill, built in 1909, is pictured in the foreground. Behind it, constructed much earlier between 1846 and 1848, the Lawrence Machine Shop (now known as the Stone Mill) made most of the machinery and machinists' tools used in the mills and also built railroad locomotives for a time. In *History of Massachusetts Industries: Their Inception, Growth, and Success*, historian Orra Stone wrote, "The city manufactures a wider variety of paper-making machinery than any other one center; a larger total volume than any other city in the United States." Lawrence's Russell Paper Mills are seen below around 1895.

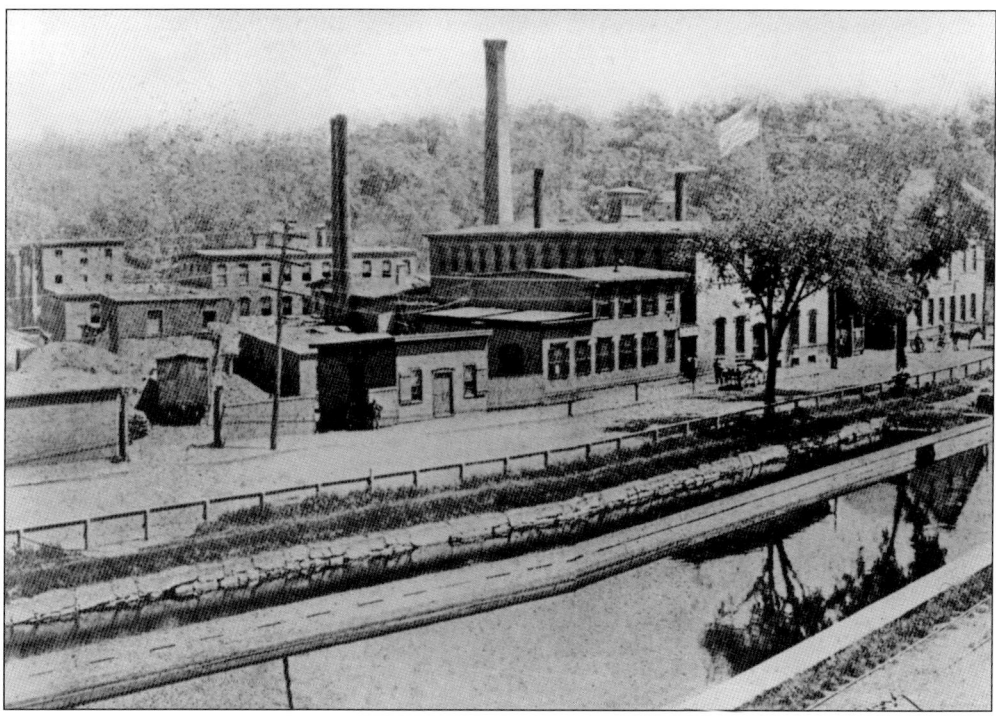

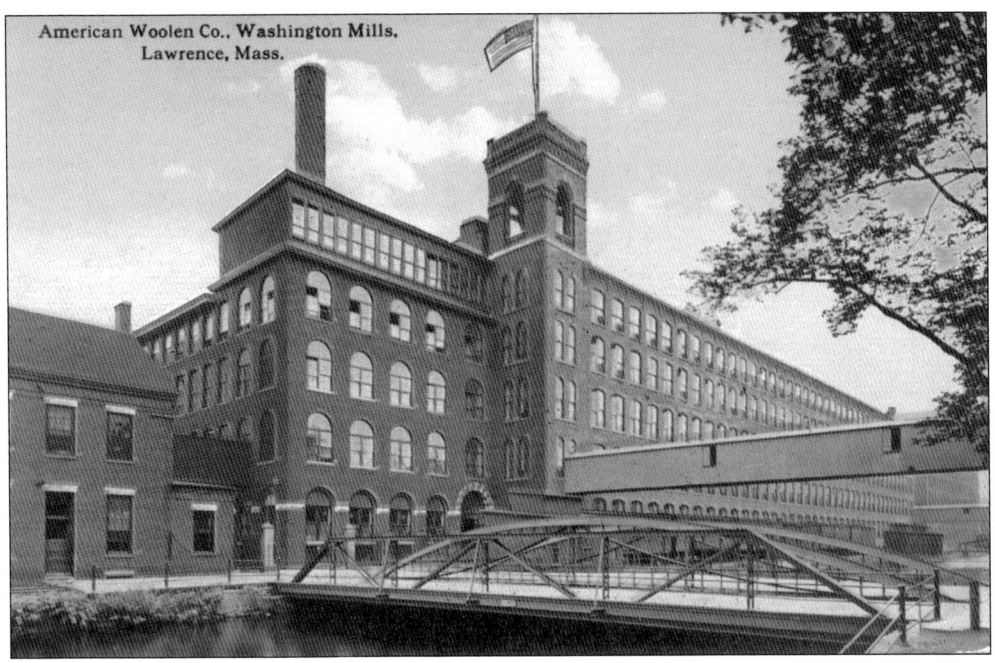

American Woolen Co., Washington Mills. Lawrence, Mass.

With the construction of the Arlington Mills, the Pacific Mills, the Washington Mills (above), the Everett Mills, and numerous other factories, the city grew exponentially. In 1900, Lawrence produced nearly 25 percent of all the woolen cloth in the United States. The Pacific Mills had mechanical equipment capable of producing 800 miles of finished textile fabrics every working day of the year. A total of 65 percent of manufacturing output, 67 percent of all the capital invested in the city, and 52 percent of the city's wages came from the woolen mills. After only 75 years of existence, the city led the world in the production of worsted wool cloth. The phrase "We Weave the World's Worsteds" was a source of pride for the residents of the city.

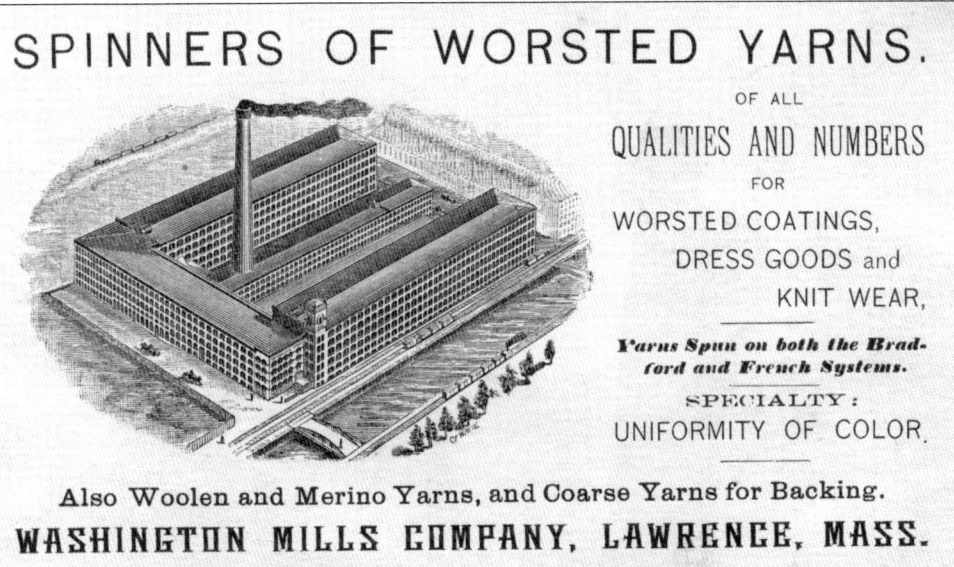

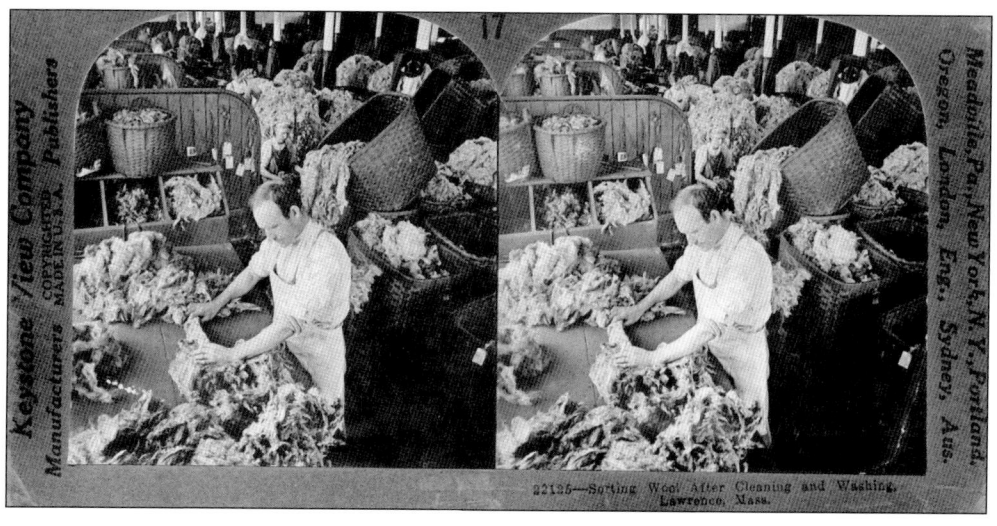

Wool sorting was a skilled job and often paid more than other positions. The sorting process is described below in text that appeared on the reverse side of the image above. The final paragraph states in part: "The first task is to divide each fleece down the back. The wool from the back and the sides of the fleece is put in Grade A basket. Grade B is from the lower parts of the fleece. Grade C is the 'rag tag' from the legs; and so on. The man in this picture [above] is busy grading wool. His senses of sight and touch are keenly alive to the value of every part of the fleece. On his judgment depends the quality of every piece of wool goods made from the material he grades."

17—(22125)
SORTING WOOL AFTER CLEANING AND WASHING, LAWRENCE, MASS.

Lat. 43° N.; Long. 71° W.

In pioneer days Grandfather sheared the sheep, and Grandmother sorted the wool and carded it. She then spun her yarn from these on a little spinning wheel that twisted the strands of wool in a smooth long cord. These threads she dyed, and then took great skeins of them to the weaving room. One set of threads she placed lengthwise in the big loom, putting them close together, till she had her strip of "cloth" the width she desired. Then she began weaving by running other threads across and over the lengthwise ones. Both sets were beaten tightly together as she went. Thus she made a strip of strong woolen cloth.

There is really no difference between the processes of cloth making as Grandmother knew them, and those of the present day. In our great factories hundreds of spinning machines fill the bobbins rapidly. Hundreds of looms take the threads so made and weave them into cloth. The work is done faster and evener than Grandma could ever have dreamed of. But the foreman of the factory would tell you that Grandma knew the chief tricks of his trade.

Here for example is the same old process of wool sorting that Grandfather knew something about. The first task is to divide each fleece down the back. The wool from the back and sides of the fleece is put in Grade A basket. Grade B is from the lower parts of the fleece. Grade C is the "rag tag" from the legs; and so on. The man in this picture is busy grading wool. His senses of sight and touch are keenly alive to the values of every part of a fleece. On his judgment depends the final quality of every piece of woolen goods made from the material he grades.

Copyright by The Keystone View Company.

Two
A Place to Live and Work

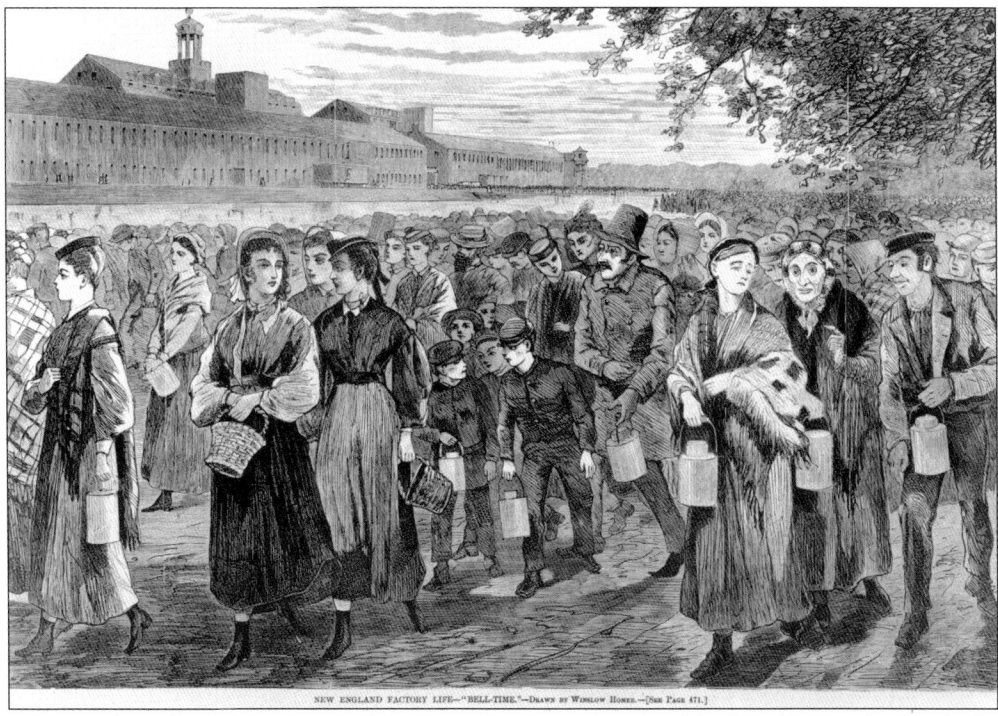

Lawrence has always been a city of immigrants. By 1912, its neighborhoods were alive with the languages and traditions of families from around the world. They came from Ireland, Quebec, Syria, Italy, Portugal, Lithuania, Poland, Russia, and elsewhere. They were spinners, weavers, and loom-fixers, mothers, fathers, sons, daughters, and grandparents. In Winslow Homer's *Bell-Time*, a cross section of the Lawrence workforce was presented to the readers of *Harper's Weekly* in 1868.

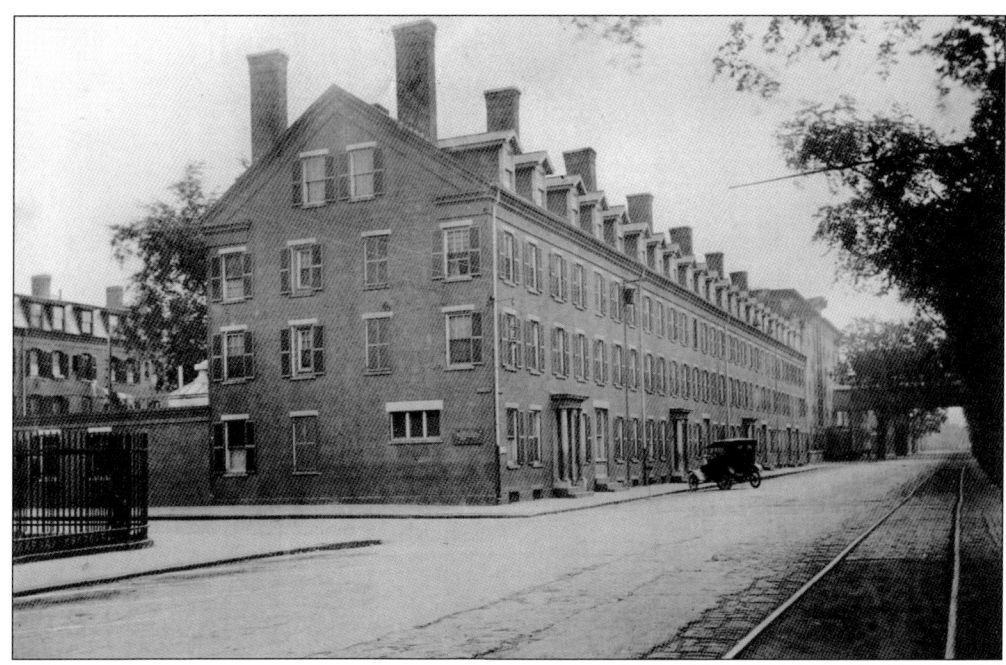

Control in the creation of Lawrence meant not only state-of-the-art mills (below), but also corporation boardinghouses on a scale large enough to enable mill owners to have sufficient sway over the behavior of their workers and to demonstrate to the world that mill workers could be accommodated in good-quality housing. Seen above is a typical factory-owned boardinghouse along Canal Street in Lawrence in 1911. The boardinghouses were home to hundreds of workers from all nationalities, just feet from the factories they worked in. According to Duncan Erroll Hay, the Essex Company also constructed Mechanics Block, "an architecturally unified set of fifty single-family brick row houses" for workers, because its directors were "concerned with getting and keeping a skilled staff of machinists."

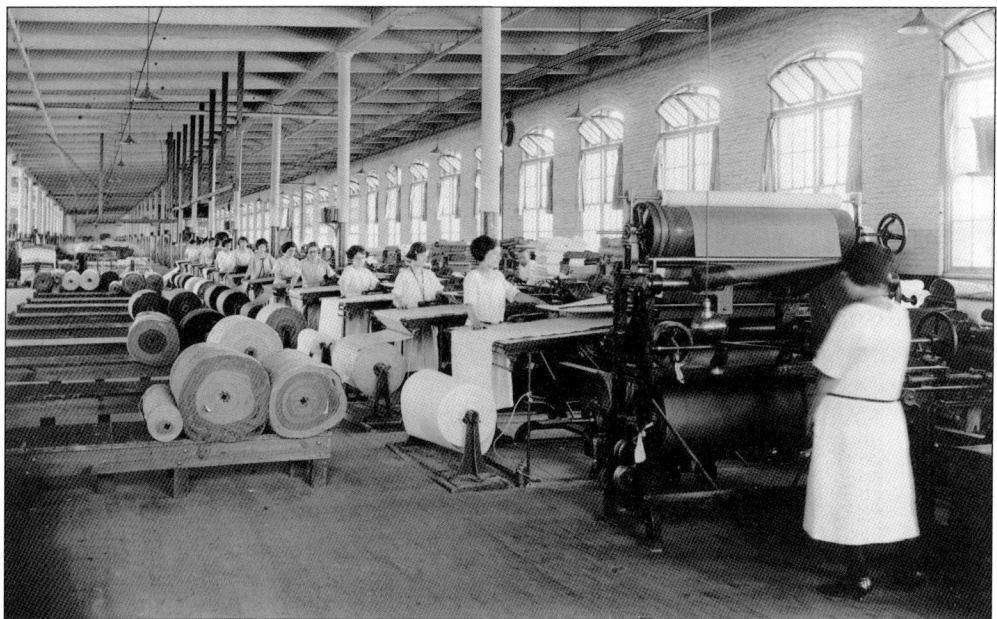

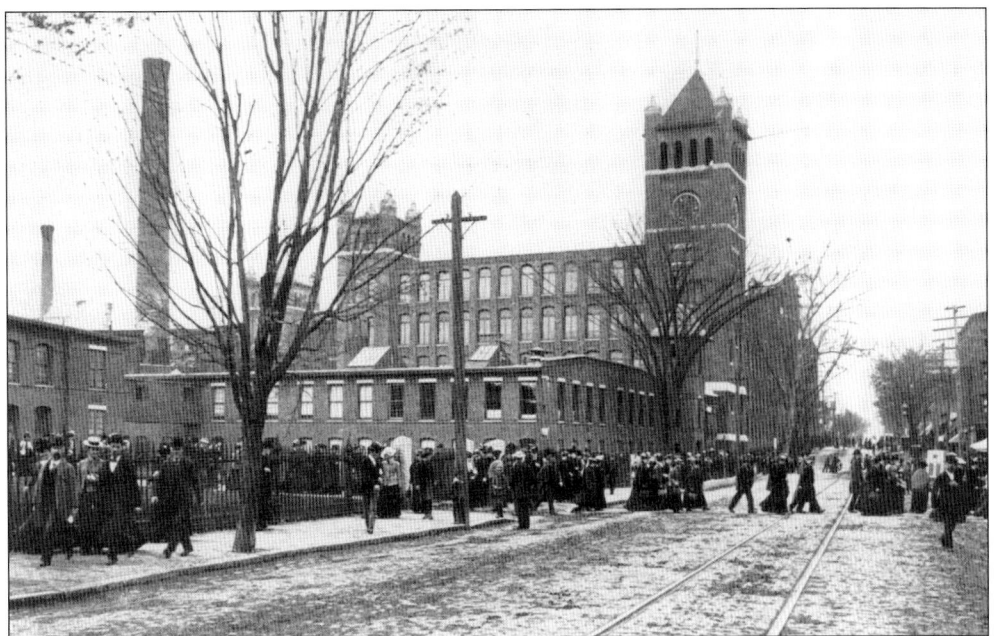

People formed communities in neighborhoods, workplaces, churches, and organizations. Lawrence is a city of factories, but by the early 1900s, it contained growing networks across these neighborhoods, which were the building blocks of the effective strike in 1912. According to Mary K. O'Sullivan, the first female organizer of the American Federation of Labor, "Catholics, Jews, Protestants and unbelievers, men and women of many races and languages, were working together as human beings with a common cause . . . It was the most unselfish strike I have ever known." Above is a scene in front of the Arlington Mills during rush hour around 1920. Men, women, and children from varying backgrounds and stations in life painted an active urban community. Below is a group of women who worked together in the Ayer Mill mending room.

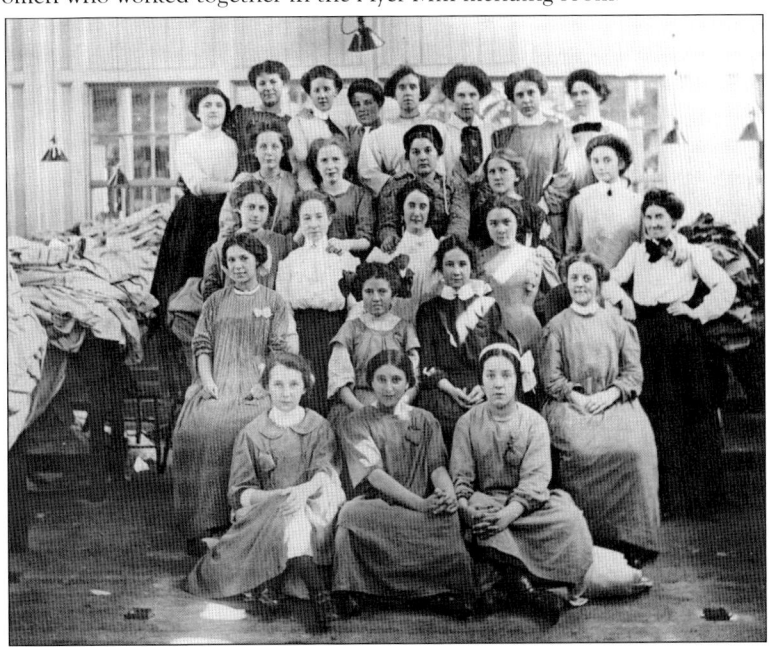

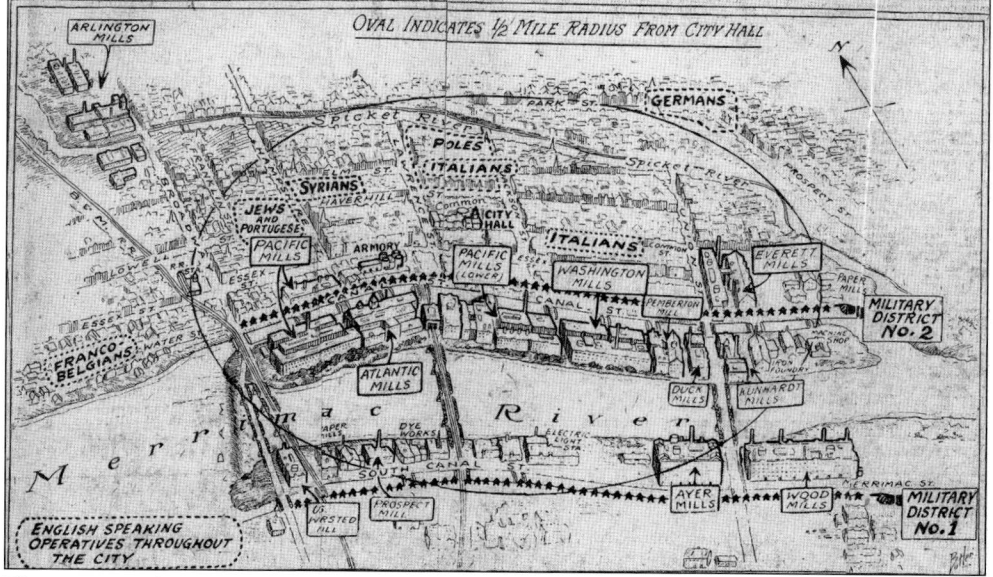

Three years after incorporation, the city contained 8,358 people. The population more than doubled by 1860, with 17,639 residents, 42 percent of them foreign-born, mostly the result of Irish immigration. Between 1845 and 1860, some one-third of Ireland's population emigrated due to famine, high employment, and mass evictions off small landholdings. According to historian Ardis Cameron, at the end of the Civil War, "the Irish accounted for more than 65 percent of Lawrence's foreign-born population . . . In 1870 some 29,000 people lived in the growing city; the number grew to just over 39,000 by 1880. At that time, Irish, Scots, and French Canadians accounted for 77 percent of the city's foreign-born population." Testifying to the growth of woolen mills and numerous supporting industries and commercial establishments, the population approached 45,000 in 1890. By then, 45 percent of the population was foreign-born, attracted by the possibilities of mill employment. The map above originally appeared in the *Boston Daily Globe*.

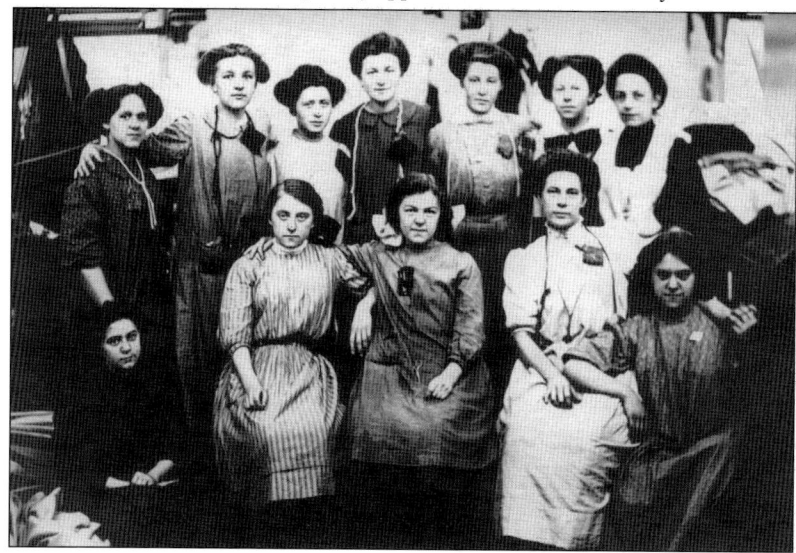

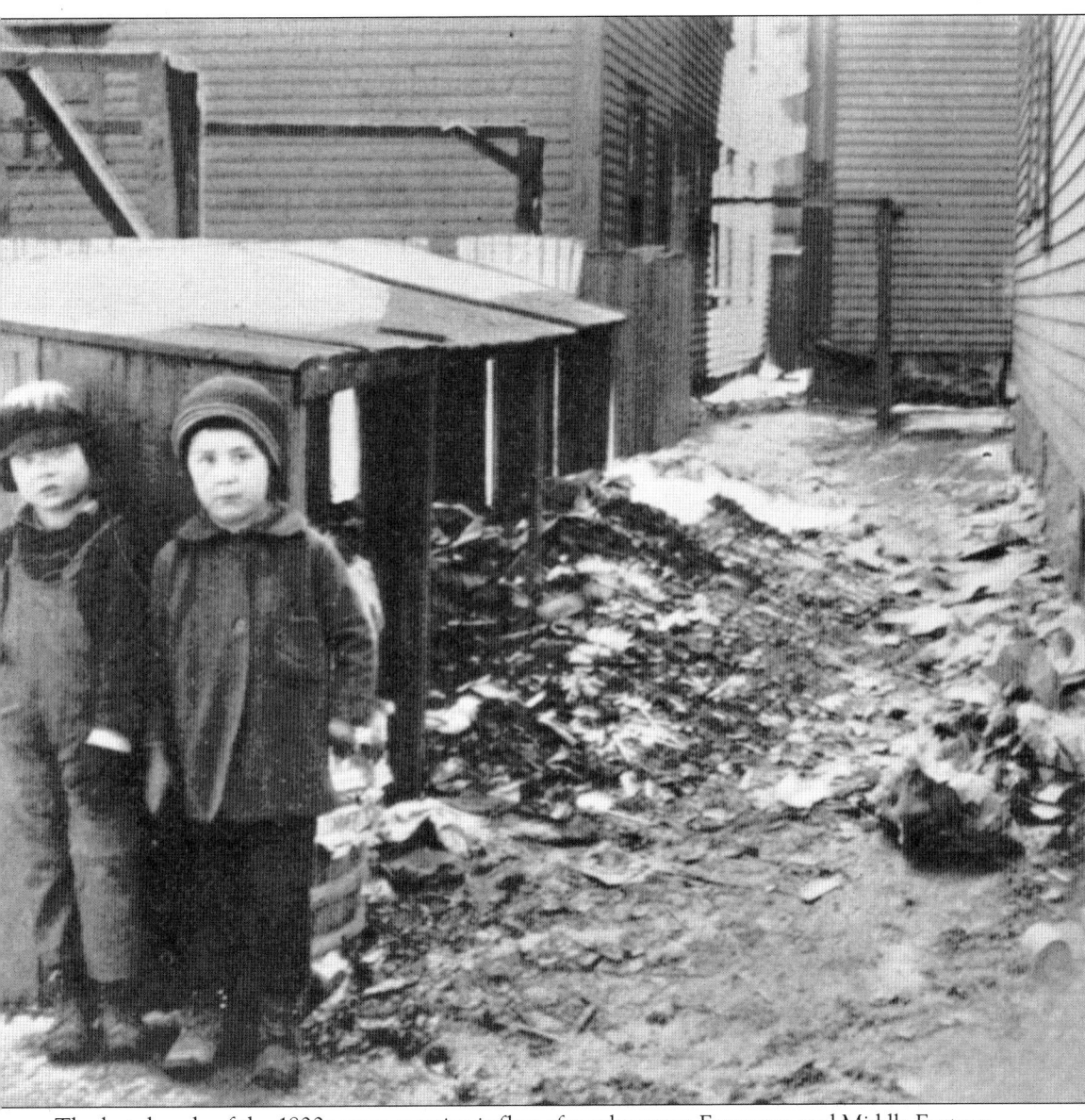

The last decade of the 1800s saw a massive influx of southeastern European and Middle Eastern immigrants, and the population in 1900 reached nearly 63,000. In 1910, a total of 85,892 people lived in Lawrence, 48 percent of them foreign-born. At that time, 74 percent of the city's total workforce of 42,526 people was engaged in manufacturing, compared to 54 percent for Massachusetts as a whole. By 1911, living conditions were challenging. In 1912, the White Fund published *The Report of the Lawrence Survey*, which stated, "Lawrence is an appendage to the textile industry . . . a tool-room attached to a workshop. . . Papers and rubbish under cellar stairs in a six family wooden house with four floors. Tenants on the second, third, and fourth floors front have egress only down the stairs over this pile. An equally great pile was seen at the next house. These houses are so situated that an uncontrolled fire in them would sweep the whole center of the city." This photograph, from *The Report of the Lawrence Survey*, shows two children in a typical alleyway between tenements.

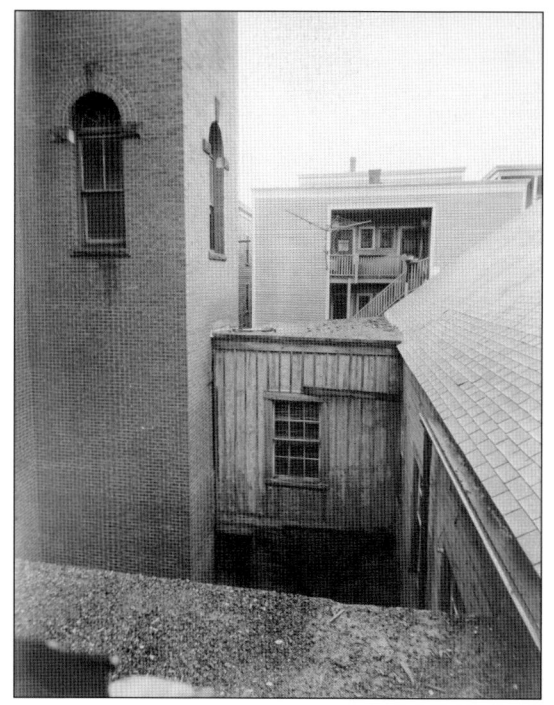

The 1912 *The Report of the Lawrence Survey* went on to say, "This is the greatest concentration of population living in wooden houses in any three acres in the state of Massachusetts. The efficiency of workers is constantly being reduced by the impaired vision and permanent injury to their eyesight that is one of the results of their living in darkened houses." The photograph at left shows the view from the roof of a Lawrence tenement, illustrating the density of workers' neighborhoods. Below, children spend time in an alleyway. In late 1911, the following was written in the *Lawrence Evening Tribune*: "The mortality in the crowded tenement districts especially in the summer reads like battle statistics."

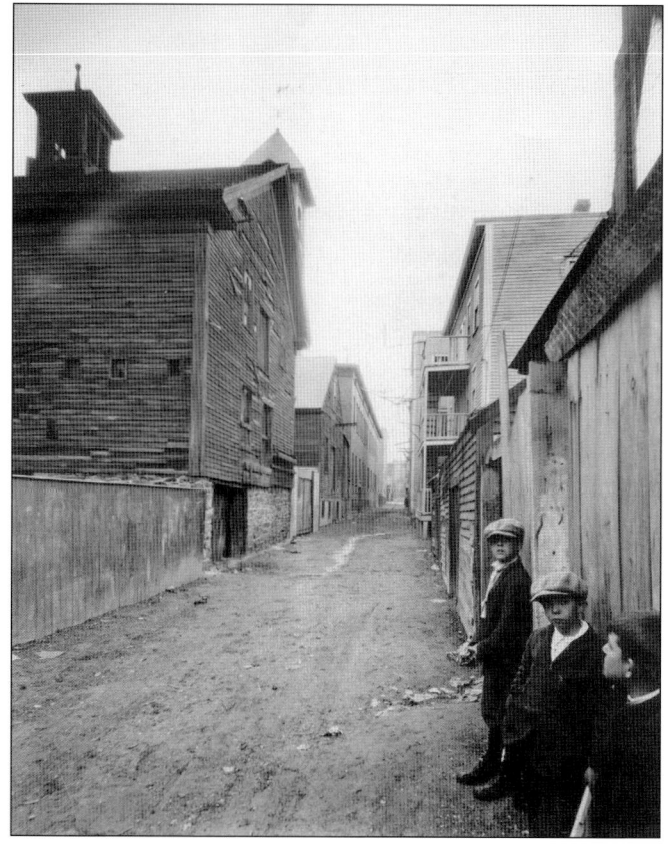

CHAPTER V.—GENERAL STATISTICS.

DEATH RATE (EXCLUSIVE OF STILLBIRTHS) OF INFANTS UNDER 1 YEAR OF AGE, PER 1,000 BIRTHS, IN REGISTRATION CITIES OF 50,000 POPULATION OR OVER, IN DESCENDING ORDER, 1908, 1909, 1910.

[Compiled from reports of the Bureau of the Census. Concerning the accuracy of birth registration in the United States and its relation to the infant mortality rate, the following statement is made by the Bureau of the Census: " * * * Owing to the very defective character of birth registration in the United States, reliable ratios of infantile mortality are not available for the country as a whole, for the registration area, or even for a single State or large city of the country. Even on the assumption, which is not always correct, that all deaths of infants are recorded, rates of infantile mortality computed on the basis of the incomplete birth returns would be somewhat higher than the actual rates."[1] "Although the birth returns are so incomplete that no thoroughly reliable rates of infant mortality can be computed for any portion of the United States nevertheless the data for certain areas in which the birth registration is believed to be conducted most efficiently may be of some service."[2]]

1908		1909		1910	
City and State.	Death rate of infants under 1 year of age per 1,000 births.	City and State.	Death rate of infants under 1 year of age per 1,000 births.	City and State.	Death rate of infants under 1 year of age per 1,000 births.[3]
Manchester, N. H.	212	Manchester, N. H.	263	Lowell, Mass.	231
Lowell, Mass.	202	Holyoke, Mass.	231	Holyoke, Mass.	213
Holyoke, Mass.	182	Fall River, Mass.	186	Manchester, N. H.	193
Fall River, Mass.	178	Lowell, Mass.	185	Fall River, Mass.	186
Scranton, Pa.	176	Detroit, Mich.	176	Detroit, Mich.	179
Detroit, Mich.	175	Pawtucket, R. I.	173	New Bedford, Mass.	177
Allentown, Pa.	164	Lawrence, Mass.	172	Lawrence, Mass.	167
Washington, D. C.	157	Johnstown, Pa.	162	Johnstown, Pa.	165
White	110	Erie, Pa.	155	Washington, D. C.	152
Colored	261	Washington, D. C.	148	White	105
Lawrence, Mass.	155	White	105	Colored	244
Pittsburgh, Pa.	152	Colored	243	Pittsburgh, Pa.	150
Pawtucket, R. I.	150	Waterbury, Conn.	147	Waterbury, Conn.	149
Boston, Mass.	149	Scranton, Pa.	146	Scranton, Pa.	148
Philadelphia, Pa.	149	New Bedford, Mass.	143	Wilkes-Barre, Pa.	146
New Bedford, Mass.	144	Allentown, Pa.	141	Saginaw, Mich.	145
Wilkes-Barre, Pa.	144	Pittsburgh, Pa.	141	Allentown, Pa.	144
Reading, Pa.	139	Bridgeport, Conn.	138	Portland, Me.	144
Portland, Me.	137	Portland, Me.	136	Reading, Pa.	142
Saginaw, Mich.	134	Philadelphia, Pa.	135	Philadelphia, Pa.	138
Providence, R. I.	133	Providence, R. I.	135	Worcester, Mass.	137
Waterbury, Conn.	132	New York, N. Y.	130	Harrisburg, Pa.	129
New York, N. Y.	129	Bronx Borough	105	Boston, Mass.	126
Bronx Borough	120	Brooklyn Borough	119	New York, N. Y.	125
Brooklyn Borough	107	Manhattan Borough	140	Bronx Borough	96
Manhattan Borough	136	Queens Borough	135	Brooklyn Borough	117
Queens Borough	126	Richmond Borough	152	Manhattan Borough	135
Richmond Borough	169	Harrisburg, Pa.	129	Queens Borough	122
Bridgeport, Conn.	128	Saginaw, Mich.	125	Richmond Borough	138
Erie, Pa.	124	Worcester, Mass.	121	Springfield, Mass.	124
Johnstown, Pa.	121	Boston, Mass.	120	Bridgeport, Conn.	123
Cambridge, Mass.	118	New Haven, Conn.	120	Grand Rapids, Mich.	122
Altoona, Pa.	117	Wilkes-Barre, Pa.	119	Altoona, Pa.	119
Harrisburg, Pa.	116	Brockton, Mass.	116	Cambridge, Mass.	119
Worcester, Mass.	114	Altoona, Pa.	114	Hartford, Conn.	119
Lynn, Mass.	111	Springfield, Mass.	110	Erie, Pa.	115
New Haven, Conn.	111	Reading, Pa.	107	New Haven, Conn.	108
Hartford, Conn.	110	Hartford, Conn.	102	Somerville, Mass.	101
Grand Rapids, Mich.	102	Cambridge, Mass.	102	Brockton, Mass.	99
Somerville, Mass.	98	Grand Rapids, Mich.	101	Lynn, Mass.	97
Brockton, Mass.	97	Lynn, Mass.	99	Pawtucket, R. I.	(4)
Springfield, Mass.	96	Somerville, Mass.	84	Providence, R. I.	(4)

[1] Bureau of the Census, Bulletin 109, p. 14.
[2] Idem, p. 17.
[3] Based on provisional figure for births.
[4] Returns of births not received from the State board of health in time for inclusion.

Much was written about infant mortality in Lawrence. Charles Neill's 1912 *Report on the Strike of Textile Workers in Lawrence* stated: "We know that in 1910 Lawrence ranked among the top ten cities in the country for deaths of infants under age one and for deaths of children under age five." According to Bruce Watson's *Bread and Roses*, "Diseases now easily cured—diarrhea, measles, whooping cough, croup—killed hundreds, most of them children. During the year preceding the strike, 1,524 people died in Lawrence. Almost half were under the age of six, and more than 500 had not yet reached their first birthday . . . When mill workers died, word spread through the tenements along a network linked by clotheslines and gossip, a network largely ignored by men and nurtured by women. Even before news reached the papers, women heard the names, just as they heard every time another infant died . . . in a single week: Cara Meola, age one year and five months. Patricia Madden, 16 days old. Margaret Burns, three months old. Ida Kappanan, nine months."

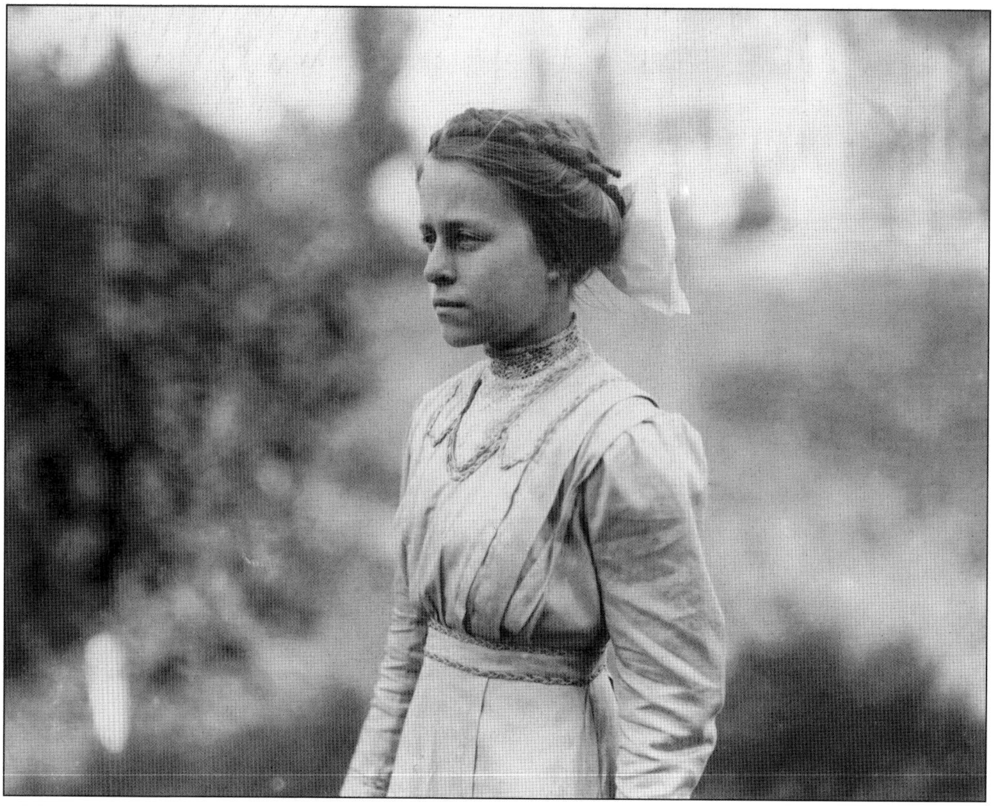

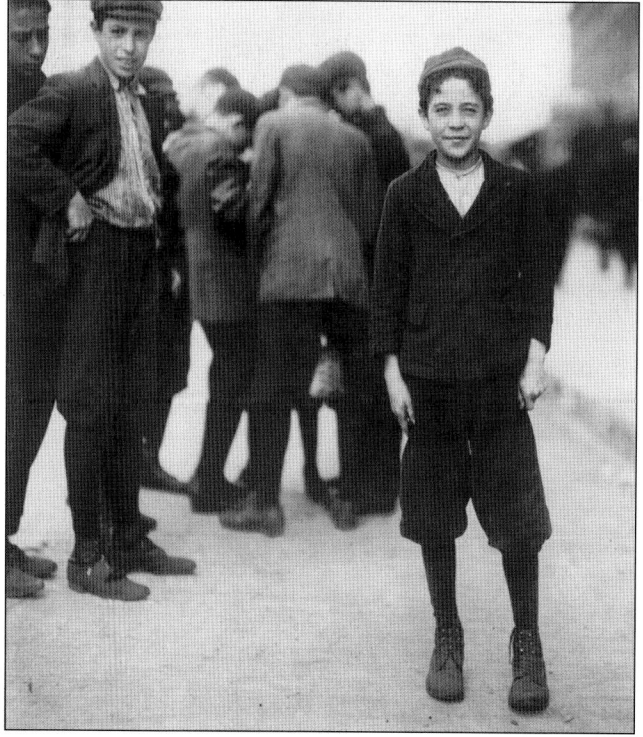

The faces of Lawrence's child mill workers were captured by photographer Lewis Wickes Hine in 1910 and 1911. The National Child Labor Committee hired him in 1908 to take photographs of children in or near their workplaces, in order to expose their plight to as many influential people as possible. The organization had thousands of members all over the country who were on the lookout for factories that employed young children, often in violation of state child labor laws that were meager and infrequently enforced. Eva Tanguay (above) was 15 years old and a doffer in a spinning room in the Ayer Mill. Sam Gangi (left) was also 15 and a worker in the Ayer Mill. (Both, courtesy of LOC.)

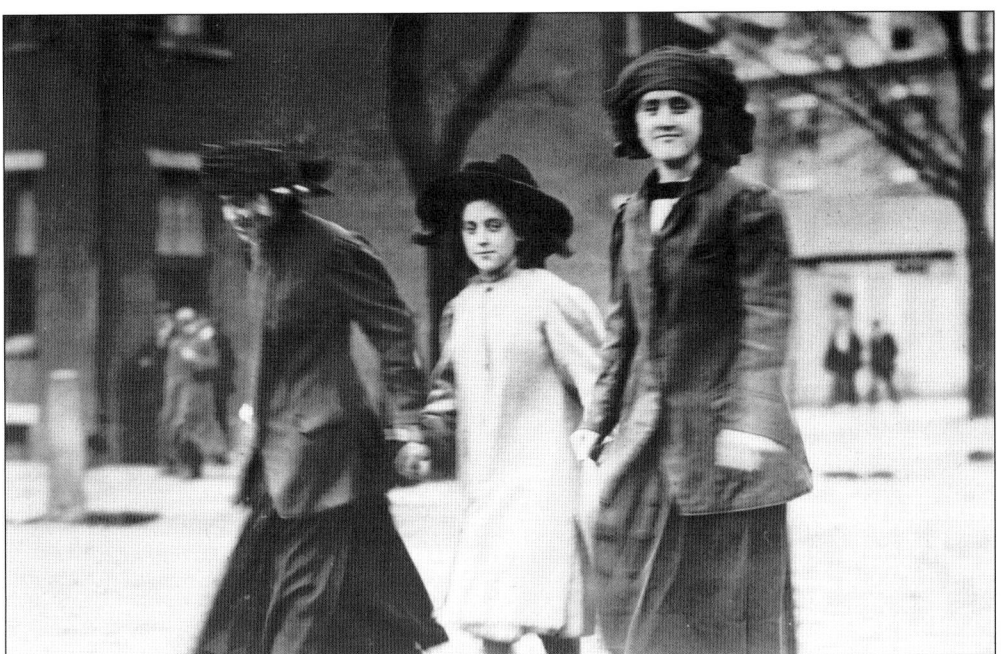

The women in the 1911 Hine photograph above are on their way to work at the Pacific Mills. They went to work every day at 12:00 p.m. and worked until approximately 8:00 p.m. They were working there at the time of the strike. Seen below are Ida Descheues and her family. Lewis Hine's notes accompanying the photograph read, "Ida has half hour ride in crowded stuffy cars to and from work each day. Leaving home at 6:00 a.m. and returning at 6:30 p.m. The doffing work is much of it standing, stooping and reaching." (Both, courtesy of LOC.)

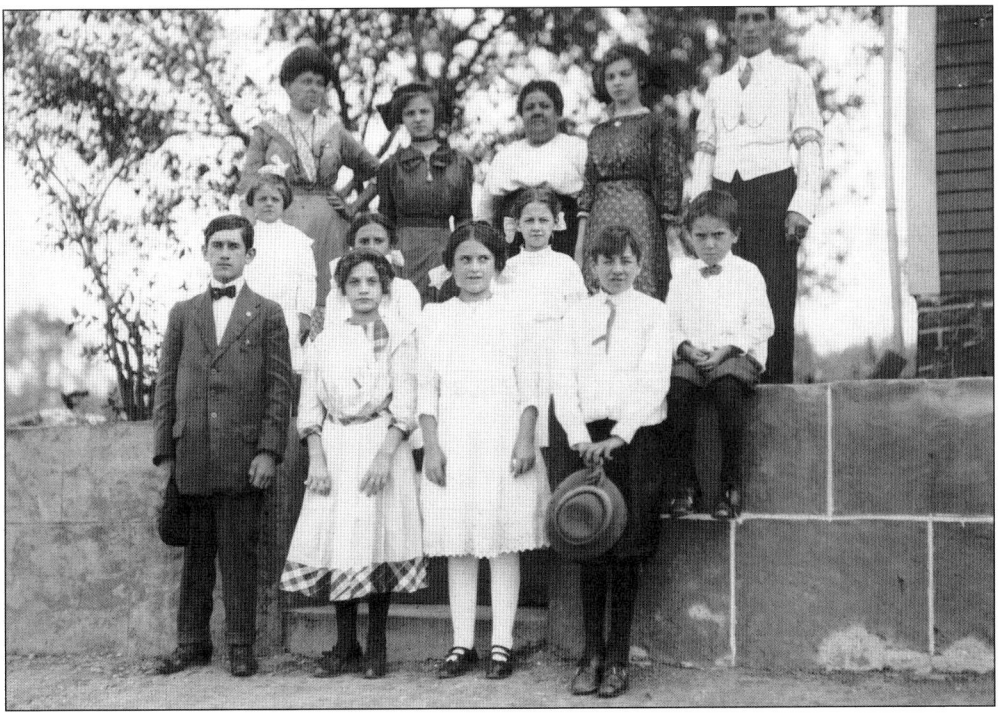

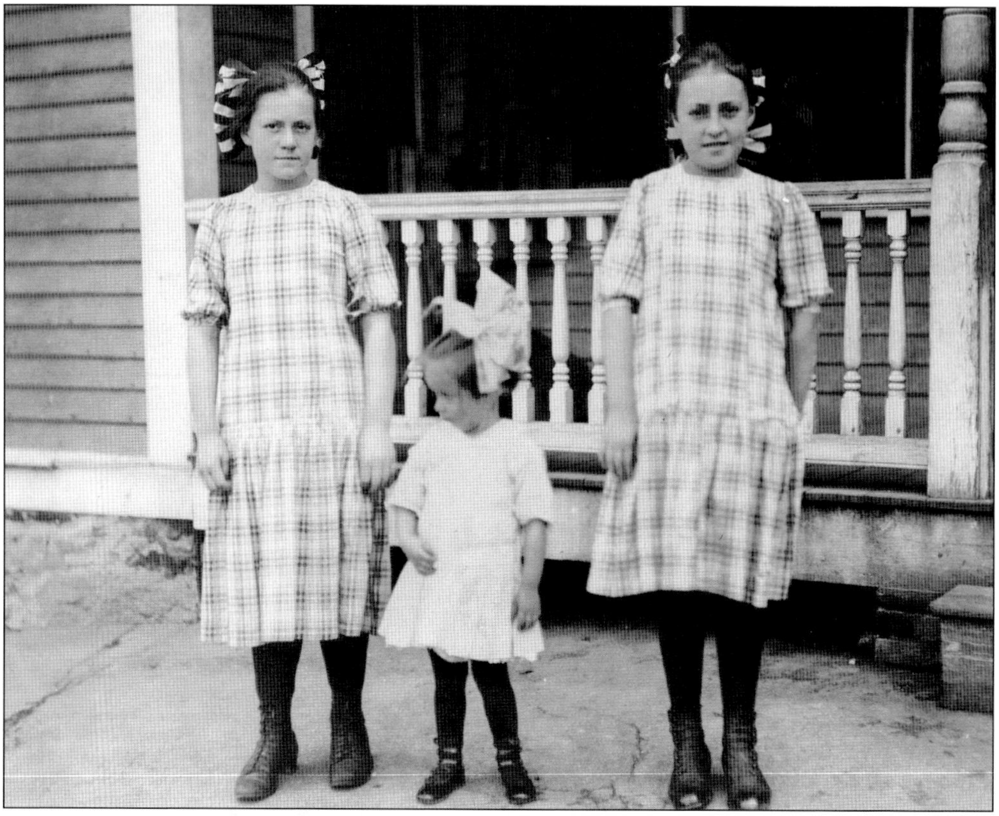

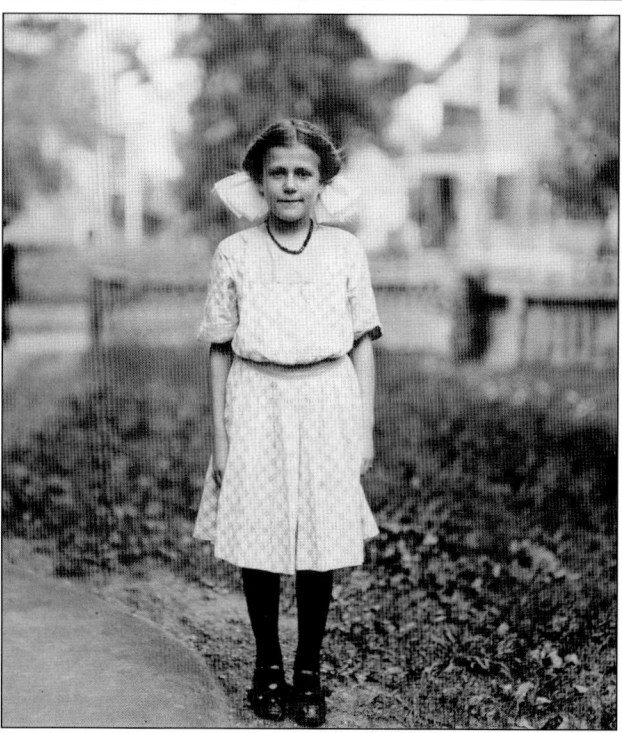

Alice (above, left) and Antoinette Deon (above, right) are seen with their young sister. Alice and Antoinette worked in the Ayer Mill. The average mill wage for a woman over 18 was 14¢ per hour, equal to $3.31 per hour today. The sisters were likely paid 11¢ or 12¢ per hour because they were 14 and 16. Antoinette Pothier (left) also worked in the Ayer Mill, and reported walking nearly 30 minutes each way to work and back home. She left home at 6:00 a.m. and returned at 6:30 p.m. Just months after this photograph was taken, she and others shut down their machines during the strike, a landmark moment in labor history. Both of these photographs were taken by Lewis Hine in late 1911. (Both, courtesy of LOC.)

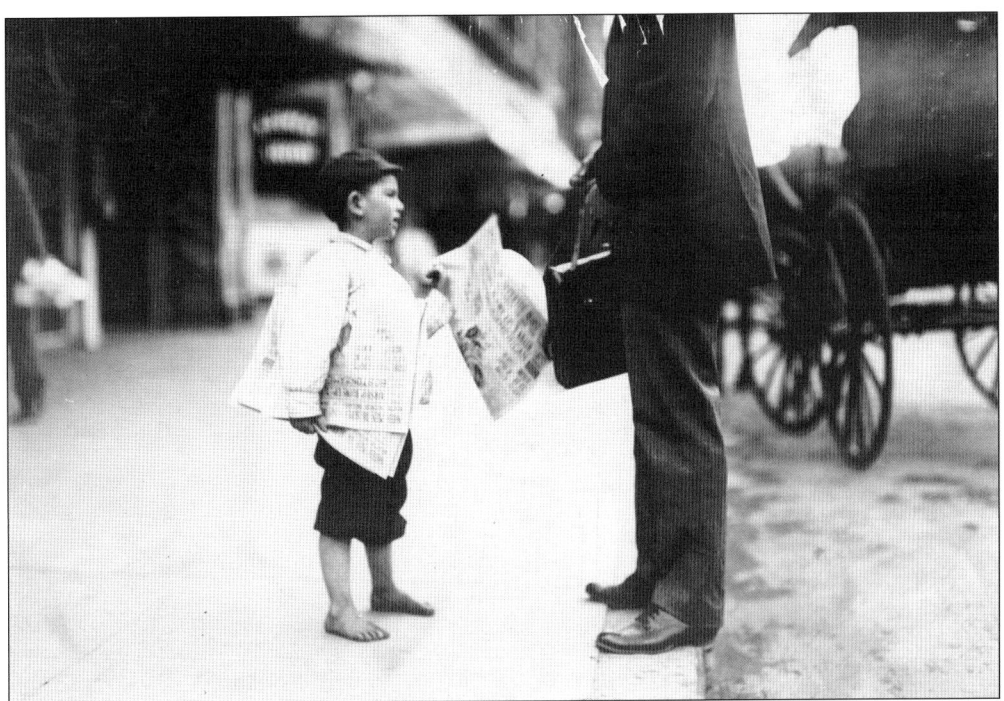

In his *Report on the Strike of Textile Workers*, Charles Neill writes, "In some instances the children are taken out on Sunday afternoons to the country and left there [with relatives or friends] until the following Saturday, then during the Saturday afternoon holiday the parents go out and bring children back home and keep them until the afternoon of the following day. The usual practice is, however, for the father and mother to take the children, before going to work at 6:30 a.m., to a neighboring family, in whose charge they are left during the day." The Lewis Hine photograph above shows Hyman, a six-year-old "newsie" who said he sold newspapers until 6:00 p.m. At right is a poster decrying the use of child labor in textile mills. (Above, courtesy of LOC; right, courtesy of WSU.)

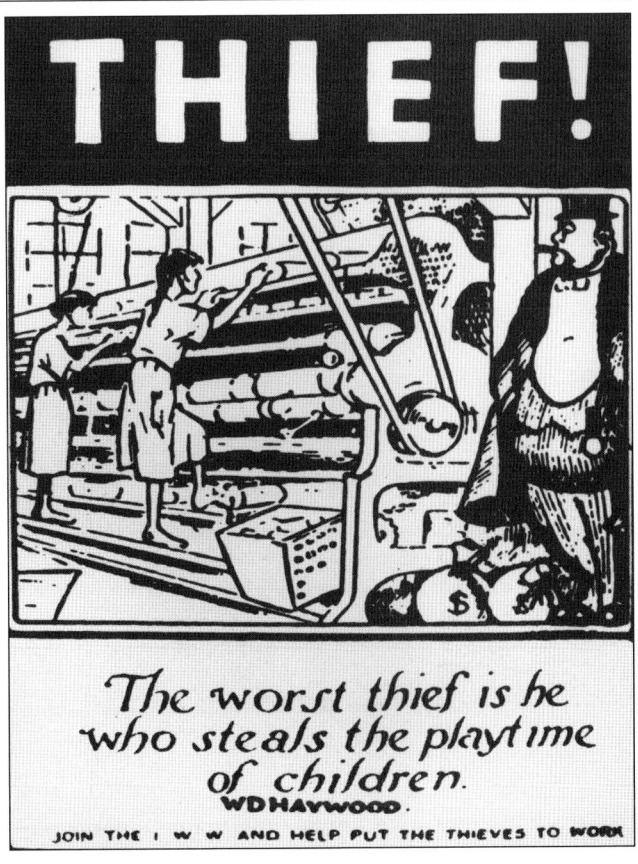

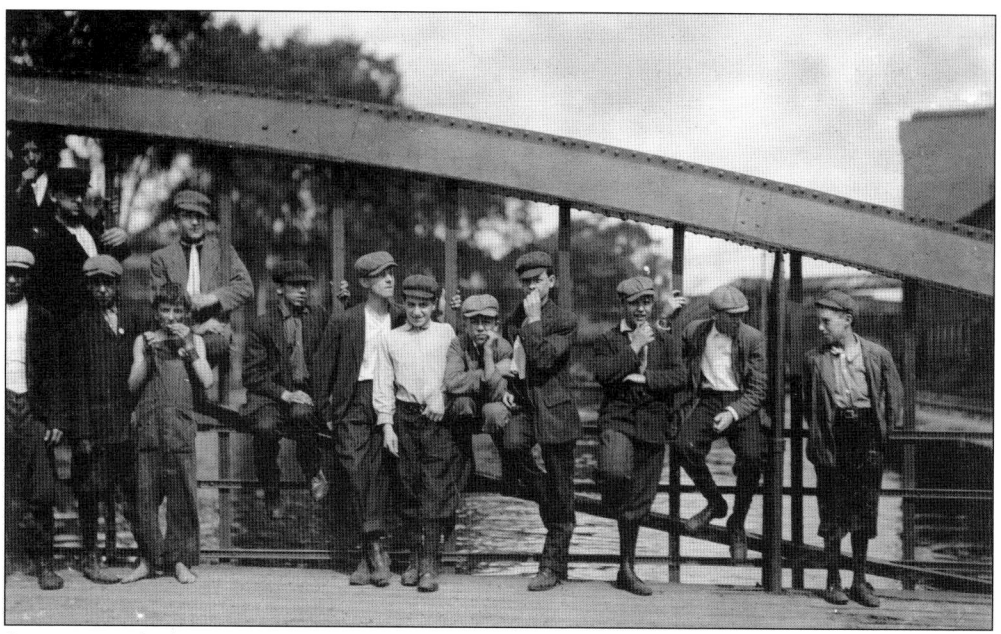

Spinners worked in extremely damp and humid rooms and were vulnerable to tuberculosis and pneumonia. The Lewis Hine photograph above shows Washington Mill spinning room workers in the fall of 1911. In the years before the 1912 strike, one-third of Lawrence's spinners died before they had worked 10 years. The photograph below, from the Lawrence History Center's collection, was taken of male workers in the Wood Mill. Conditions were such that, just days before the strike commenced, on Saturday, January 6, a worker from the Wood Mill walked into a store on Essex Street and dropped dead. No one knew whether the cause was stress, factory fatigue, tuberculosis, or something else. Three days later, a 14-year-old boy had his leg crushed in an elevator at the Arlington Mill; he died the next day. (Above, courtesy of LOC.)

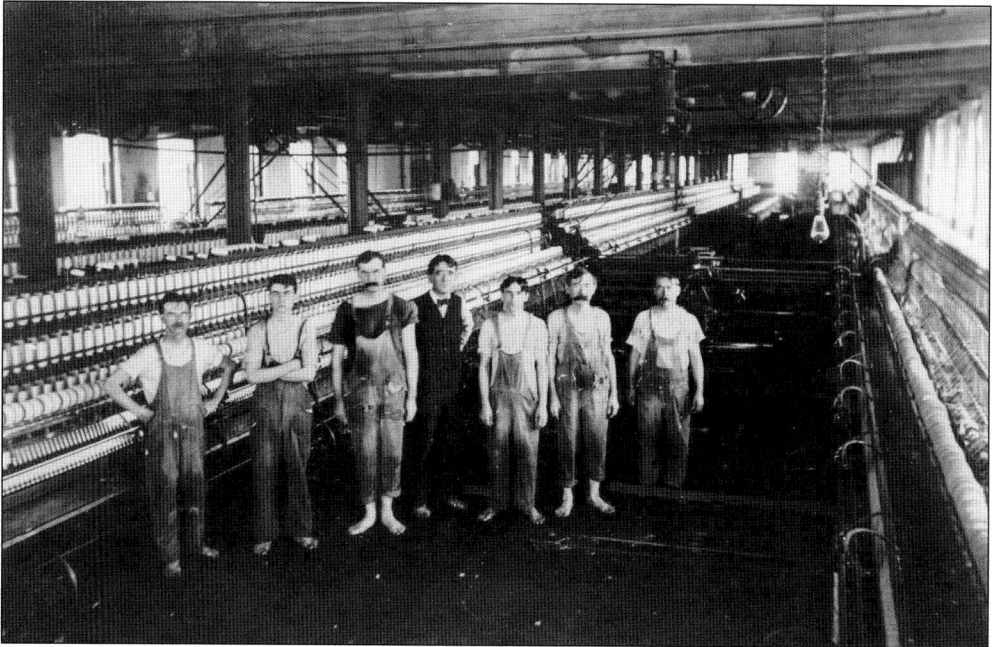

In an article indicative of the anti-immigrant attitudes in Massachusetts at the time of the strike, the *Boston Globe* informed its readers of the following in mid-January: "The textile operatives in many of the mills number a larger percentage of foreigners—Italians, Syrians, Poles, Portuguese, and Armenians—than of any English-speaking race. Having been encouraged to come to Lawrence, these classes of men and women now overrun the place." Such workers, the newspaper concluded, "are ignorant and easily deceived and more readily excited." According to the 1910 federal census, 65 percent of Lawrence mill workers had lived in the United States for less than 10 years, and 47 percent of them for less than five years. A Belgian woman, Marie Lingier, is seen at right in the Prospect Mill. Carpenters from diverse backgrounds are seen below in the Washington Mill in 1901.

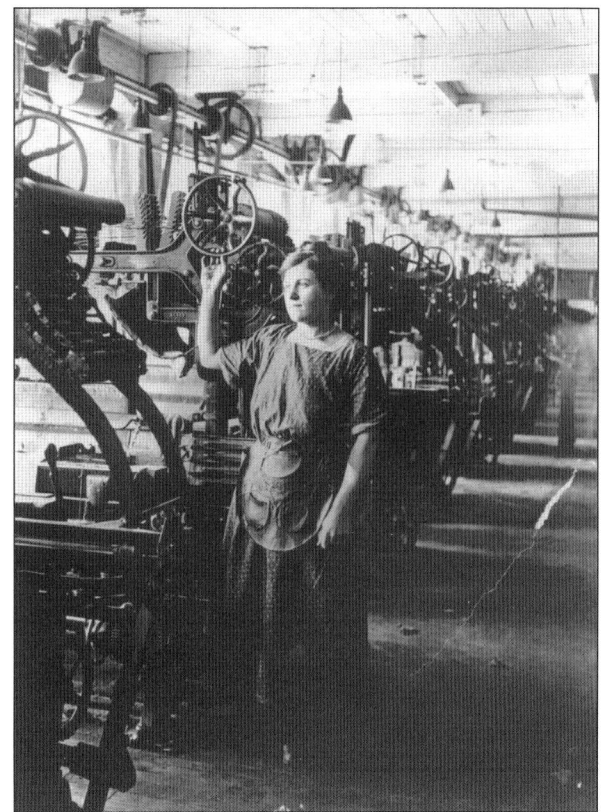

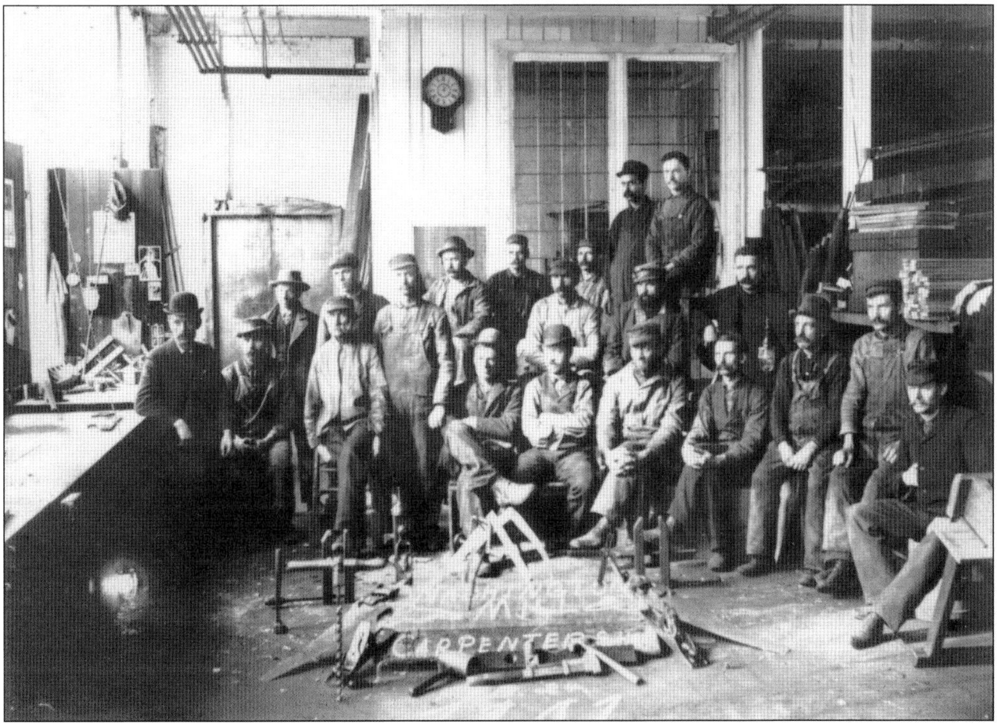

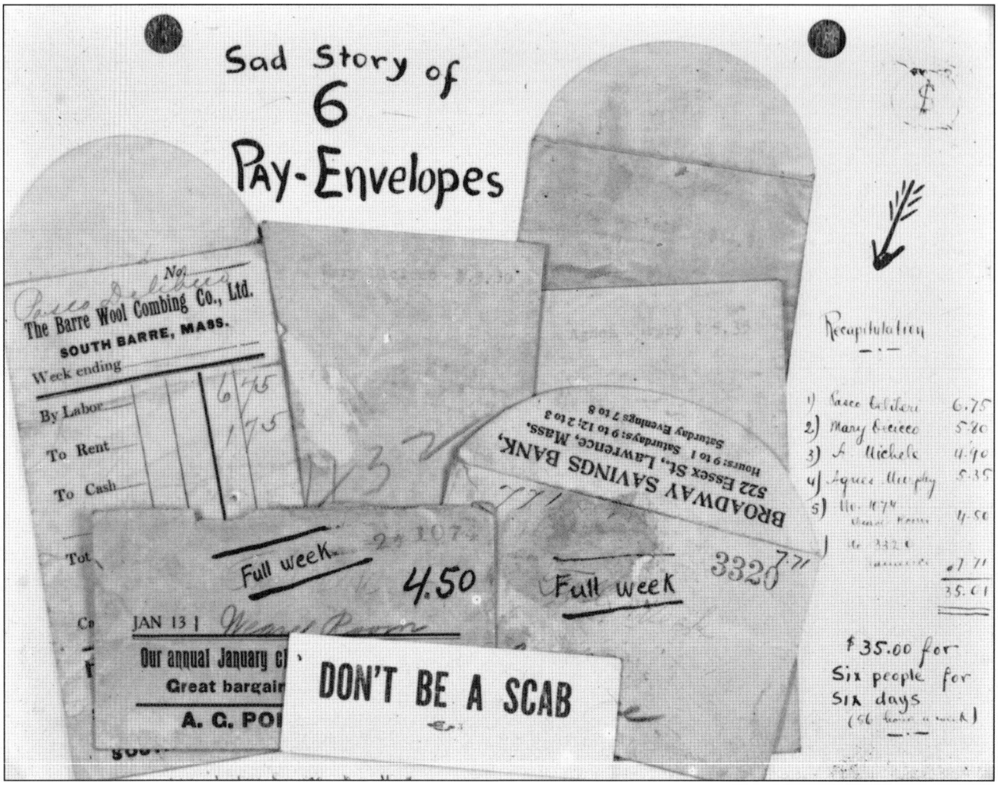

Rent per week varied from $1 to $6, but the amount most commonly paid was $2 to $3 for a four-room apartment and $3 to $3.50 for a five-room apartment. Wages could not be stretched far enough to cover rent, food, and medicine when needed. Charles Neill's *Report on the Strike of Textile Workers* noted that because of low wages, unless at least one child was old enough to work, it became necessary for mothers to work. In cases where children were so young as to necessitate the mother remaining at home, extreme hardship resulted. The image above reveals five Lawrence pay envelopes and one from South Barre, Massachusetts, where Lawrence solidarity work led to a strike over local issues in March 1912. (Both, courtesy of UNH.)

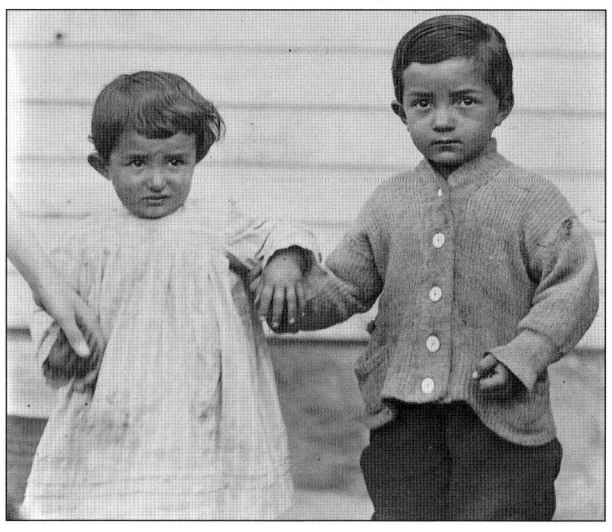

Three

THE 1912 STRIKE

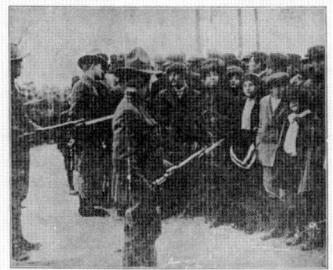

Effective January 1, 1912, a Massachusetts law reduced the maximum workweek for women and children from 56 hours to 54 hours. When paid on January 11, Polish and Lithuanian women weavers at the Everett Cotton Mills realized their wages had been reduced by approximately 32¢. Stopping their looms, they left the mill shouting "short pay, short pay!" On January 12, thousands more workers join the strike.

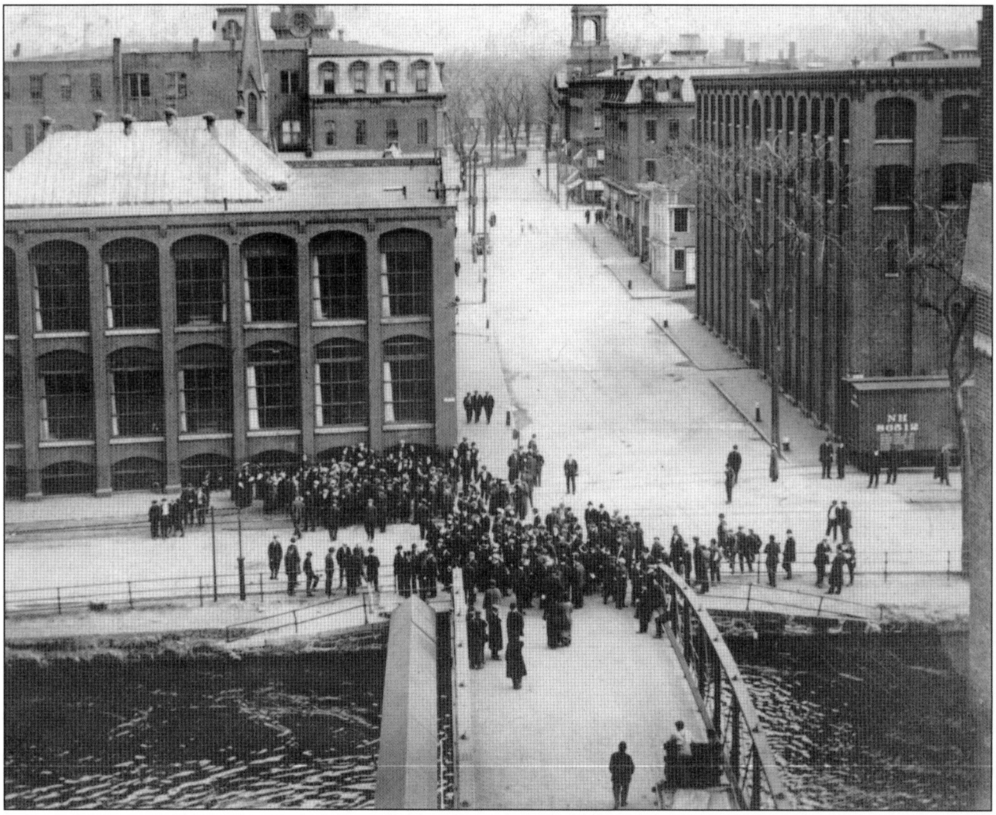

The *Lawrence Eagle Tribune* reported the following about a strike meeting held on January 11: "Voting unanimously to walk out if their pay for 54 hours is less than that received for 56 hours, several hundred Italians, Poles, and Lithuanians, who are employed in the local mills, met last evening at Ford's Hall. A majority of those who attended the meeting will receive their pay today. A mass meeting will be held Saturday afternoon at 2 o'clock in the City Hall at which speakers in English, Italian, Polish, and French will be present." The walkout was well underway. Above, strikers gather at the corner of Appleton and Canal Streets. City hall and the Lawrence Common are in the background. Below, the militia enters the Everett Mills.

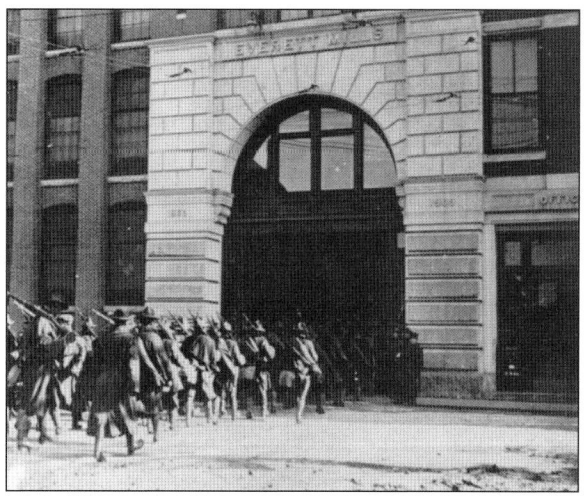

36

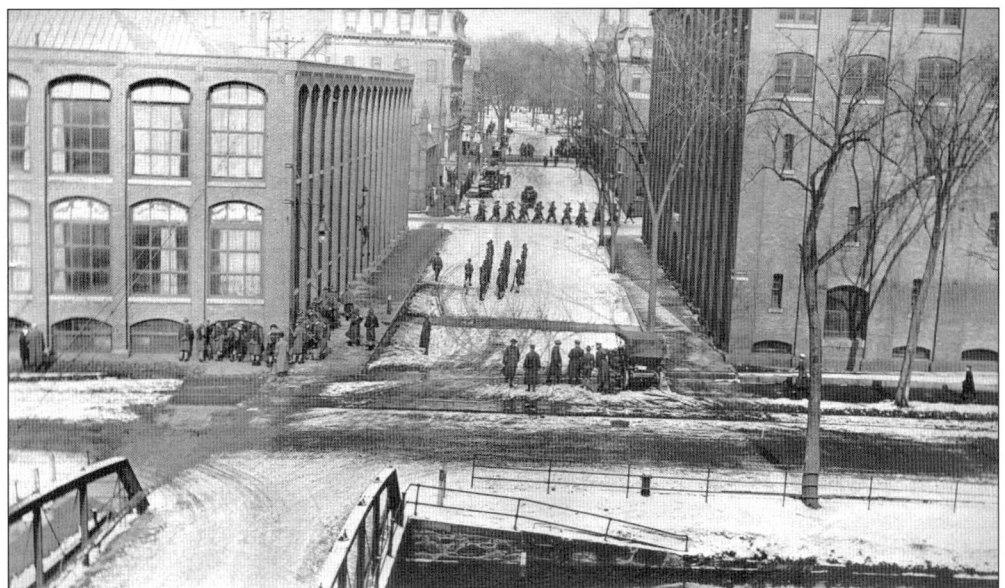

As the strike entered its first full week, mill owners expected things to return to normal on Monday, January 15. Instead, lines hardened. More militia companies arrived to patrol the streets, as seen above. Strike leaders issued this call for others in the city to join them: "To all Workers of Lawrence, as long as the fight was confined to the mills of Lawrence and appeared not to extend any further we deemed it unnecessary to appeal to other classes of workers; but now that the combination of capitalists have shown the unity of all our adversaries, we call on you as brothers and sisters to join hands with us in this great movement. Our cause is just." Below, textile workers, mostly women and children, stand outside of an unidentified mill during the strike. (Below, courtesy of WSU.)

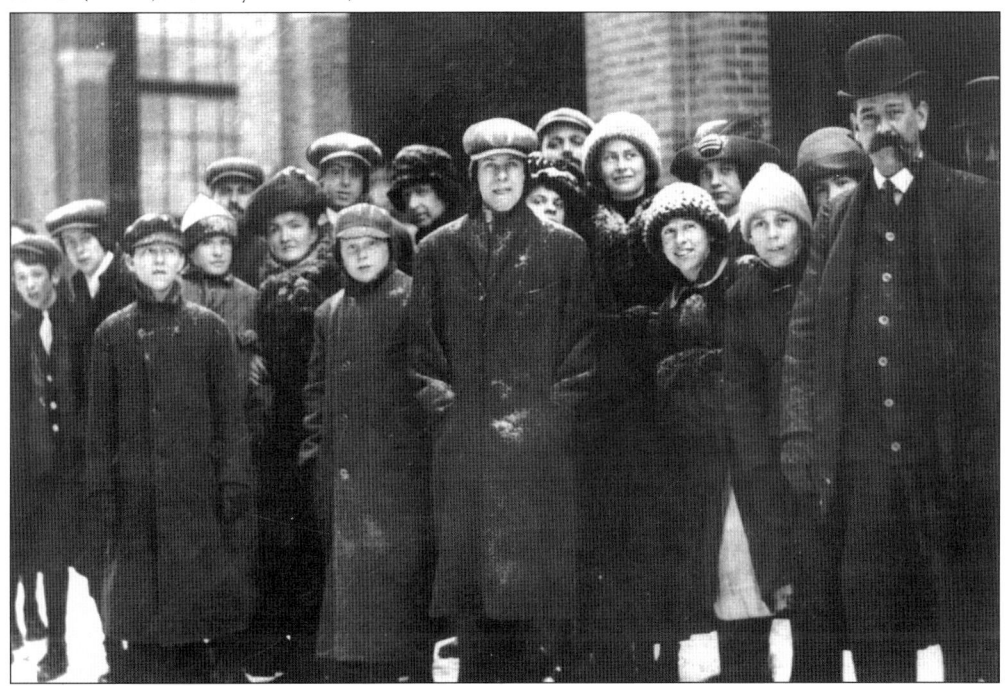

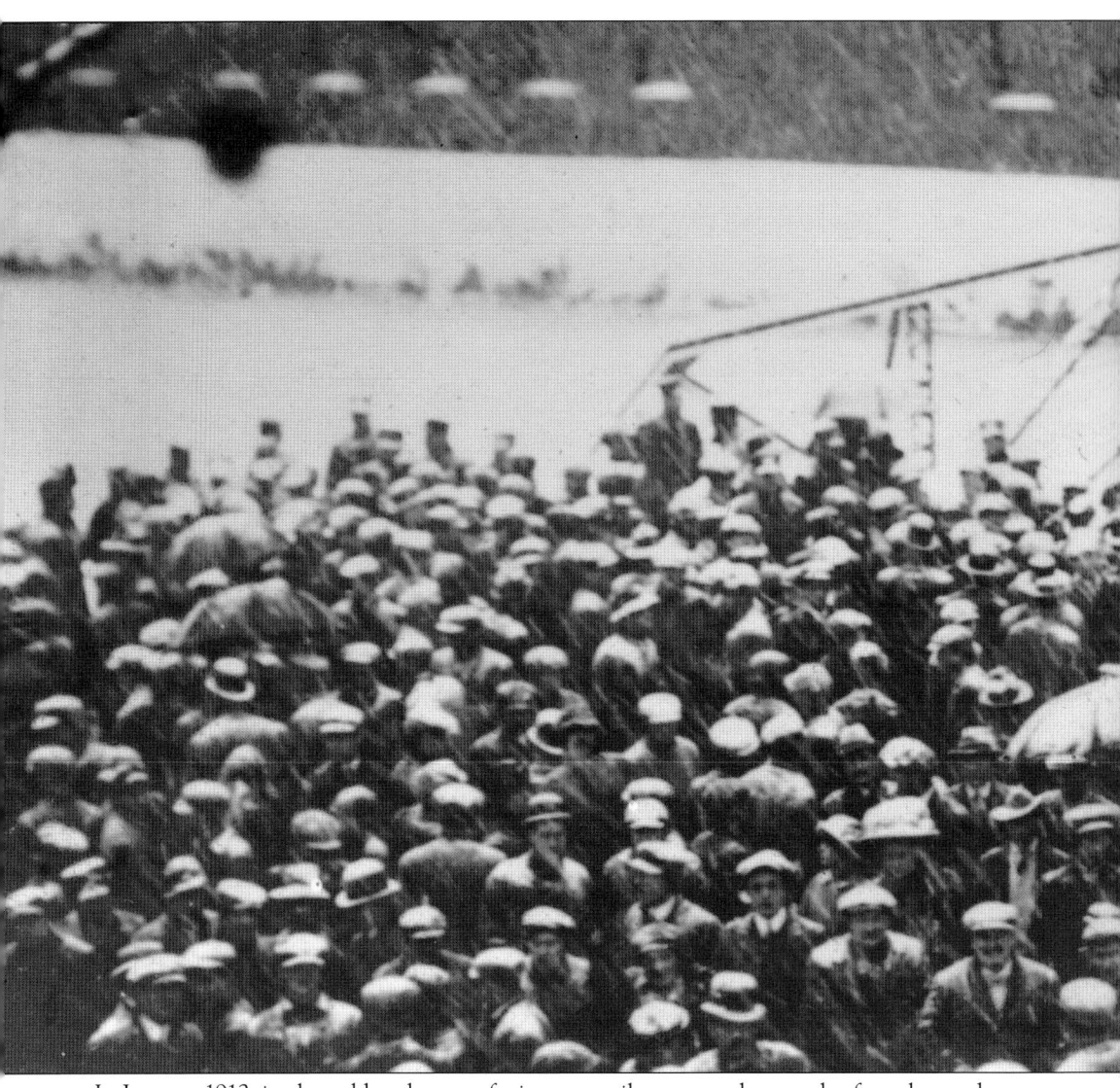

In January 1912, in the cold and snow of winter, a strike among thousands of woolen and cotton mill workers in Lawrence forced the nation to face questions about community, immigration, organized labor, and the harsh realities of American industry. In *Bread and Roses*, Bruce Watson writes that at the Washington Mill at 9:00 a.m. on Friday, January 12, the paymaster witnessed

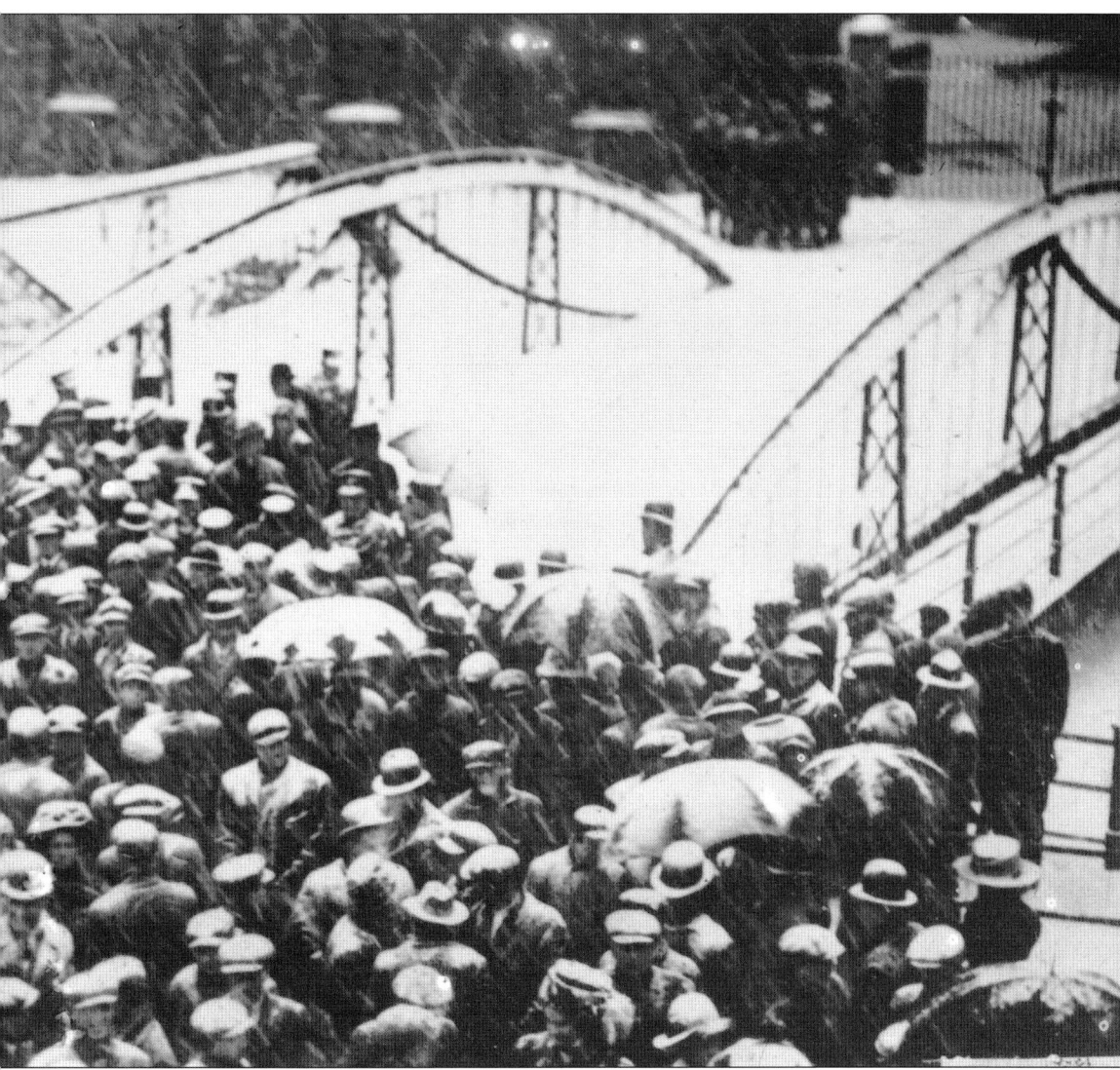
"a blur of arms and backs surging through the mill gates and into the courtyard. He immediately called the police. Nightstick in hand, the lone cop on the local beat arrived a few minutes later to find two thousand people swarming outside the mill." (Courtesy of UNH.)

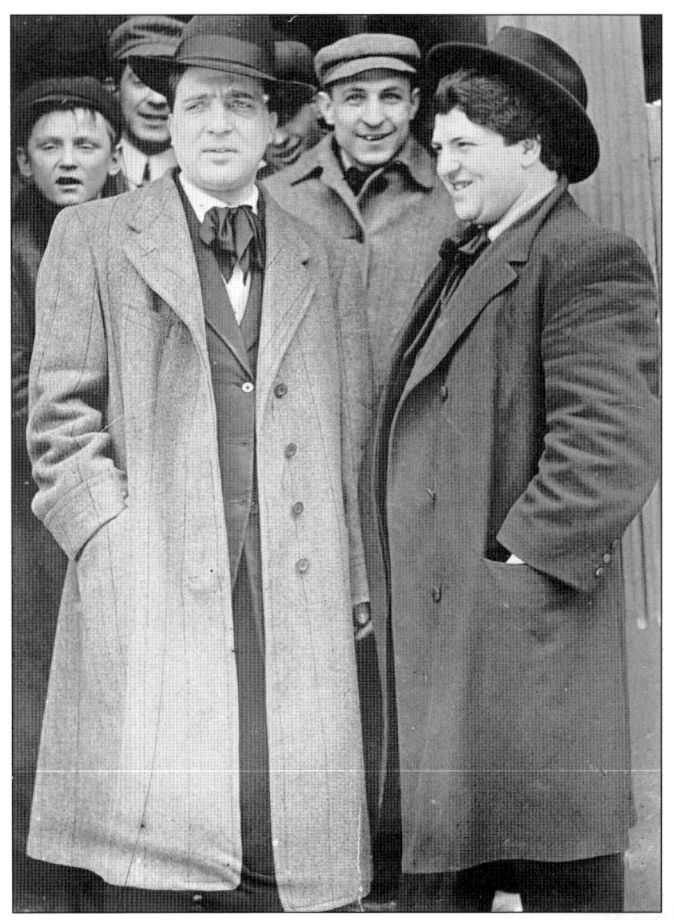

On January 13, Industrial Workers of the World (IWW) organizer Joseph Ettor arrived in the city. He spoke to workers at city hall, saying, "If the workers of the world want to win, all they have to do is recognize their own solidarity. They have nothing to do but fold their arms and the world will stop. The workers are more powerful with their hands in their pockets than all the property of the capitalists. As long as workers keep their hands in their pockets the capitalists cannot put theirs there. With passive resistance, with the workers absolutely refusing to move they are more powerful than all the weapons and instruments that the other side has for protection and attack." At left, Ettor (right) is seen with Arturo Giovannitti. (Left, courtesy of UNH.)

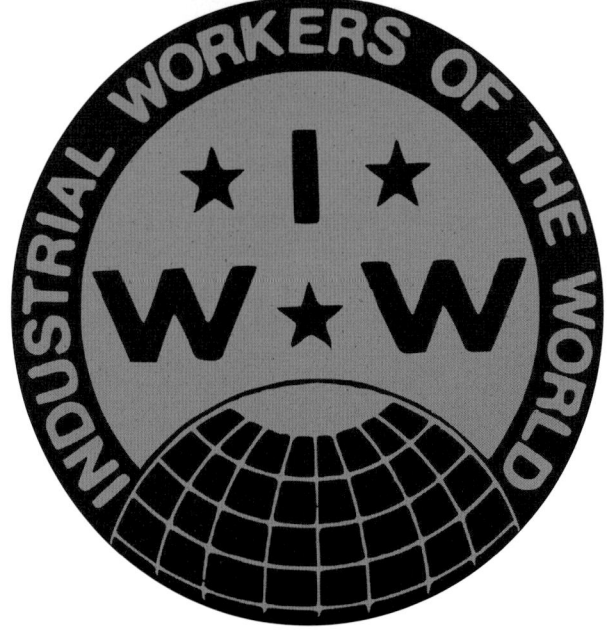

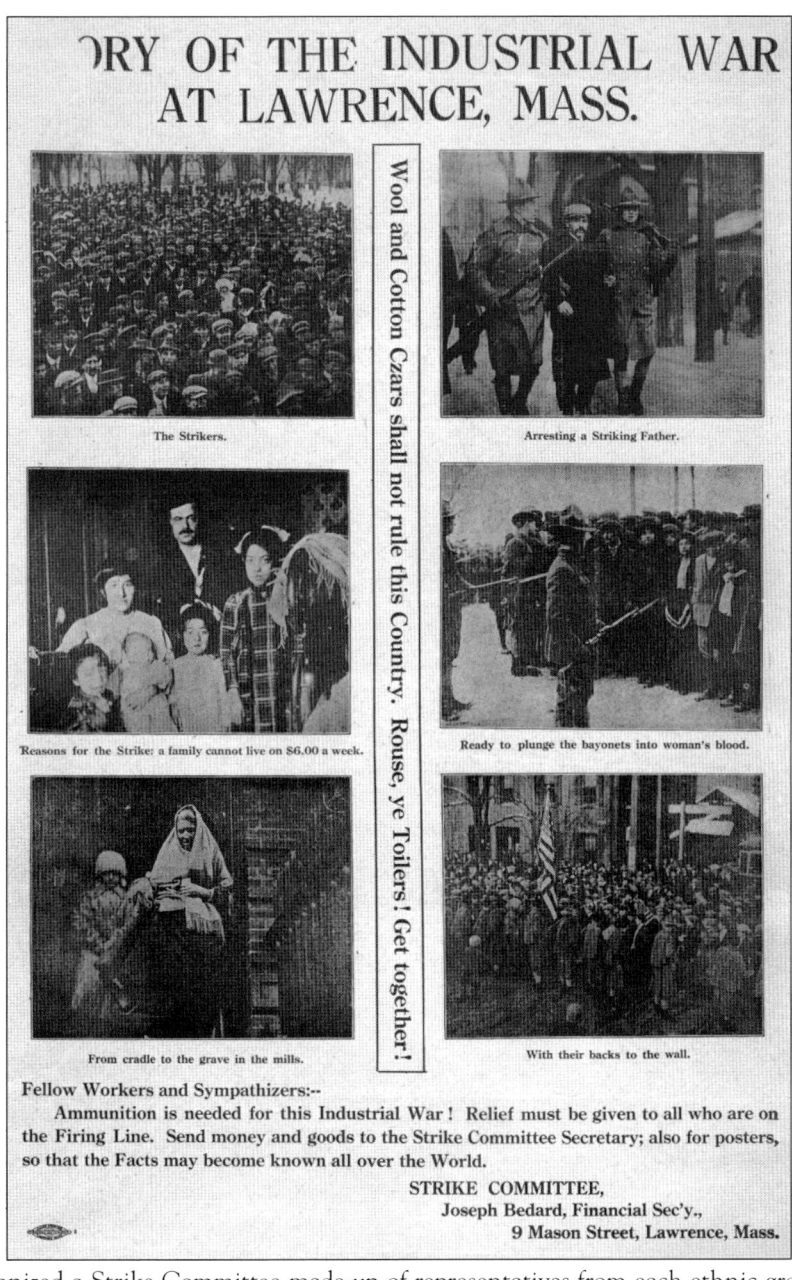

Ettor organized a Strike Committee made up of representatives from each ethnic group in the mills. Called the Committee of Ten, the group included nine Lawrence textile workers and Ettor of the IWW. The group had the responsibility for making certain its strike meetings were translated into numerous languages and for conducting negotiations directly with the American Woolen Company and company president William Wood. Some members of the committee paid a price for their work on behalf of the strike even though the agreement that ended the strike included assurances that there would be no retaliation against strikers. Two were blacklisted and lost their textile jobs in 1914. And the lone female member of the committee, Canadian-born Annie (Steindl) Welzenback, was harassed to the extent that she could no longer find work in Lawrence, and she and her husband left the city.

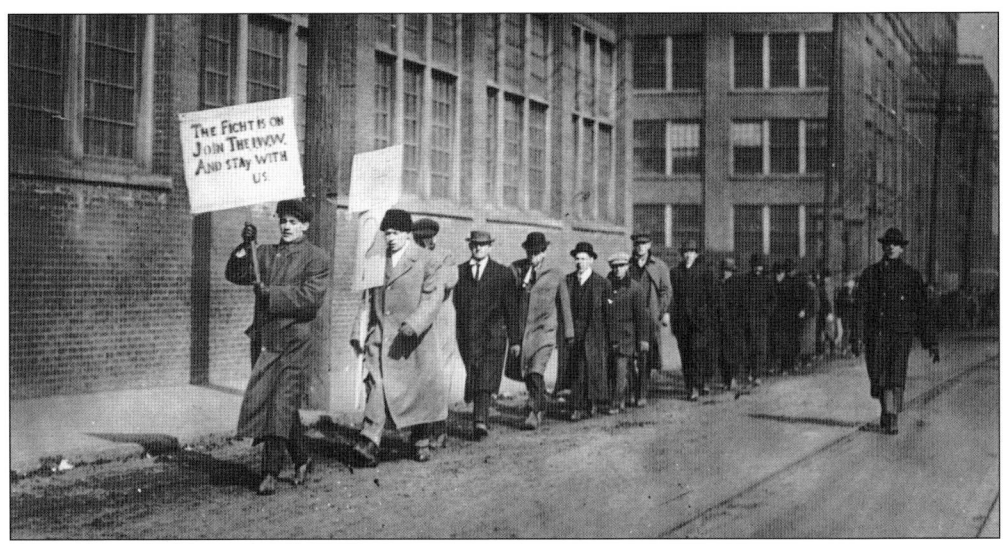

Above, a man in Lawrence carries a sign that reads, "The Fight is on. Join the IWW and Stay with US." Formed in 1905 in Chicago, the IWW was the radical wing of the United States labor movement. The American Federation of Labor, the mainstream of the labor movement, focused on organizing mainly skilled, white, male workers, mostly native-born Americans or men of northern European descent. The IWW organized workers regardless of race, ethnicity, gender, religion, language, or skill level. It is therefore not surprising that Lawrence mill workers invited the IWW to help organize the strike. Seen below is a group of IWW organizers, some of whom were in Lawrence in 1912. They are, from left to right, E. Stobins, Ted Boyd, Pat Lumbar, Thomas Lotta, Adolph Lessig, Bill Haywood, Ewald Koettgen, and Arturo Giovannitti. (Both, courtesy of WSU.)

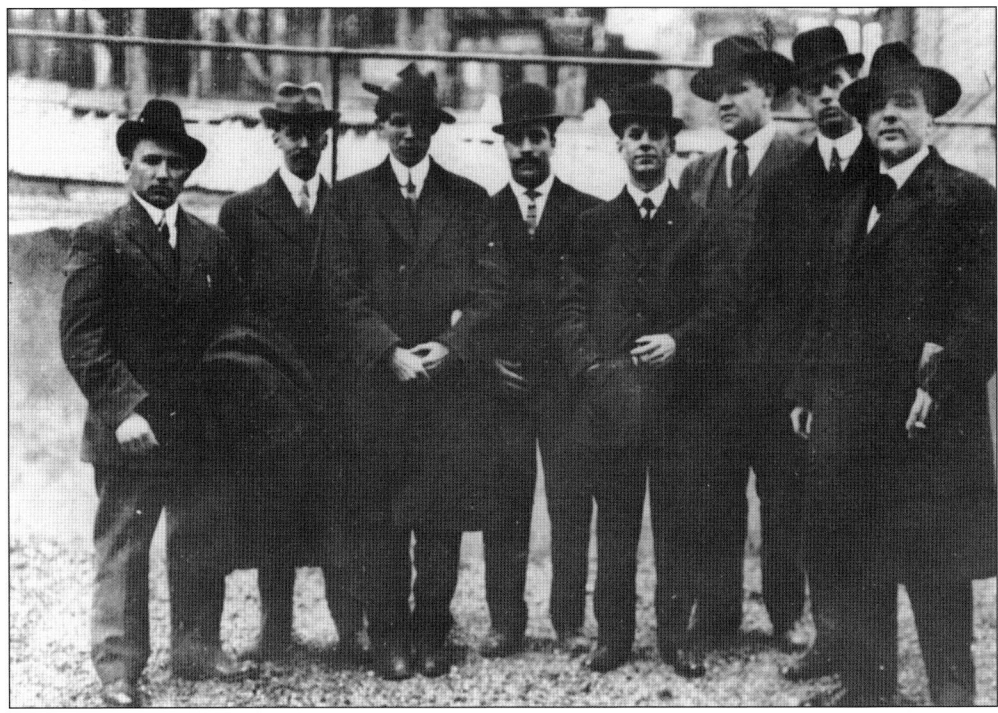

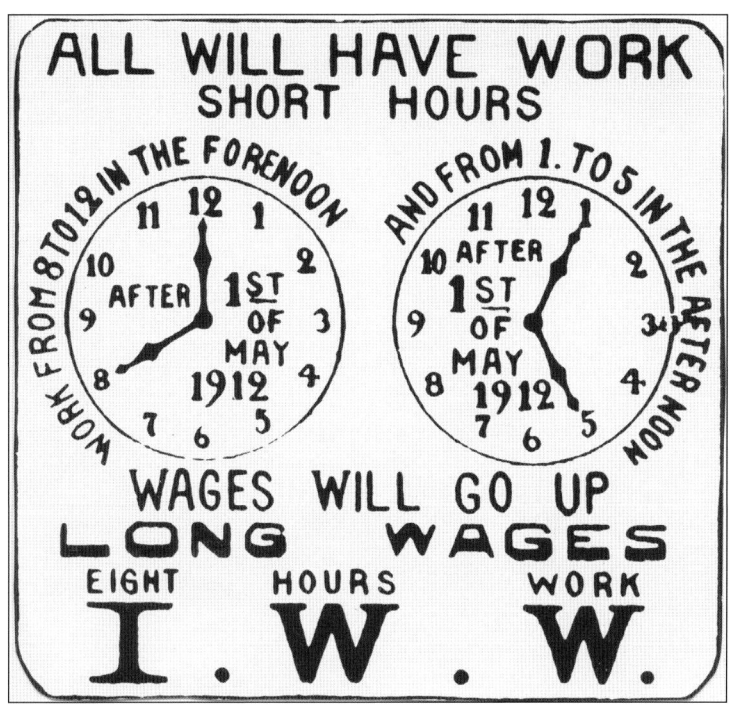

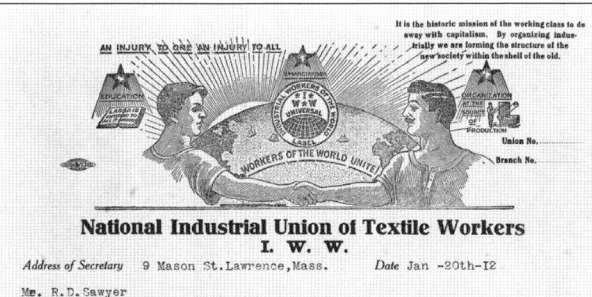

The IWW was a force to be reckoned with in Lawrence during the strike. With over 20 active foreign-language chapters in the city, Lawrence's IWW members had skillfully built the broad-based community organization needed to make the massive strike succeed. Joe Ettor told workers: "You cannot make shoes without shoemakers. Your shoe factories may be ever so well built and stocked. Your machinery may be of the very latest kind. You may have the best brains in the world directing your plant. Still you cannot make shoes. To make shoes requires shoe workers. The shoe workers are the shoe industry, and to them should the whole industry belong." Lawrence's mill workers got the point. At left is a letter from Ettor to Rev. Roland D. Sawyer rejecting arbitration. More about Sawyer and his ongoing role can be found on page 102. (Both, courtesy of UNH.)

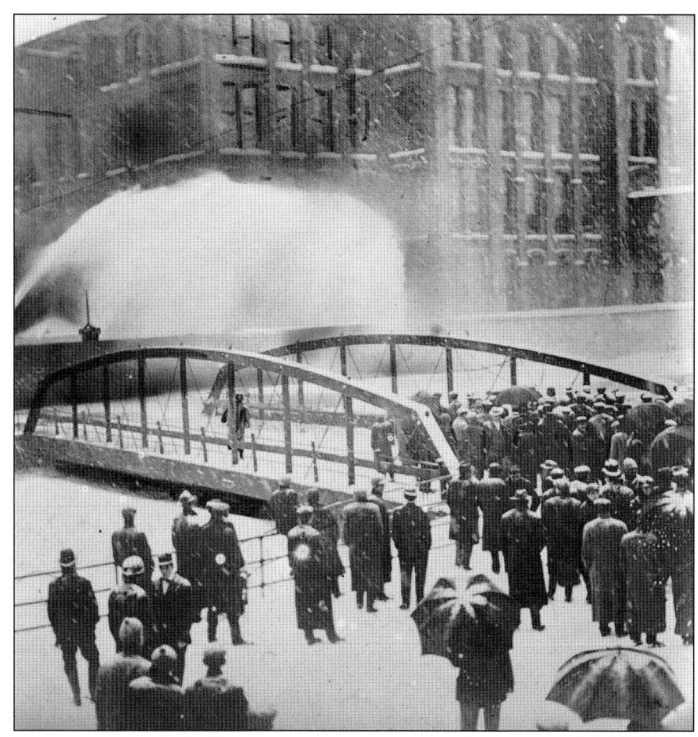

Civil liberties were sharply curtailed during the strike. On January 15, Pacific Mill watchmen turned fire hoses on the strikers. The head of the militia, Col. E. LeRoy Sweetser, stated, "I will allow no mass meeting. I will allow no parades. We are going to look for trouble. We are not looking for peace now." Lawrence mayor Michael Scanlon said, "We will either break this strike or break the strikers' heads." For emphasis, an American Woolen shareholder told *Collier's* reporter Richard Child, "The way to settle this strike is to shoot down 40 or 50 of 'em." (Left, courtesy of UNH.)

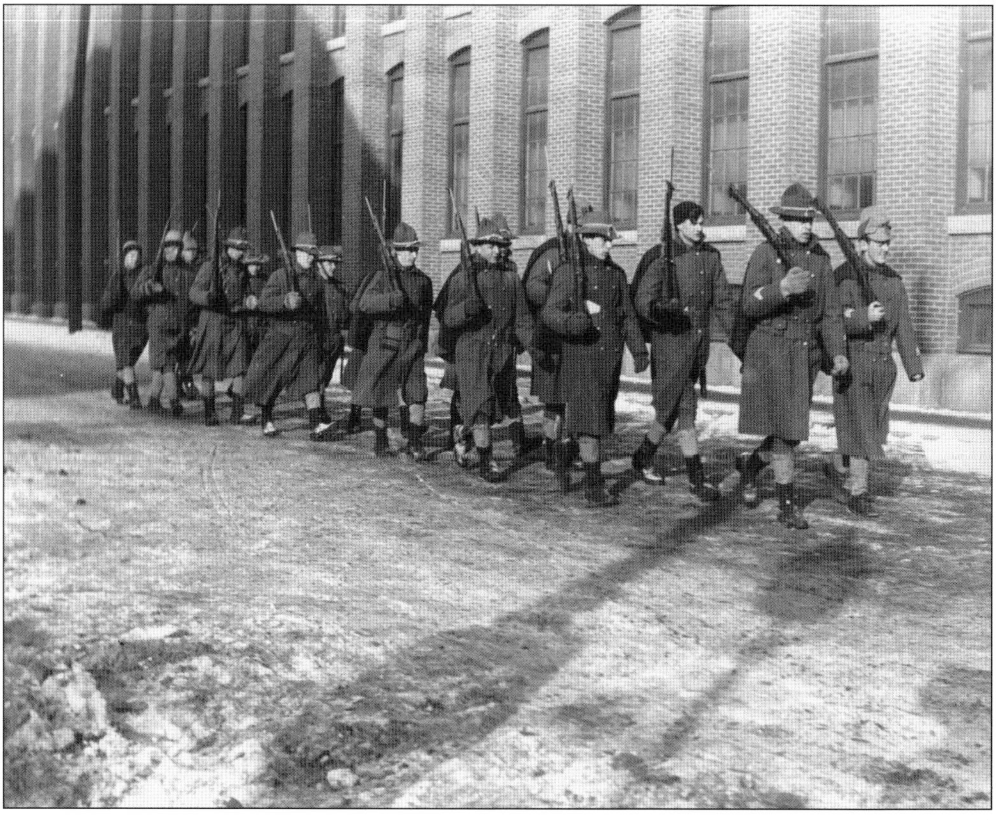

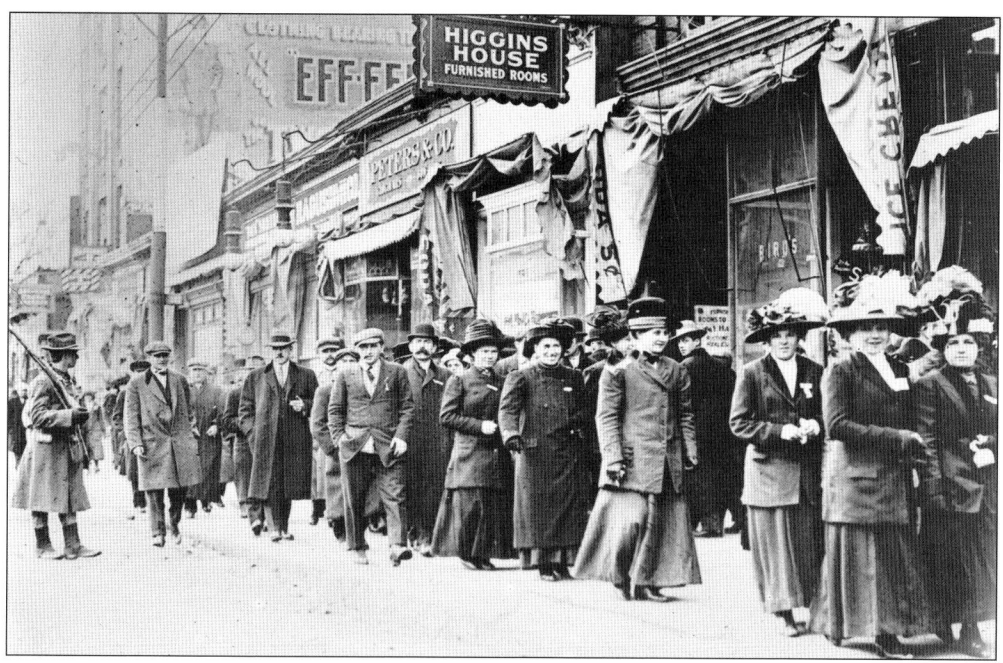

When Lawrence mayor Michael Scanlon called in the state militia, it became difficult for strikers to congregate in front of large mill buildings. Thousands of workers joined singing, chanting picket lines that snaked through the city's commercial and mill districts. In a January 17, 1912, *Lowell Courier-Citizen* article titled "Strikers Issue a Burning Proclamation," strikers were quoted as saying, "We, striking textile workers, who in the past have suffered untold exploitations, outrages and insults, have reached the limit of human resignation and endurance. We had to rebel because we had drained the cup to the very dregs. Our enemies are making an effort to blind the issue by making a cry of 'foreigners, rioters' to which we make reply, we were not considered foreigners when we meekly consented to being robbed of our labors and opportunities." (Above, courtesy of UNH; below, courtesy of LOC.)

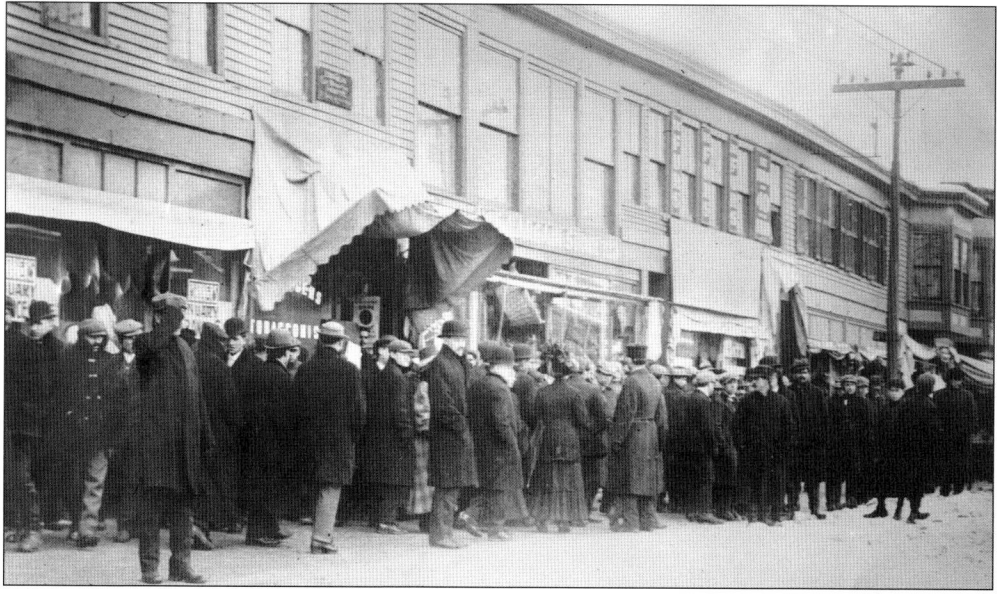

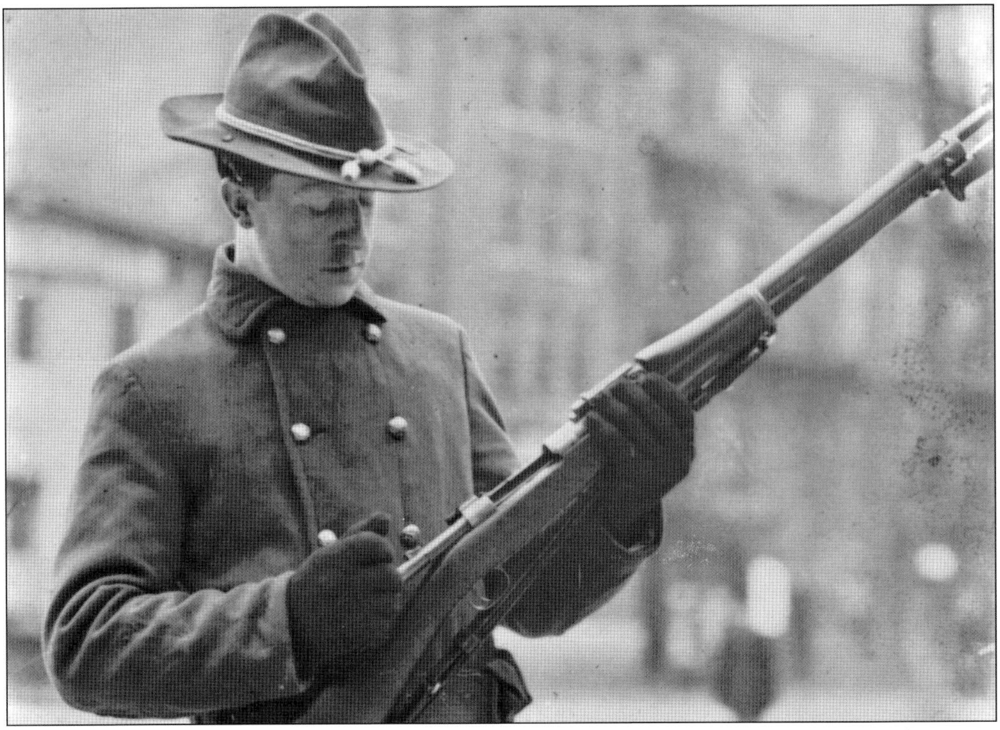

Sent by *Harper's Weekly* to report on the strike, journalist Mary Heaton Vorse wrote of the scene: "All the mills were guarded with troops. Young boys patrolling high brick walls with guns over their shoulders. We looked at each other and we did not speak, but walked on down the cold, pale street, which was so unnaturally quiet and which looked so menacing. It was the first time I'd seen a town where the troops had been called out against the workers; and suddenly Lawrence, a familiar New England town, seemed strange and alien. Everywhere stood the uniformed boys with their guns guarding streets, guarding mills. High brick walls and guns." Above, a member of the militia loads his rifle. Below, young men patrol the mill district. (Above, courtesy of UNH.)

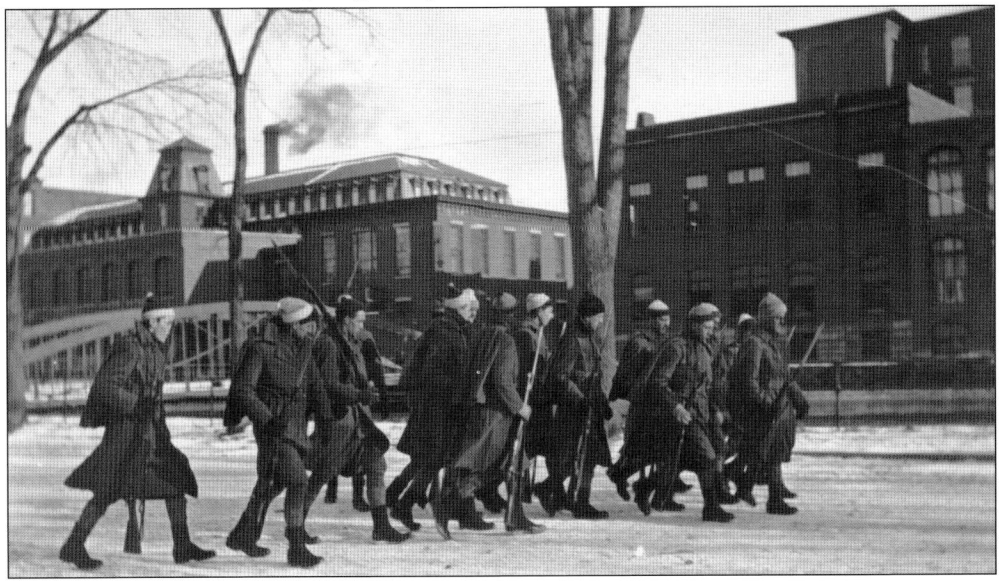

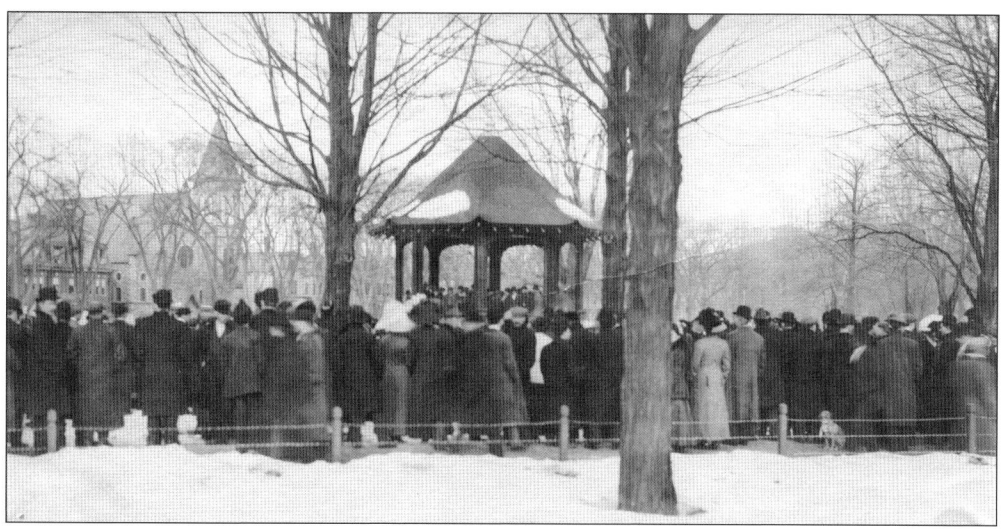

The photograph above shows a diverse gathering of strikers at a meeting on the Lawrence Common on January 23, 1912. On February 10, 1912, the *Outlook*, a weekly New York City magazine, wrote, "There are almost as many nationalities here in Lawrence as there are in your Babel of New York. The workers are American, English, Scotch, Irish, German, French, Flemish, French-Canadian, Polish, Italian, Syrian, Russian, Armenian. I heard speeches in six languages. You might not suspect that a common sentiment could animate these diverse groups and weld them into a fighting unit. Nevertheless they have struck—struck as a single homogenous body." Workers also sang songs in a variety of languages. Seen below is one of the marching bands that played before meetings and in the streets.

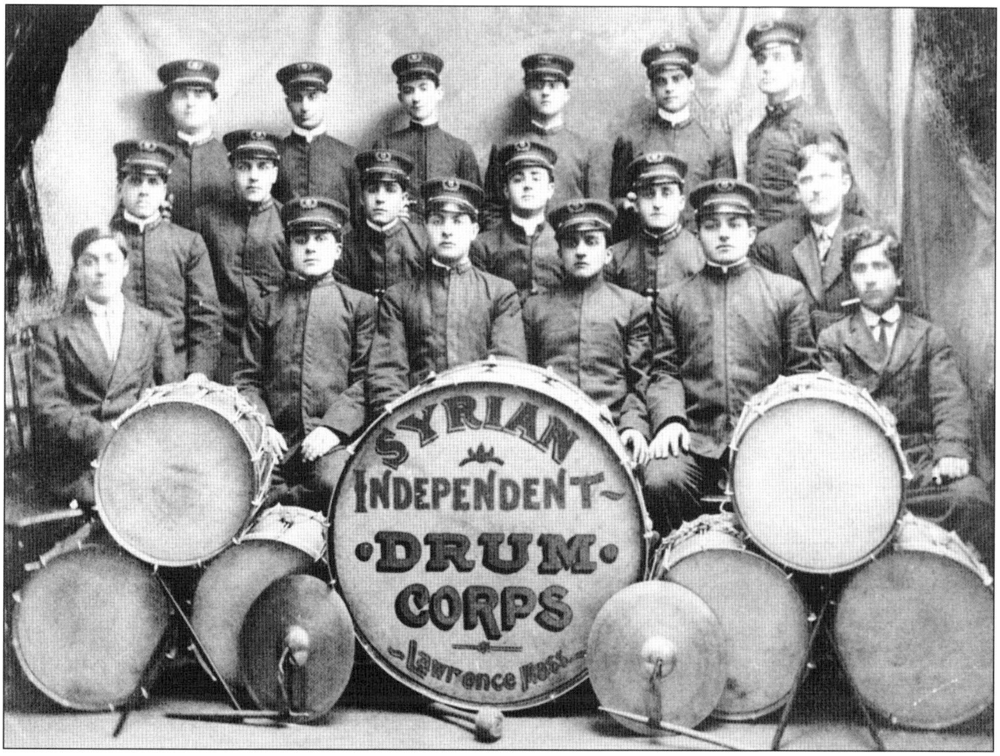

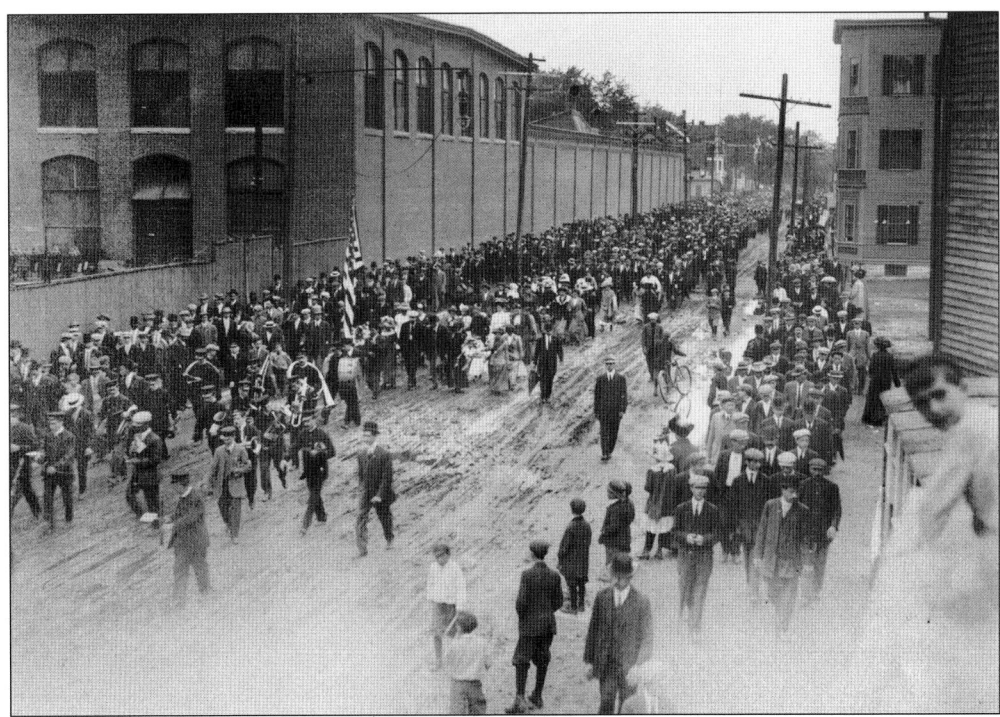

The strike became known as the "singing strike," as demonstrations often included a band. In May 1912, journalist Ray Stannard Baker wrote in the *American Magazine*: "It is the first strike I ever saw which sang. I shall not soon forget the curious lift, the strange sudden fire of the mingled nationalities at the strike meetings when they went into the universal language of song. And, not only in the meetings did they sing, but in the soup houses and in the streets. I saw one group of women strikers who were peeling potatoes at a relief station suddenly break into the swing of 'The Internationale.'" Even the National Guardsmen stationed in Lawrence during the strike gathered for song during their downtime. (Above, courtesy of ATHM; below, courtesy of WSU.)

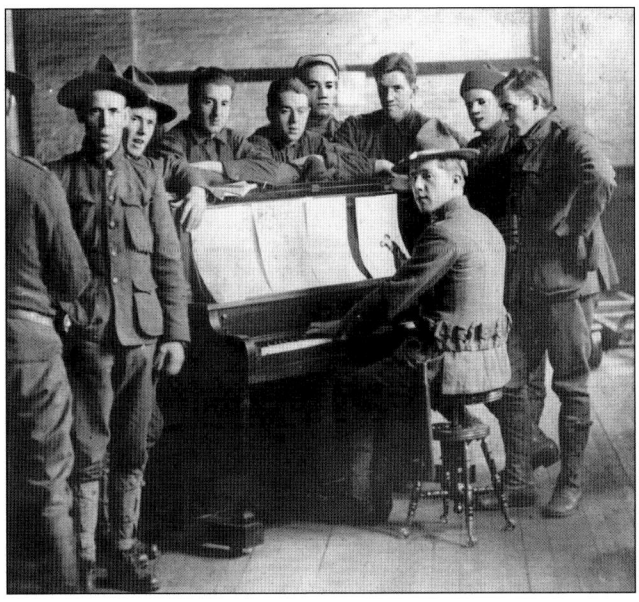

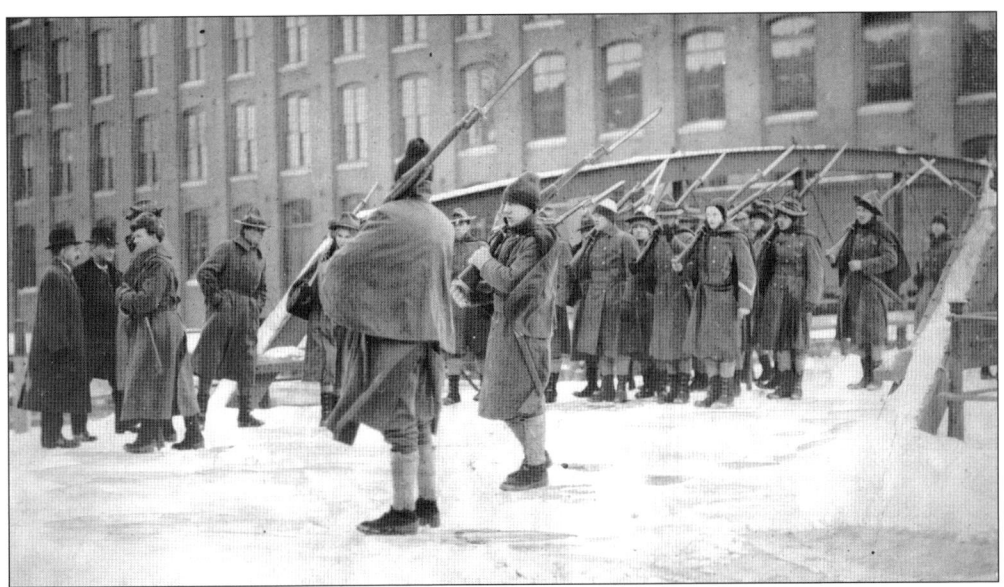

The photograph above shows the changing of the guard at a mill during the strike, which happened every two hours. On January 22, the Strike Committee of the striking textile workers of the American Woolen Company inquired of company president William M. Wood: "We, the committee, would like to know if the militia, the special policemen, and the Pinkerton detectives brought into this city, know anything about the textile industry except to bayonet and club honest workingmen into submission?" Ernest Calderone, a child sent away to Barre, Vermont, during the strike, recalled the time of the strike in his oral history in the Lawrence History Center collection, saying, "I remember seeing the cops beat people on the bridge . . . hit them over the head with a billy on horseback. Oh, I tell you, it was terrible. It was terrible." (Above, courtesy of WSU; below, courtesy of LPL.)

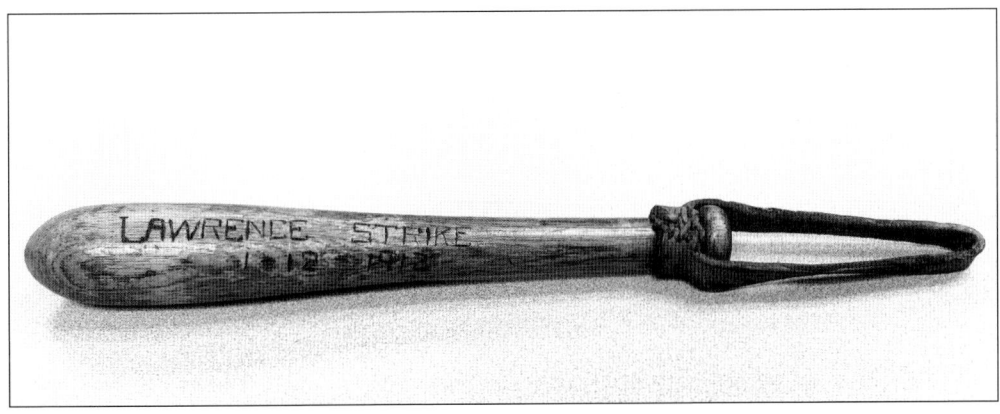

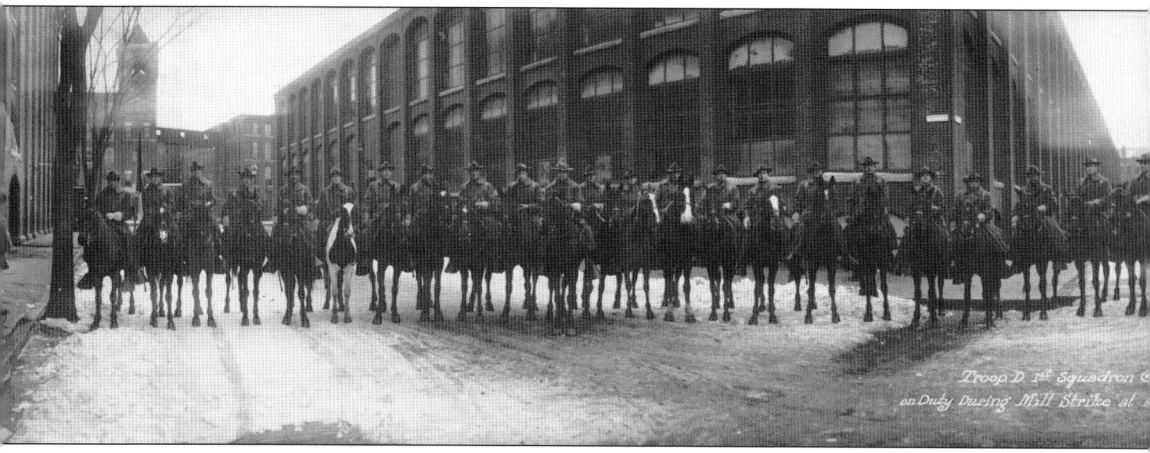

On January 15, 1912, Lawrence mayor Michael Scanlon sent a letter to Capt. Louis Cox, the head of Battery C of the Massachusetts State Militia. Scanlon wrote, "A body of men are acting together and threaten by force to violate the laws of the Commonwealth in our city of Lawrence . . . a tumult is threatened." This *Washington Post* headline from January 16 captured the mood: "Bayonets Awe City: Mill District of Lawrence is Under Martial Law." Headlines from Lawrence

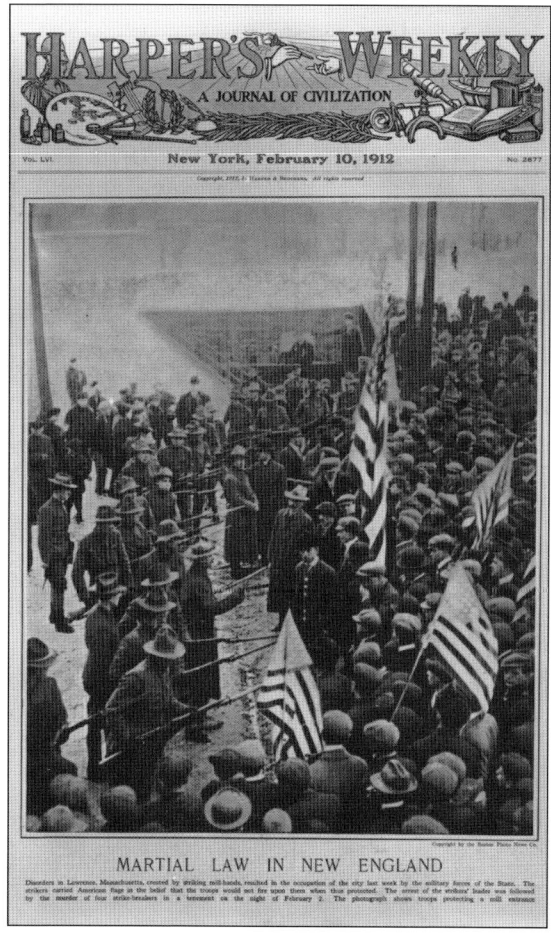

The February 10, 1912, *Harper's Weekly* cover declares "Martial Law in New England."

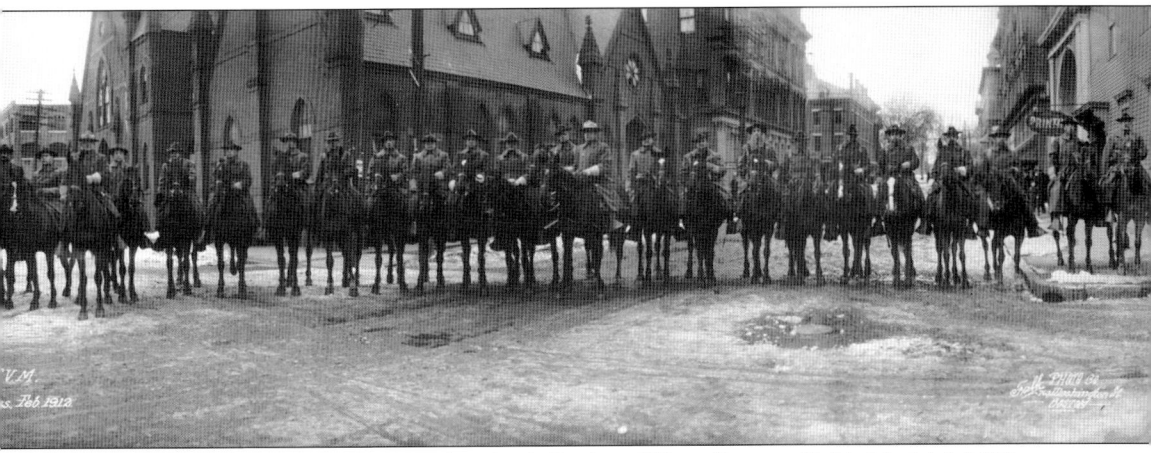

newspapers captured a similar mood: "Heads Broken When Battery Holds Up Mob," "Three Thousand Strikers March on Soldiers," "Bloodshed Narrowly Averted," and "Bayonets Bar Path of Big Parade." Above, Troop D of the 1st Squadron Cavalry is seen at the ready. (Courtesy of Bob Frishman.)

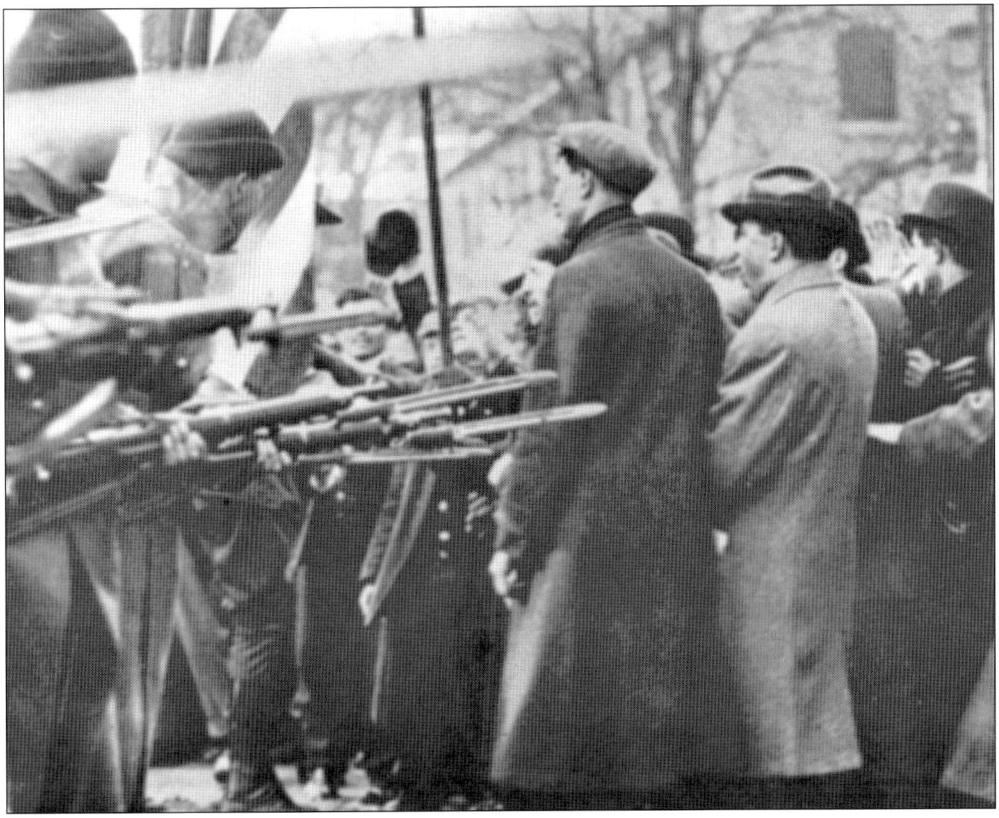

Pictured above is a standoff between the militia and the strikers.

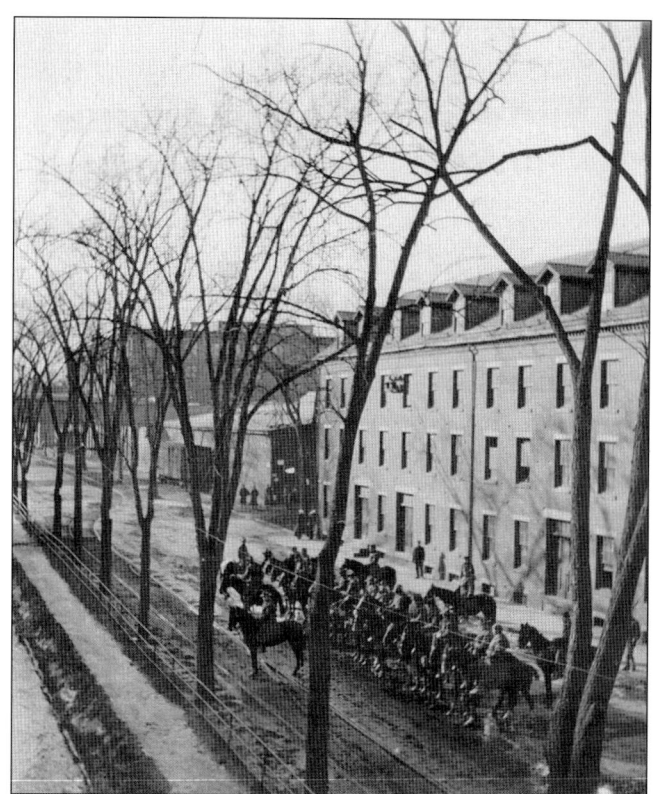

As the strike progressed through January and February, militia patrols requested by Lawrence mayor Michael Scanlon arrived on the streets of the city. The increased militia presence in the city resulted in tense standoffs. Police and militia came from Lowell, Haverhill, Lynn, Newton, Wakefield, Stoneham, Charlestown, Waltham, and Boston and even from Harvard University. Harvard students who volunteered were let out of their mid-year examinations to gallop on horseback down Essex and Common Streets (left). A troop of Boston Metropolitan Police and a number of sharpshooters from the US Marine Corps were present as well. Below is a *New York Call* cartoon spoofing the Harvard students' role in the militia. (Left, courtesy of ATHM; below, courtesy of UNH.)

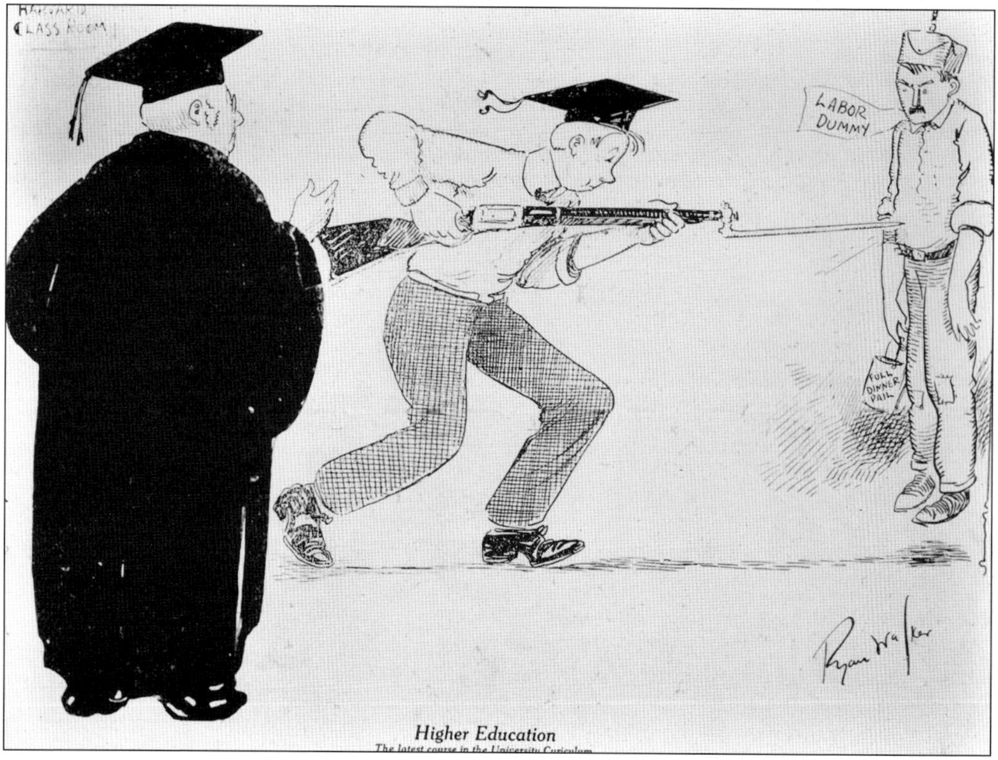

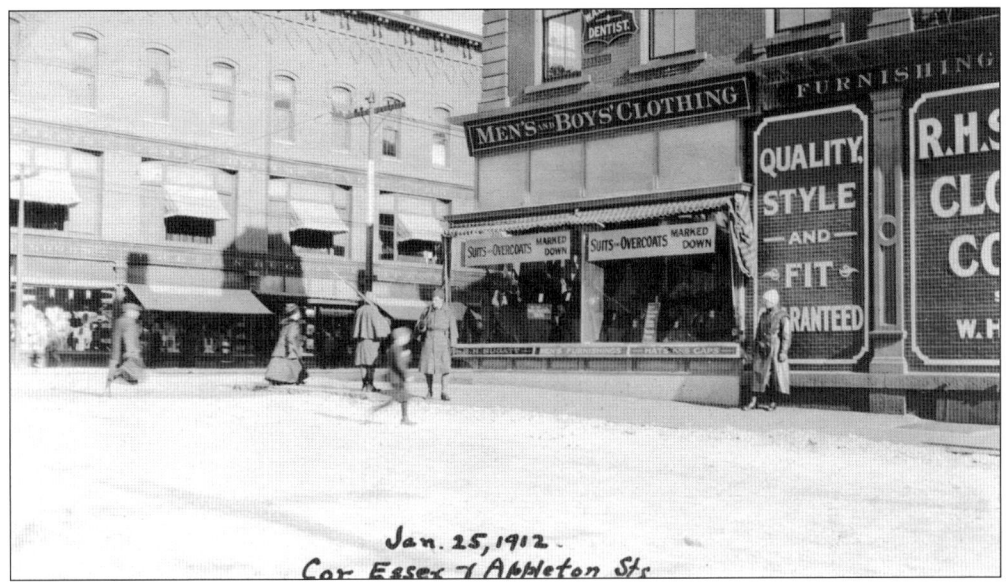

Jan. 25, 1912.
Cor Essex & Appleton Sts

Days into the strike, civil liberties were suspended, strikers were tossed in jail on the flimsiest of charges, and scores of militia on foot and on horseback tried intimidating strikers. The *Outlook*, a weekly magazine published in New York City, reported regularly on the strike. The February 10, 1912, issue included the following: "The impression of Lawrence which I gained during my first evening was that of a besieged city. The militia armed with guns and bayonets, guarded the streets and bridges in the mill district and challenged all comers. The hulking factories, with their massive gates and iron doors, appeared in the semi-darkness like fortresses, and along the face of these mills there played a strange, trembling light from the search lanterns opposite."

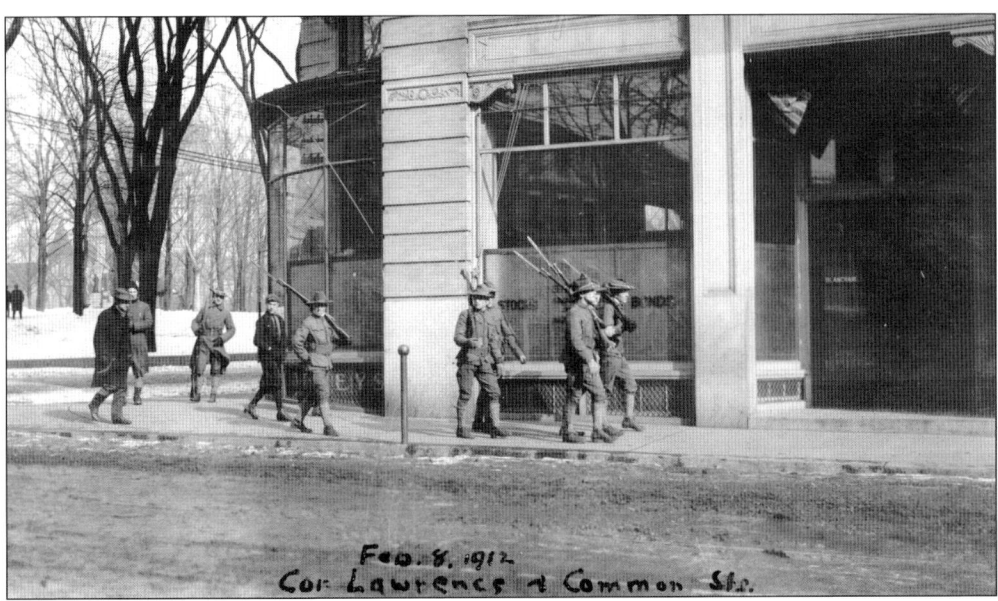

Feb. 8, 1912
Cor Lawrence & Common Sts.

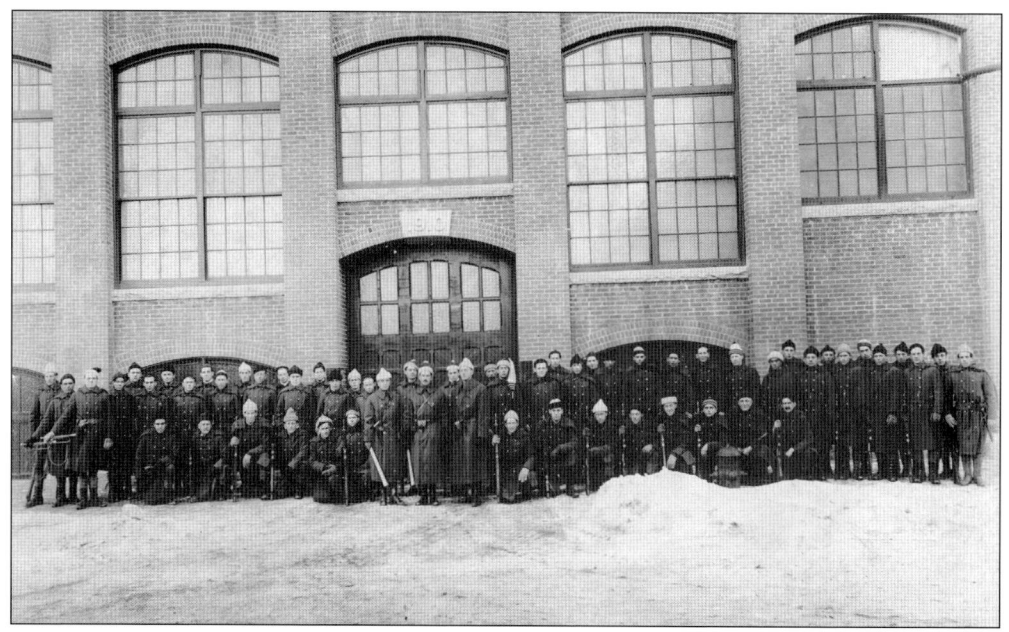

Early on in the strike, the *Lowell Courier-Citizen* carried the headline "More Troops Ordered to Report at Lawrence." The troops were called after English-speaking operatives voted to join the strike. Mill owners who once banked on divisions between native-born workers, second-generation workers, and recent immigrant workers urged Lawrence's mayor and the governor to mobilize the state militia to protect their mills. The city's police force, supplemented by the militia, became quite aggressive. According to one news report, "Squads of police tonight are patrolling the streets in the mill district, guarding the property. For more than three hours today police fought Italian strikers who left their places in the mills of the American Woolen Company." Yet, even this impressive show of force—troops on horseback in tight marching formations with bayonets at the ready—failed to shake the solid strike organization across the city's immigrant neighborhoods, as organization and solidarity bested money and muscle. (Both, courtesy of ATHM.)

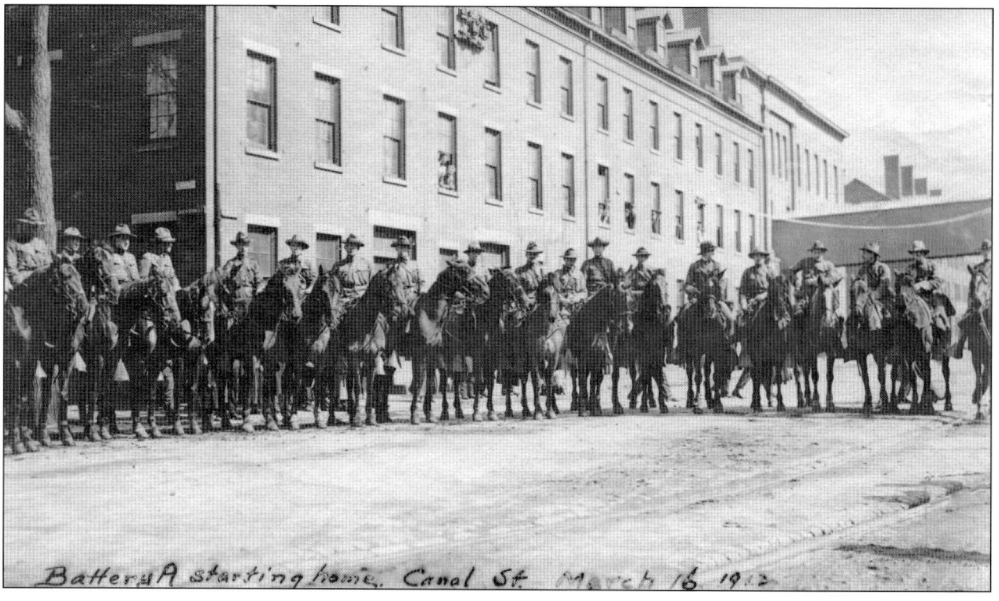

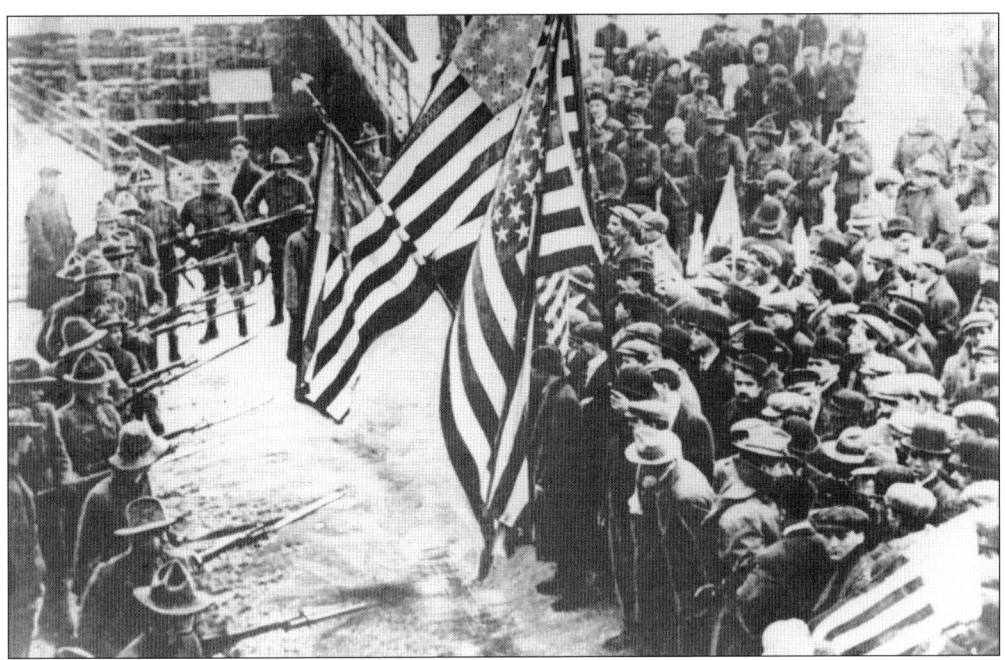

Newspaper articles during the 1912 strike reveal that the militia pushed strikers along the streets of Lawrence with fixed bayonets. The caption "Monster Parade of Strikers" appeared in the *Lowell Courier-Citizen* on January 19. Noting the irony, a reporter wrote that several times each day confused-looking militia units stopped their own marching and saluted as a loud group of strikers approached waving American flags. These street confrontations were a constant throughout the walkout, with hundreds of workers arrested for defying a ban on meetings of three or more strikers on city streets. In the face of horses, rifles, and bayonets, workers perfected the fine art of the moving picket line. Mill owners had the money and the support of the state militia, seen in these photographs, while neighbors, workers, and progressives around the world supported the strikers.

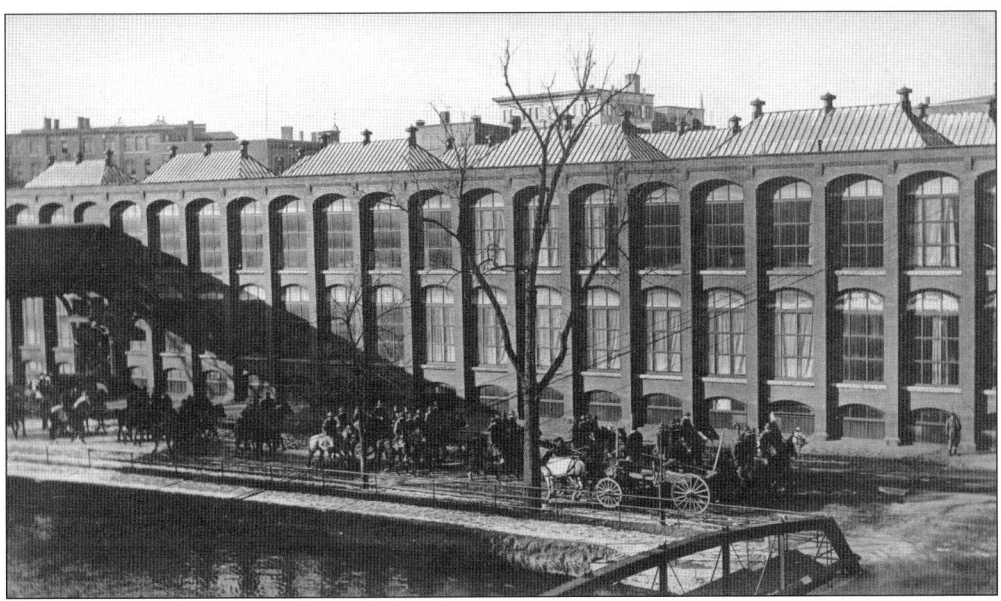

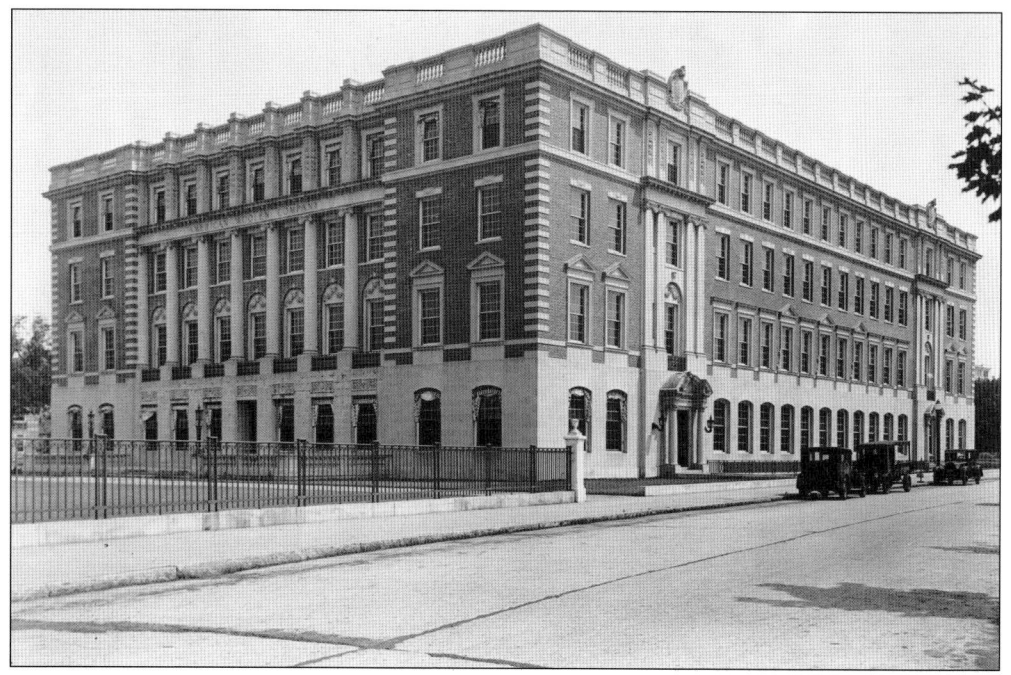

American Woolen Company was established in 1899 under the leadership of William M. Wood and his father-in-law, Frederick Ayer, through the consolidation of eight financially troubled New England woolen mills. By the 1920s, they owned and operated 60 woolen mills across New England. Their executive offices in neighboring Andover are pictured here.

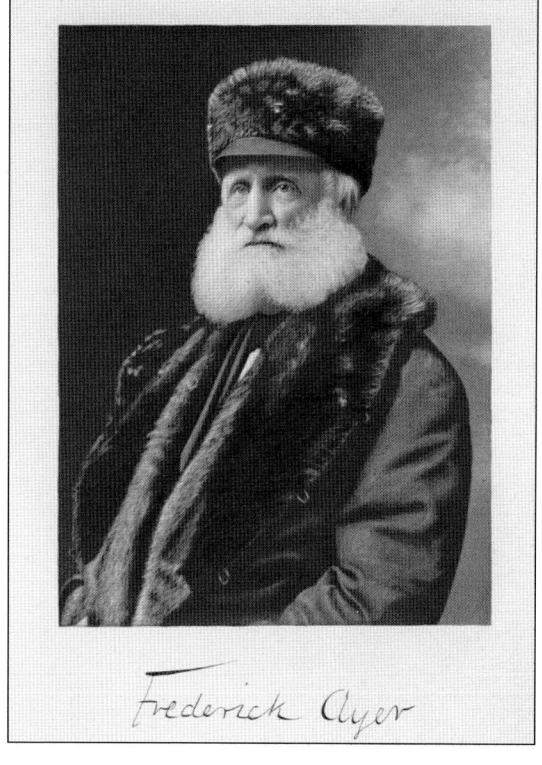

When Frederick Ayer (1822–1918), an American businessman and the younger brother of patent-medicine tycoon Dr. James Cook Ayer, purchased the Washington Mill, he hired his son-in-law William M. Wood to run it. Wood had already turned around a bankrupt mill in Fall River. With Ayer's financial backing, Wood brought together underperforming mills to reduce competition and increase prices for his products. Ayer also owned the Tremont and Suffolk mills in nearby Lowell.

William M. Wood was born in 1858 in Edgartown, Massachusetts, on the island of Martha's Vineyard. His parents, Grace (Emma) Wood and William Wood Sr., were Portuguese immigrants from the Azores. Wood Sr., a crewman on a New Bedford whaling ship, died from consumption in 1871. The younger Wood was 12 years old when his father died, and he dropped out of school to provide for his mother and younger siblings. In 1923, he told a reporter from the *American Magazine*, "I started to work. That was where my good fortune began. Work is whatever you make it: hardship or happiness, a punishment or a pleasure. I have worked practically all my life and I love it. A man who doesn't work not only shirks his duty but misses the greatest satisfaction."

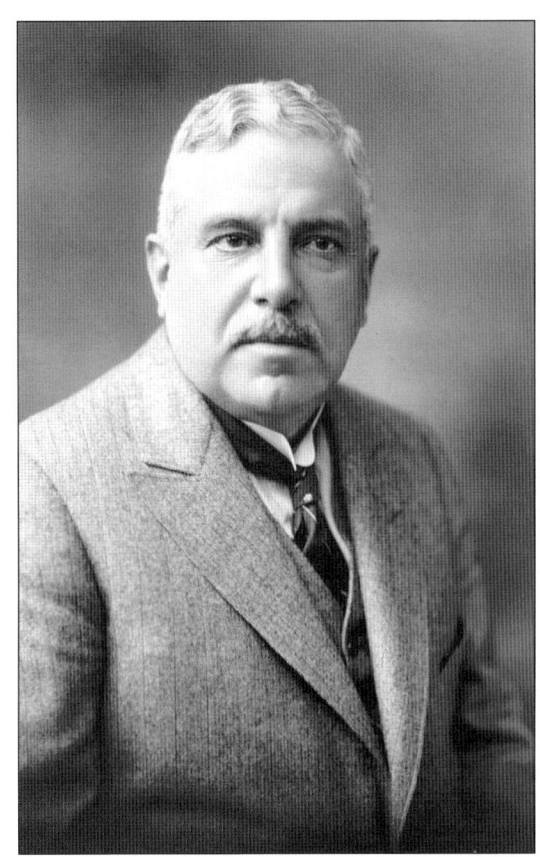

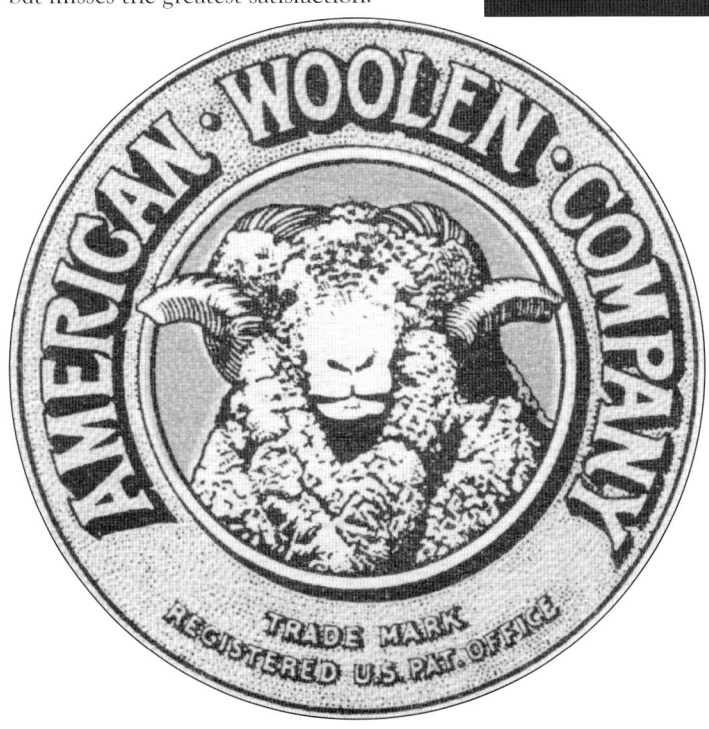

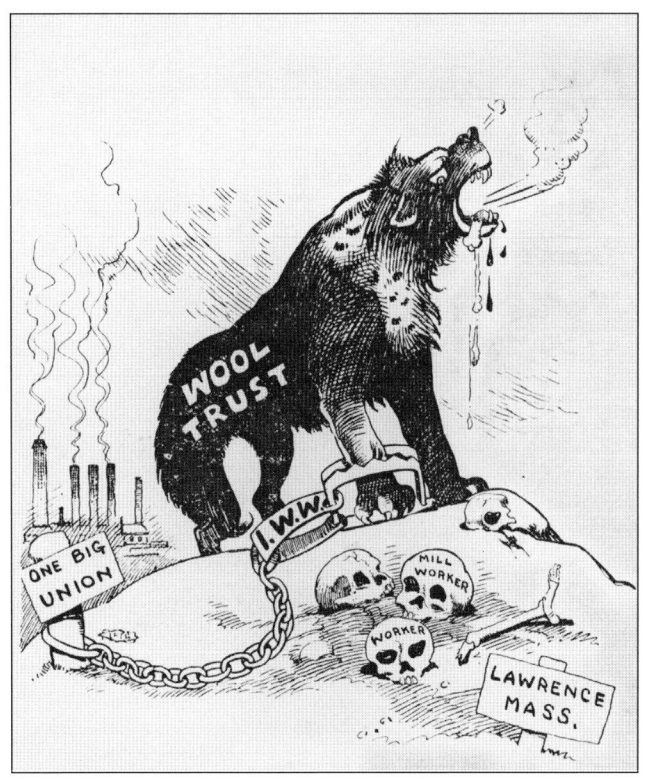

William Wood wrote a public letter to workers that was released on January 19. In it, he wrote that the strike was a total surprise to him and that a raise was not possible because the company could not afford it. "I am an employee of the company as you are," he said. But he enjoyed all the trappings of the wealth produced in his mill. In response, a letter by the Strike Committee to Wood on January 22 read, in part, "You must bear in mind the fact that these men, women, and children have not gone on strike for light or transient causes, but because they no longer could bear up under the burdens laid upon their shoulders." The illustration depicts the Wool Trust as a beast caught in a trap set by the IWW. Pictured below is a female worker in the Wood Mill. (Left, courtesy of WSU.)

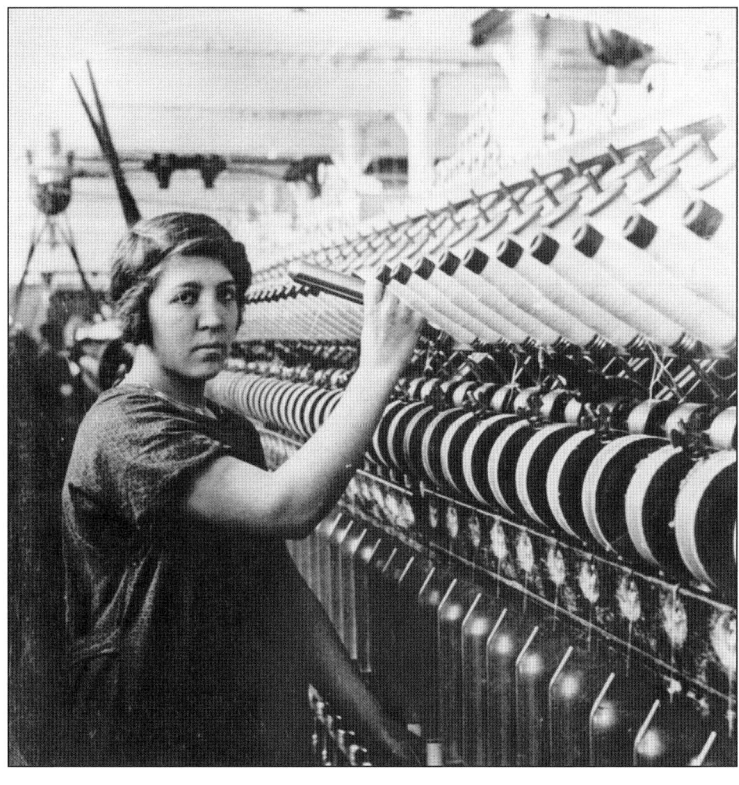

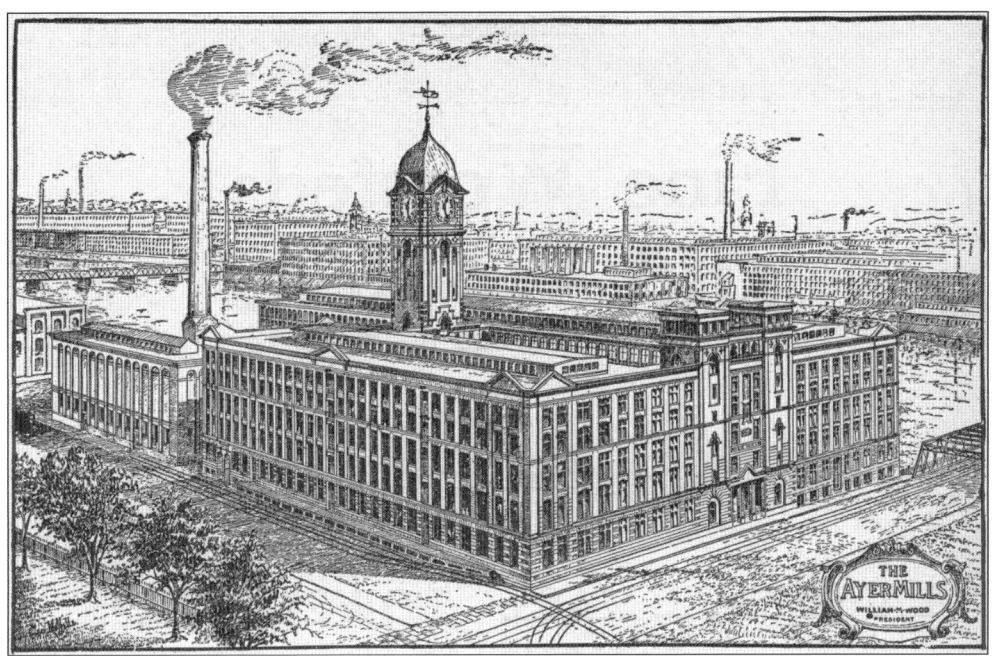

The full weight of the American Woolen Company was arrayed against the Lawrence strikers. When the new $3.5 million Wood Mill opened in 1905, it was the largest mill in the world. It had two parallel wings, each just over 1,900 feet long. Inside were 16 miles of aisles with nearly 1,500 state-of-the-art power looms. The mill employed 5,000 hands, while the Ayer Mill employed 3,500 workers. American Woolen's products were protected by a high tariff that made foreign woven goods more expensive when they came into the United States. According to Bruce Watson, "the Wood Mill was to textiles what Pittsburgh was to steel—the very symbol of consolidation and power."

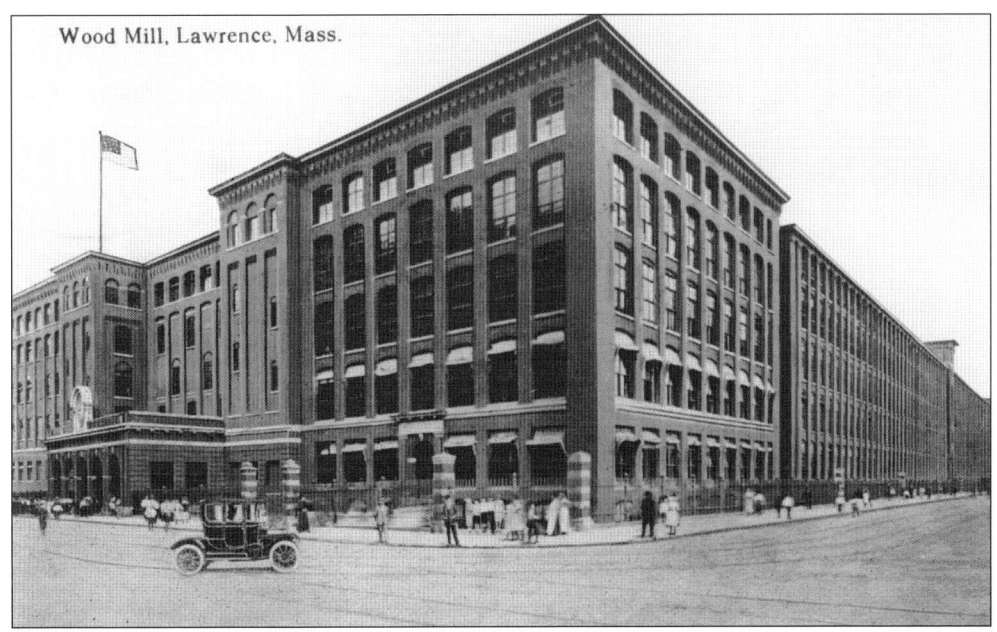

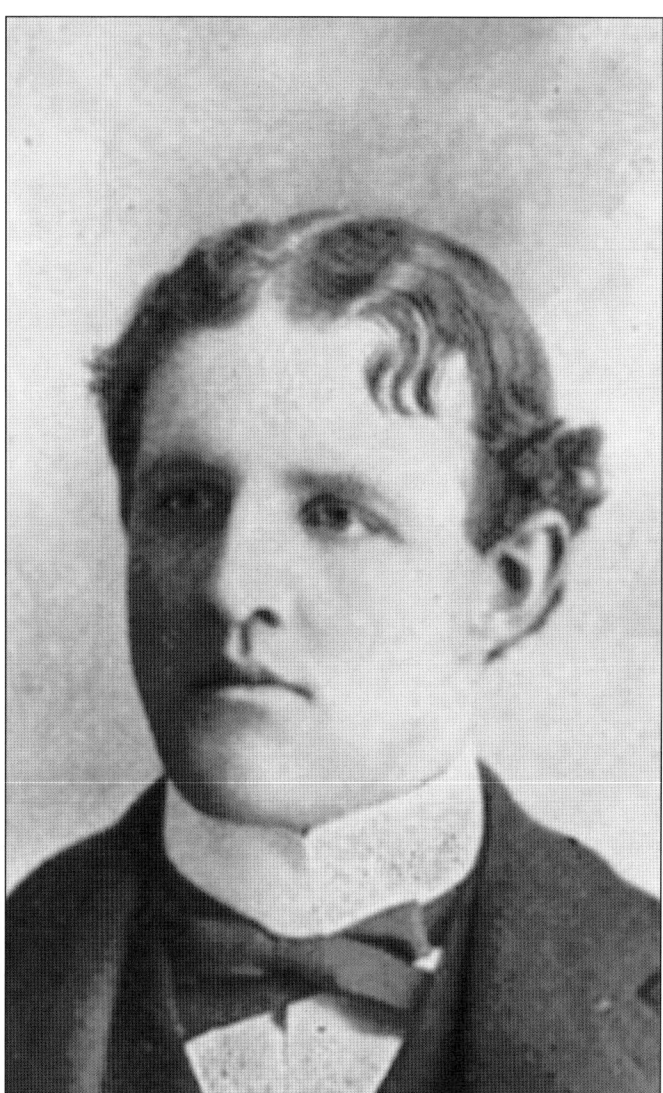

On January 20, police discovered dynamite planted in three popular meeting locations to discredit strikers, including in Urbano Di Prato First Class Shoe Repair. Undertaker John Breen Jr. (left), the son of Lawrence's first Irish American mayor, who was an ex-alderman and a current school committee member, was arrested on Monday, January 29, 1912, and accused of planting the dynamite. Upon the initial discovery of the explosives, strikers were arrested; however, they were exonerated when police learned that the newspaper used to wrap the dynamite was a popular undertakers' trade journal with Breen's name on the subscription label. Released on bail, he was later tried and convicted of planting the dynamite and fined $500. Strikers learned later that Breen was an underling in an intricate conspiracy with ties to William Wood, who was, however, eventually acquitted of any wrongdoing on June 6, 1913.

John Breen, Undertaker
INCORPORATED
Automobile Service Day or Night
Carriages for Christenings, Weddings and Funerals
371 Oak Street, Corner Hampshire Street, Lawrence, Mass.
TELEPHONE 1220

At right is an exterior view of Urbano Di Prato First Class Shoe Repair in Lawrence. Dynamite was likely planted in the shoe repair shop because it shared a doorway with Colombo's print shop (below), where the IWW's Joseph Ettor received his mail, where strike literature was printed in many languages, and where occasional worker meetings were held. A Catholic newspaper, the *Brooklyn Tablet*, reported that Ettor kept the peace by telling workers to keep their hands in their pockets while on the picket line. "He had a personality that was winning in its way. He spoke English and Italian fluently. He soon had all the active spirits in the strike believing in him absolutely." (Both, courtesy of WSU.)

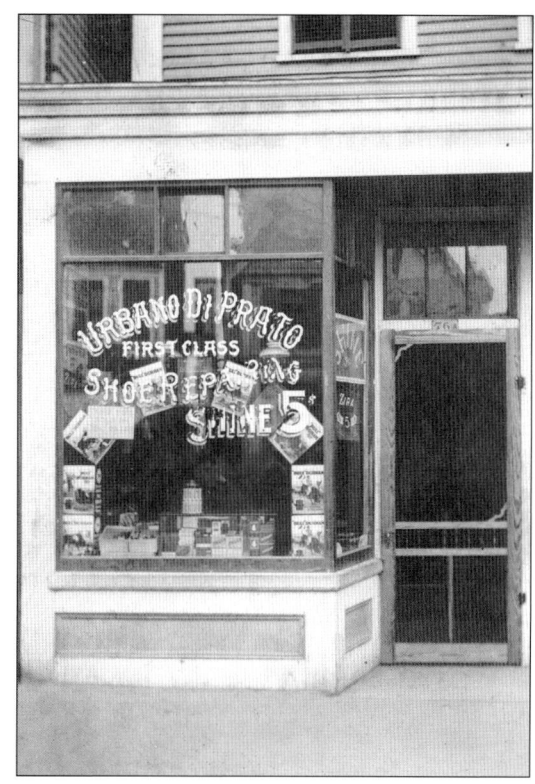

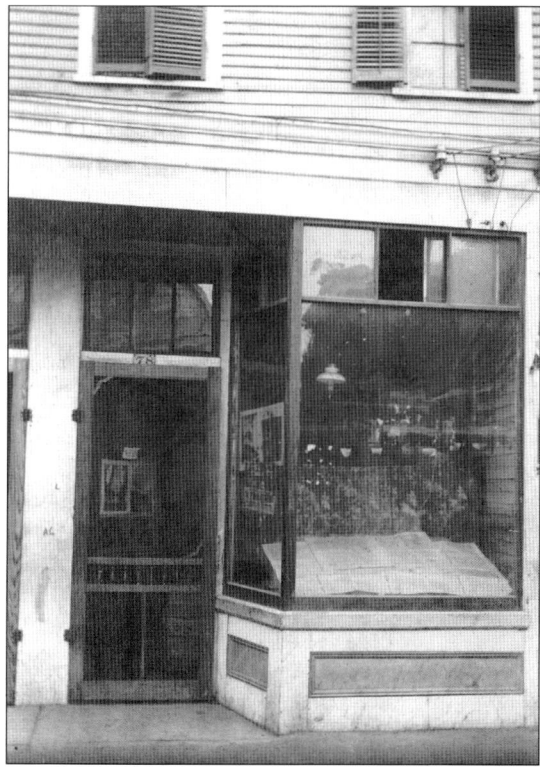

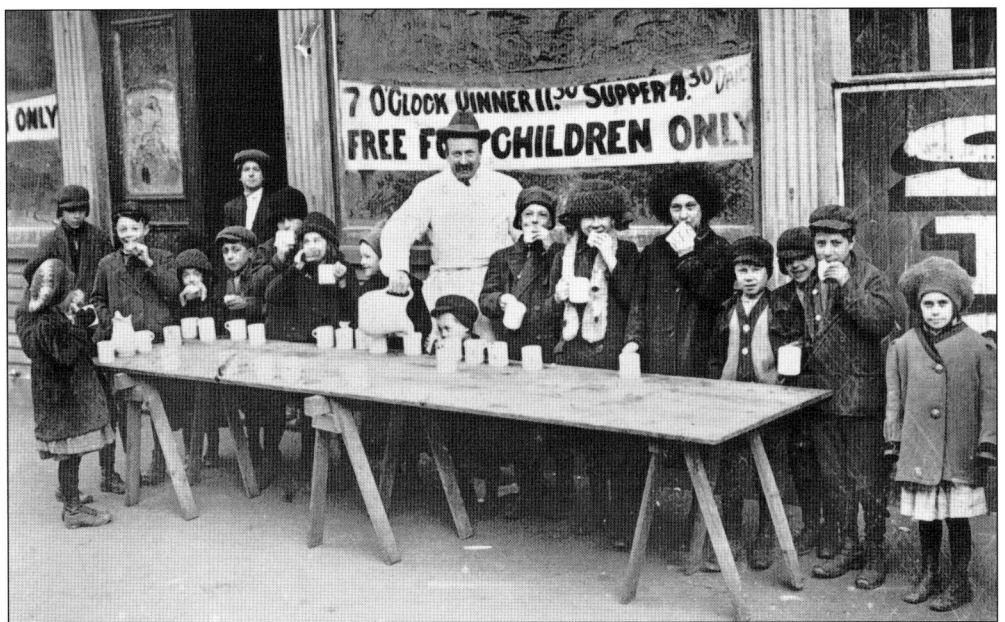

Realizing that a wage cut at the start of 1912 was probable, multiethnic community support networks were set up in late 1911. On January 23, relief stations opened to serve the strikers' children, feeding them as the larger community unified to support the walkout. Material support was also received from surrounding towns. Elizabeth Gurley Flynn, an IWW organizer who spent considerable time in Lawrence during the walkout, noted in her autobiography that "the workers of Lowell, a nearby textile town, led a cow garlanded with leaves, to the strikers of Lawrence. I felt sorry for her with her festive appearance and her mild eyes. But she had to be slaughtered to feed hungry children. Her head was mounted and hung up in the Franco-Belgian Hall." (Both, courtesy of UNH.)

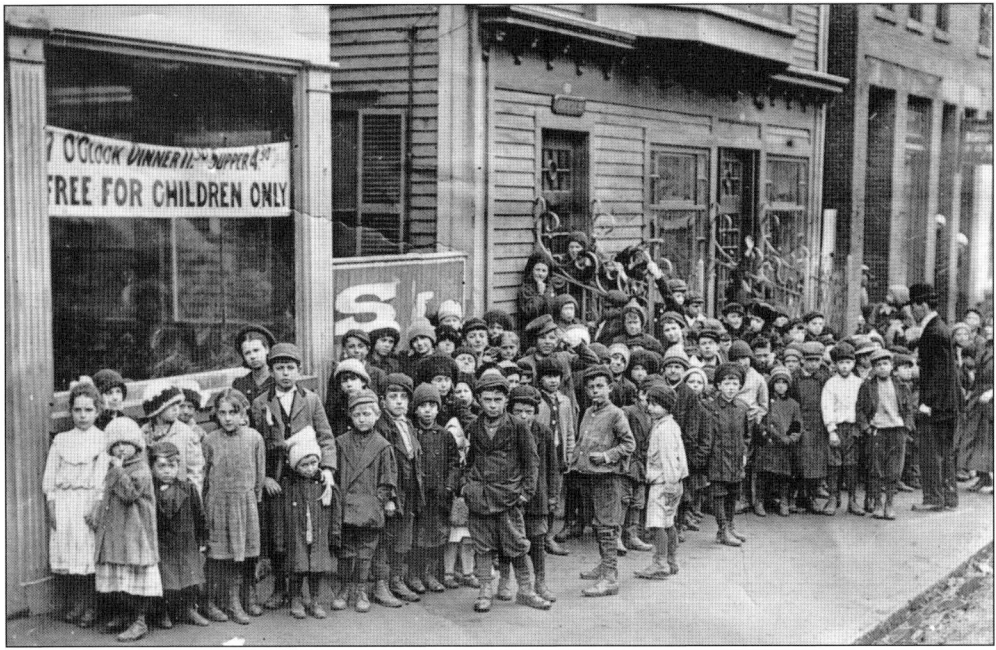

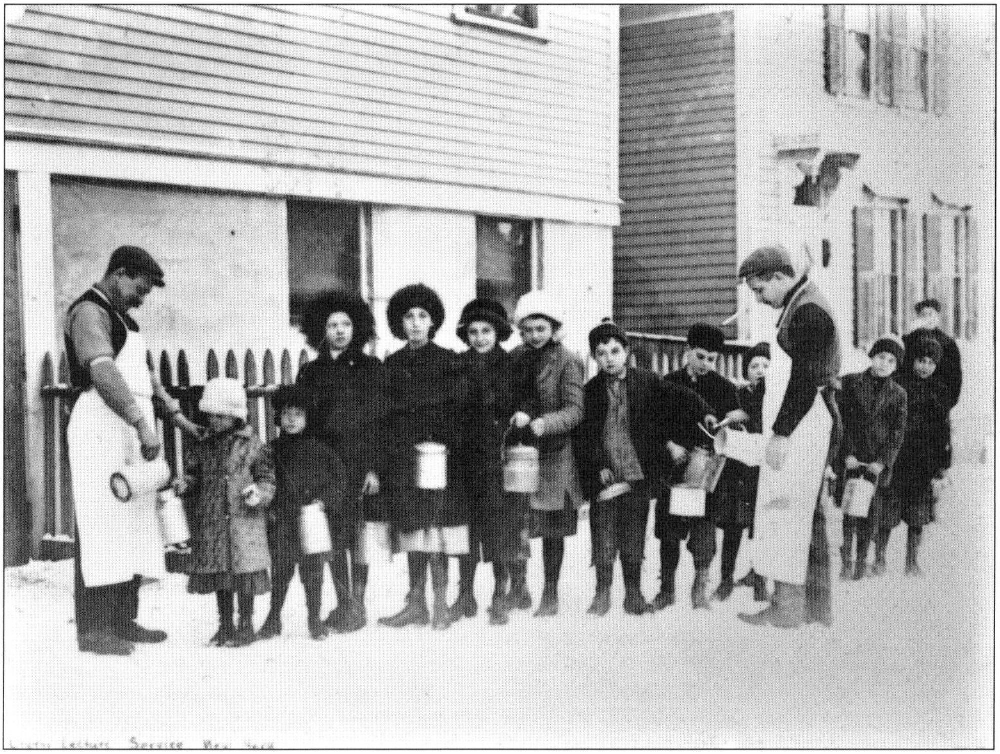

Above, children stand in line at the Franco-Belgian Hall awaiting much-needed nourishment. Franco-Belgians had a cooperative in place and relationships with area farmers; using their contacts, they helped feed thousands. The soup kitchen run by the cooperative opened on January 22 and fed 1,300 workers twice a day regardless of nationality. During the strike, the hall fulfilled its role as a support system for the IWW and became the general strike headquarters, provided meeting places for Finnish, Lithuanian, and Russian workers. According to Janelle Bourgeoise, accounts of the strike recognized that "there is something substantial about the primitive custom of meeting in the presence of food to thresh out social questions." There, "workers met to discuss their problems and to obtain renewed courage." (Above, courtesy of UNH.)

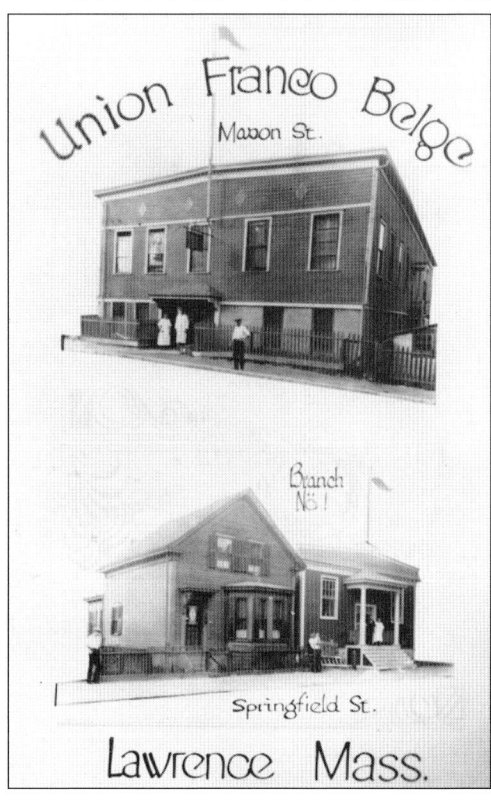

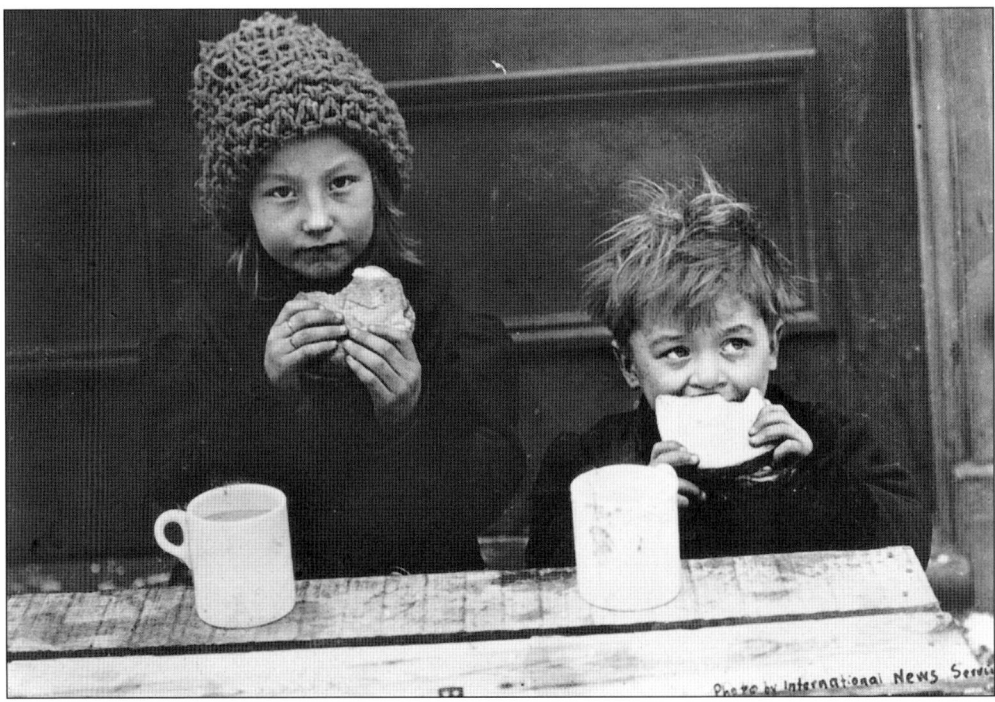

Soup kitchens and cooperatives like the one at the Franco-Belgian Hall served thousands of Italian, Russian, Jewish, Irish, Syrian, Greek, German, Polish, and Franco-Belgian families. According to "Syndicat et Coopérative" in *L'Union des Travailleurs* on December 22, 1910, the roll of cooperatives in workers' struggles was as follows: "The Union is the place of combat. For us, the cooperative should be a financial and moral support. Its value in this role is incontestable and the worker's party of the old world owes to it a great part of its power." The children above and below were malnourished and in dire need of sustenance, as living conditions worsened during the strike. (Both, courtesy of UNH.)

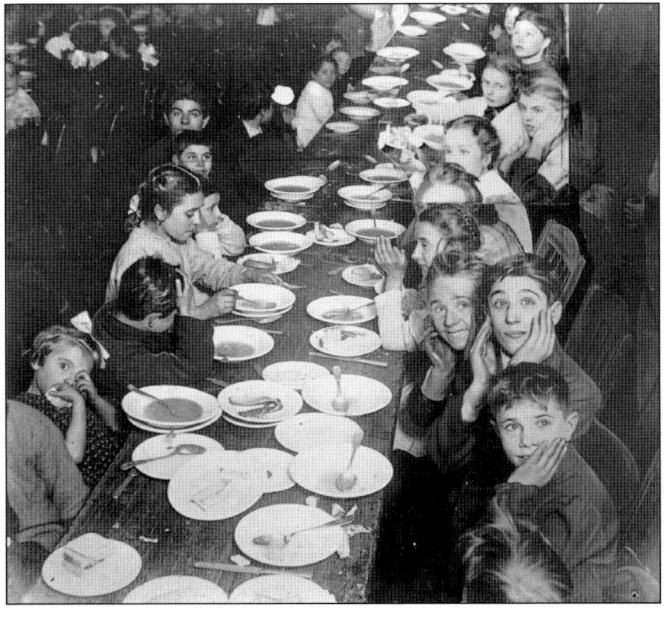

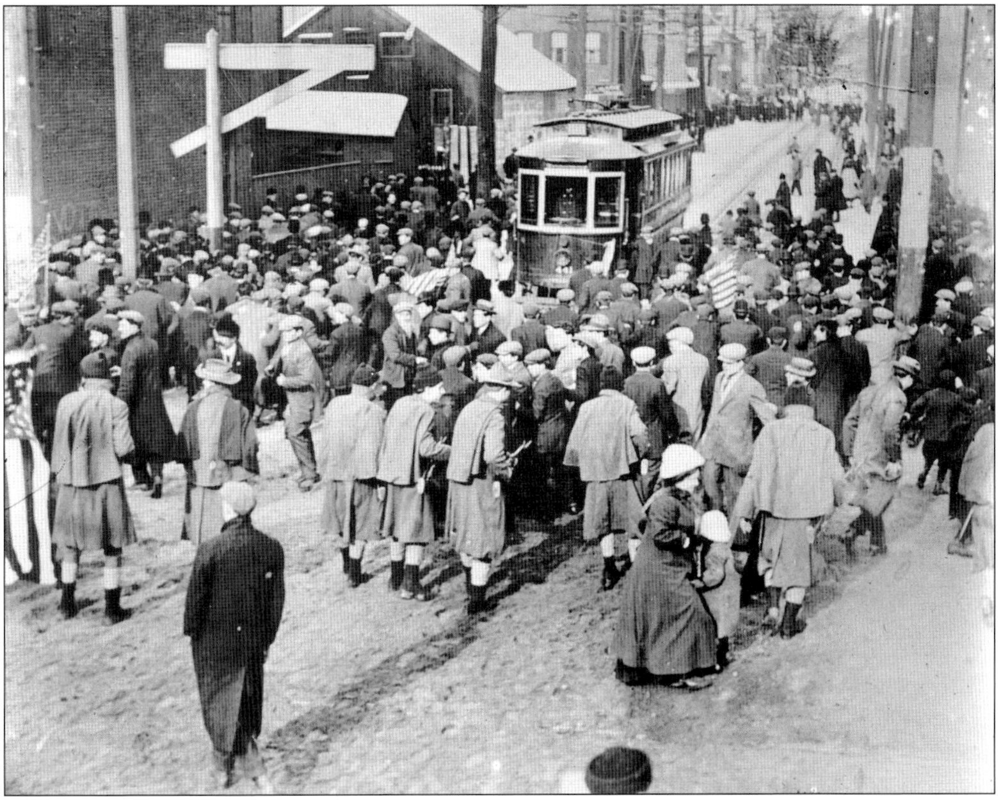

The last week of January turned violent and chaotic. On January 29, strikers gathered early in the morning and sought to keep the streetcars running along Broadway Street toward Essex Street from delivering people to work. Newspaper accounts indicate that snowballs, ice, and stones were hurled at a trolley. All that morning, skirmishes broke out between strikers and anyone they believed was trying to get into the mills. Soon, some strike leaders blamed these confrontations on provocateurs hired by mill owners to discredit the strike, a tactic that had been used elsewhere in America. Months later, alderman Cornelius Lynch, during an investigation of the dynamite plot, admitted under oath that police had provoked some of the strike violence. At right is a poster circulated by the IWW. (Above, courtesy of UNH.)

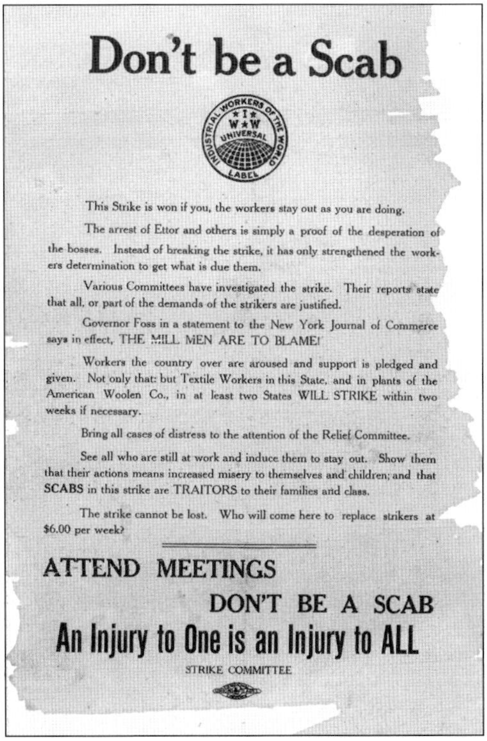

Don't be a Scab

This Strike is won if you, the workers stay out as you are doing.

The arrest of Ettor and others is simply a proof of the desperation of the bosses. Instead of breaking the strike, it has only strengthened the workers determination to get what is due them.

Various Committees have investigated the strike. Their reports state that all, or part of the demands of the strikers are justified.

Governor Foss in a statement to the New York Journal of Commerce says in effect, THE MILL MEN ARE TO BLAME!

Workers the country over are aroused and support is pledged and given. Not only that: but Textile Workers in this State, and in plants of the American Woolen Co., in at least two States WILL STRIKE within two weeks if necessary.

Bring all cases of distress to the attention of the Relief Committee.

See all who are still at work and induce them to stay out. Show them that their actions means increased misery to themselves and children; and that SCABS in this strike are TRAITORS to their families and class.

The strike cannot be lost. Who will come here to replace strikers at $6.00 per week?

ATTEND MEETINGS
DON'T BE A SCAB
An Injury to One is an Injury to ALL
STRIKE COMMITTEE

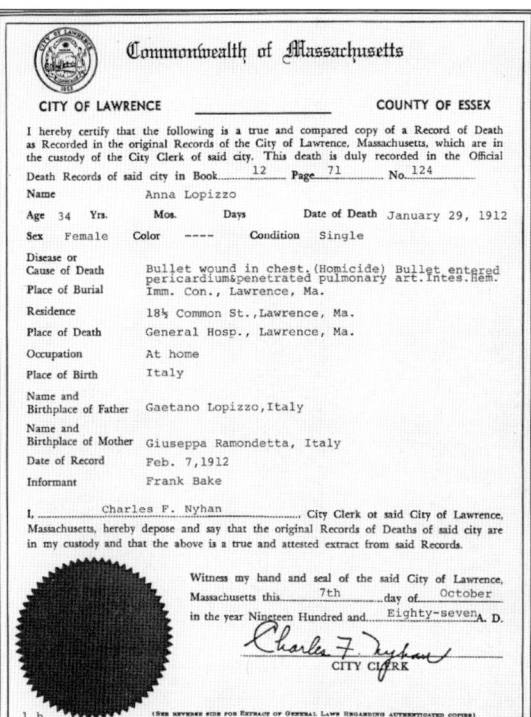

On January 29, in the early evening, the militia cornered a large group of marchers at the corner of Union and Garden Streets. After some pushing and shoving, a shot rang out, and Annie LoPizzo, a 34-year-old striker, lay dead in the street. Witnesses charged that the bullet was fired by police officer Oscar Benoit, but he and others insisted someone specifically targeting LoPizzo fired the shot from behind the police. Two important strike leaders, Arturo Giovannitti and Joseph Ettor, were arrested for murder conspiracy in her death. Striker Joseph Caruso was later arrested in April and charged with murder. The three remained in jail without bail until the end of November 1912. At left is LoPizzo's death certificate. Below, strikers decorate LoPizzo's grave on Memorial Day. (Below, courtesy of UNH.)

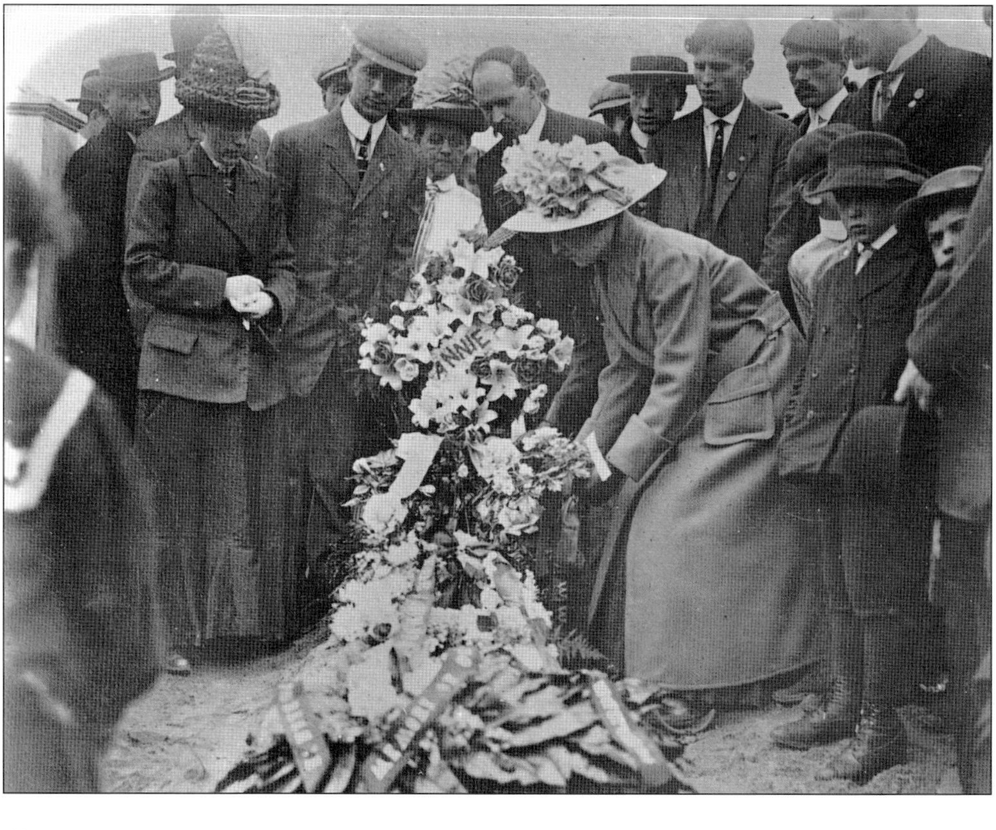

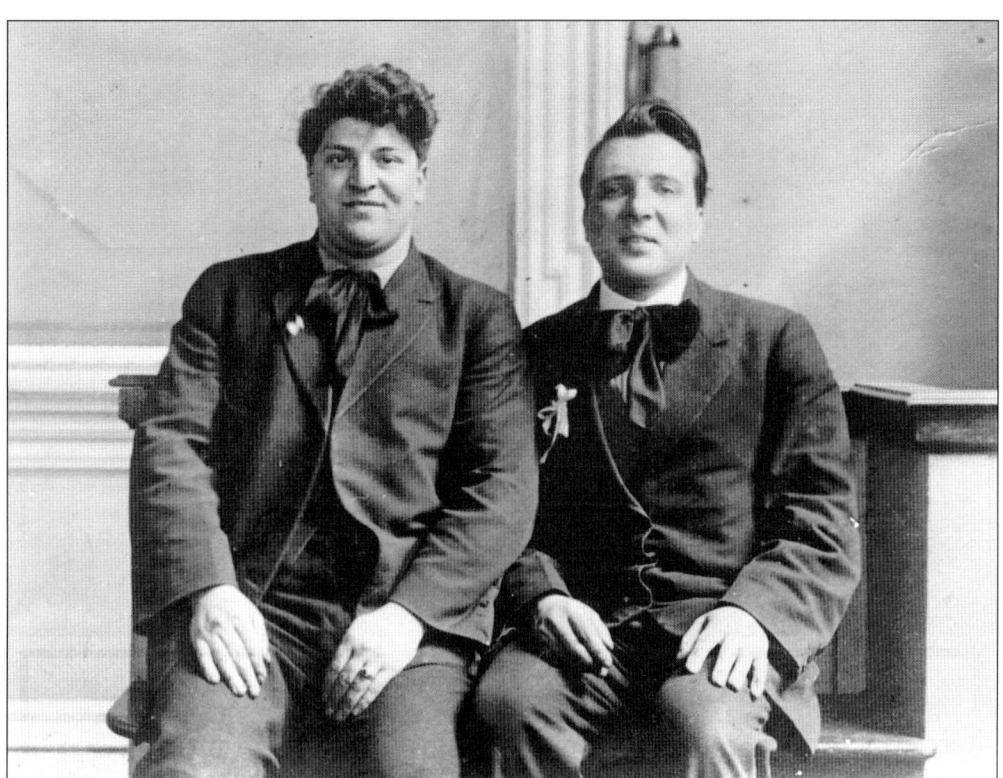

Police arrested Joseph Ettor (above, left) and Arturo Giovannitti (above, right) for their alleged involvement as accessories before the fact in the shooting death of Anna LoPizzo and for inciting a riot. At the time of LoPizzo's shooting, Ettor and Giovannitti were three miles away speaking to workers. They were denied bail and stood trial in the fall of 1912 in Salem, Massachusetts. After their arrests, IWW organizers William Haywood and Elizabeth Gurley Flynn made their way to Lawrence to help guide the strike. At right is the receiving officer's memorandum for the Essex County Jail, recording the arrest of Joseph Ettor. Each time Ettor and Giovannitti were transferred from the Essex County Jail in Lawrence to police court, it was recorded in a document like this. The Lawrence History Center has over 100 years of Essex County Jail records in its collection available to researchers. (Above, courtesy of UNH.)

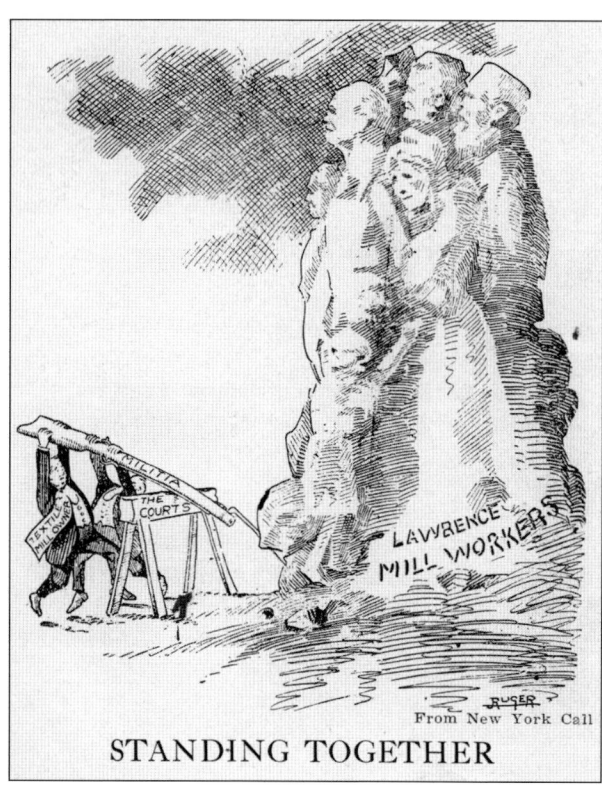

STANDING TOGETHER — From New York Call

Before his January 29 arrest, Arturo Giovannitti said the following at Lawrence's St. Anthony's Church: "Capitalism is the same in the Fatherland as it is here. Nobody cares for you; nobody is interested in you. You are considered nothing but machines. Human machines in the old country; human machines in this country. Nobody has any interest in your conditions . . . Any effort to improve your conditions and womanhood, that must come from yourselves alone . . . It is only by your own power, your own determined will, your own solidarity, that you can rise to better things." The illustration at left, which appeared in the *New York Call*, echoes this sentiment, as does the poster below, issued by the IWW. (Below, courtesy of LPL.)

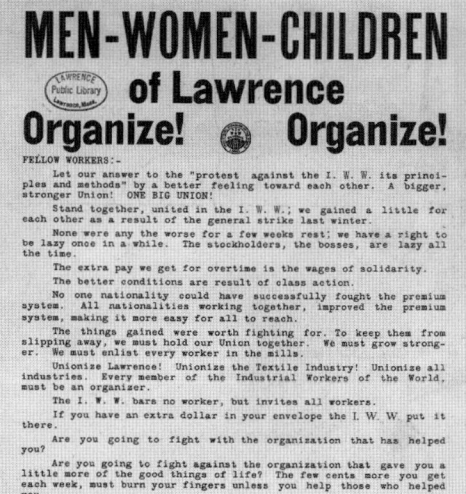

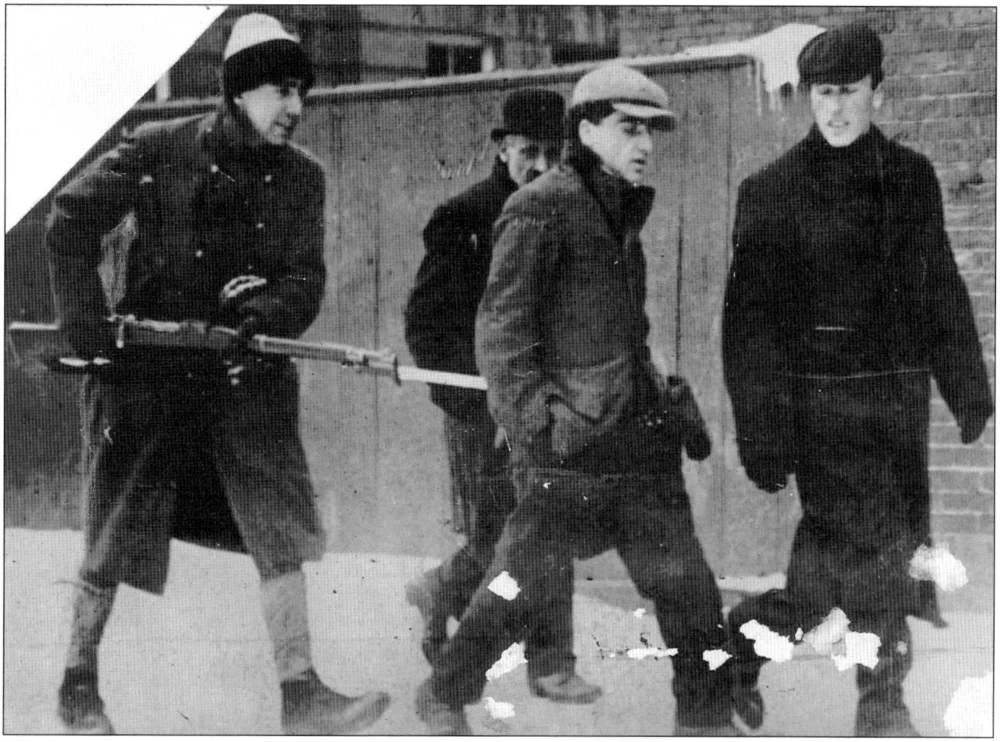

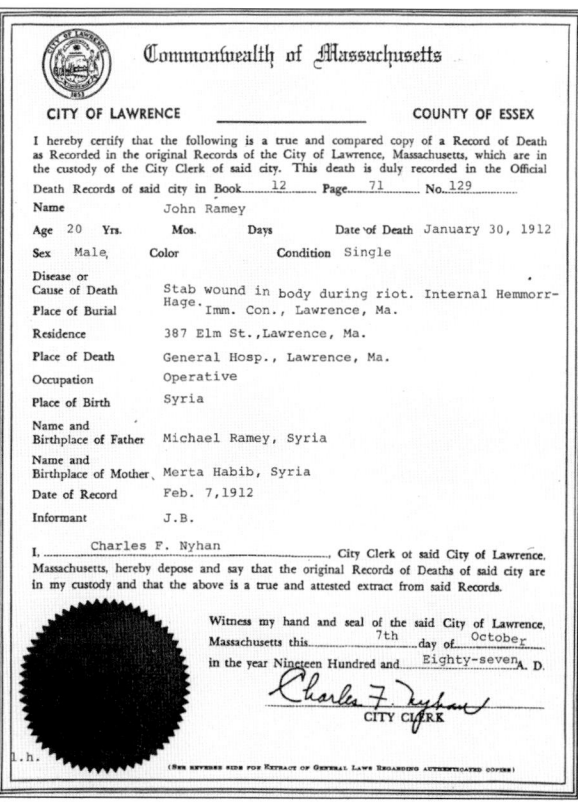

Newspaper articles during the strike reveal that the militia frequently pushed strikers along the streets with fixed bayonets, as this photograph demonstrates. John Ramey, a 17-year-old striker, lost his life in this way. On Tuesday, January 30, a large group of Lebanese strikers gathered at the corner of Oak and White Streets to prepare to demonstrate. Ramey, readying for a strikers' street parade, was practicing on his cornet. Workers often sang as they protested, usually with musicians. When the militia attacked, Ramey's back was punctured with a bayonet. He was taken to Lawrence General Hospital in critical condition and died that day. Note that, contrary to family records, the city death records have Ramey's age listed four years older at 20.

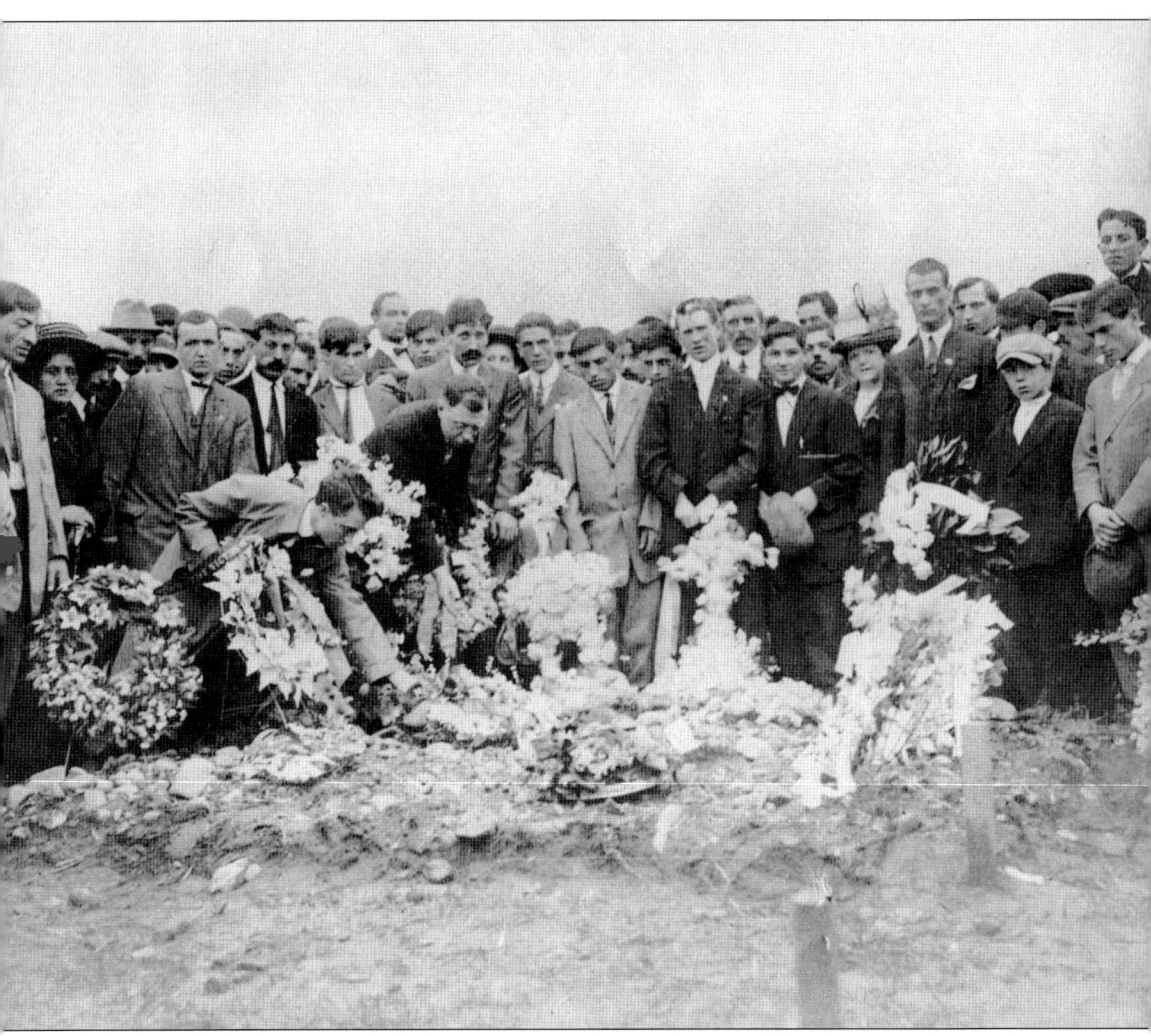

Young John Ramey's death, so close on the heels of Anna LoPizzo's passing, marked a dramatic moment in the several-days-old strike. Ramey's relatives called for militia head Col. E. LeRoy Sweetser to make a thorough inquiry, and one of Lawrence's legislators presented a "Petition of Compensation For Wrongful Death" to the committee of rules at the Massachusetts State House. According to Lawrence historian Jonas Stundzia, on Thursday, February 1, a service was held at St. Anthony's Church, followed by a 30-carriage cortege and a contingency of hundreds of Lebanese compatriots to the cemetery. Rev. Gabriel Bastany eulogized Ramey as a martyr for his family and fellow workers and called for a monument to be erected for the dead striker, with "Killed in the Lawrence Strike" inscribed on it (see page 113). In response, on February 2, William "Big Bill" Haywood, speaking at Chabis Hall, called on strikers to "remember that you are fighting more than your own fight. You are fighting for the entire working class and you must stand together." (Courtesy of ATHM.)

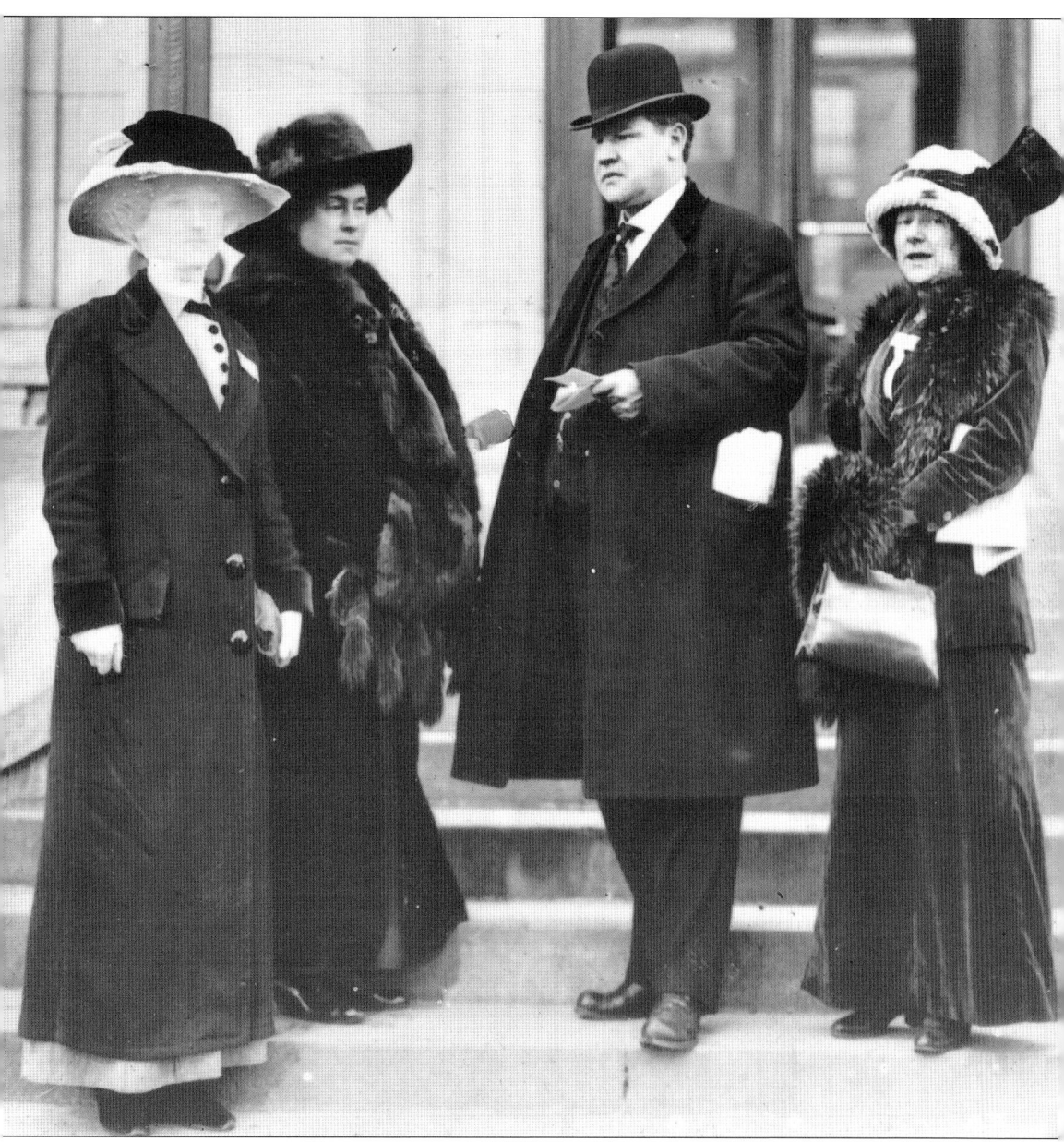

Seen here in Lawrence with the IWW's William Haywood, journalist Mary Heaton Vorse (right) remarked, "The labor movement to [Haywood] wasn't a vast faceless mass. He visualized the individual woman standing behind the loom. When he talked about the children shucking oysters or peeling shrimps, he made you see actual children, hands wrinkled with water and painful with salt-water sores. He made all of the working class of America see Lawrence textile workers through the Lawrence children." In *Harper's Weekly*, she wrote, "Things I saw in Lawrence aroused in me an indignation whose fire has never gone out. For some years before 1912, I had become more and more preoccupied with the conditions under which the work of the country was done; so while Lawrence was for me a definite turning point, the explosive force it proved to be was a logical development. Before Lawrence, I had known a good deal about labor, but I had not felt about it. I had not got angry. In Lawrence, I got angry." (Courtesy of UNH.)

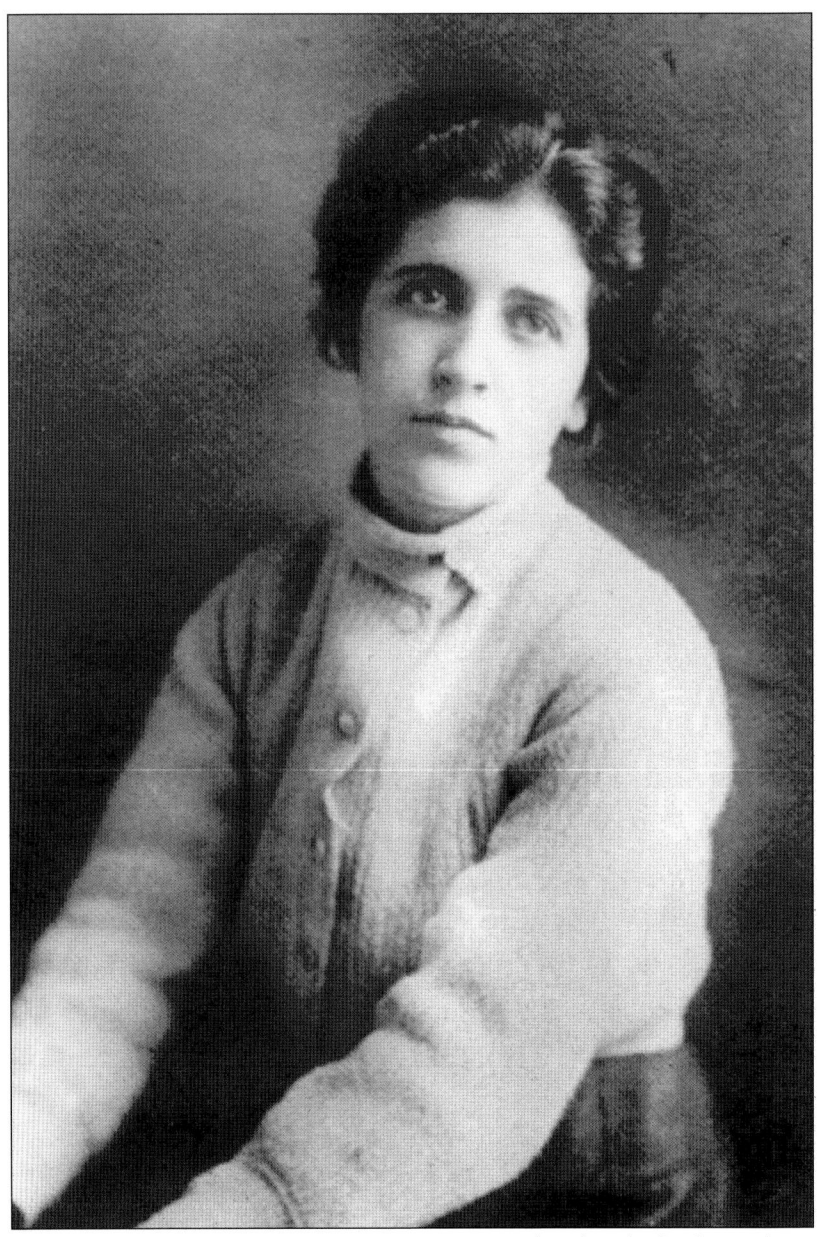

Elizabeth Gurley Flynn was a prominent IWW organizer who played a leading role in the 1912 strike. She was born in Concord, New Hampshire, in 1890. When she was 10, her family moved to New York, where she was educated in the public schools. Influenced strongly by her parents, she delivered her first speech, "What Socialism Will Do for Women," when she was just 16 years old at the Harlem Socialist Club. Her political activities ultimately caused her expulsion from high school. After the arrests of Joseph Ettor and Arturo Giovannitti, Flynn was sent to Lawrence at the end of January and was an organizer of the children's exodus. In her autobiography *Rebel Girl*, she wrote, "We talked especially to the women about the high cost of living here—how they had been fooled when they first came here when they figured the dollars in their home money. They thought they were rich till they had to pay rent, buy groceries, clothes, and shoes. Then they knew they were poor."

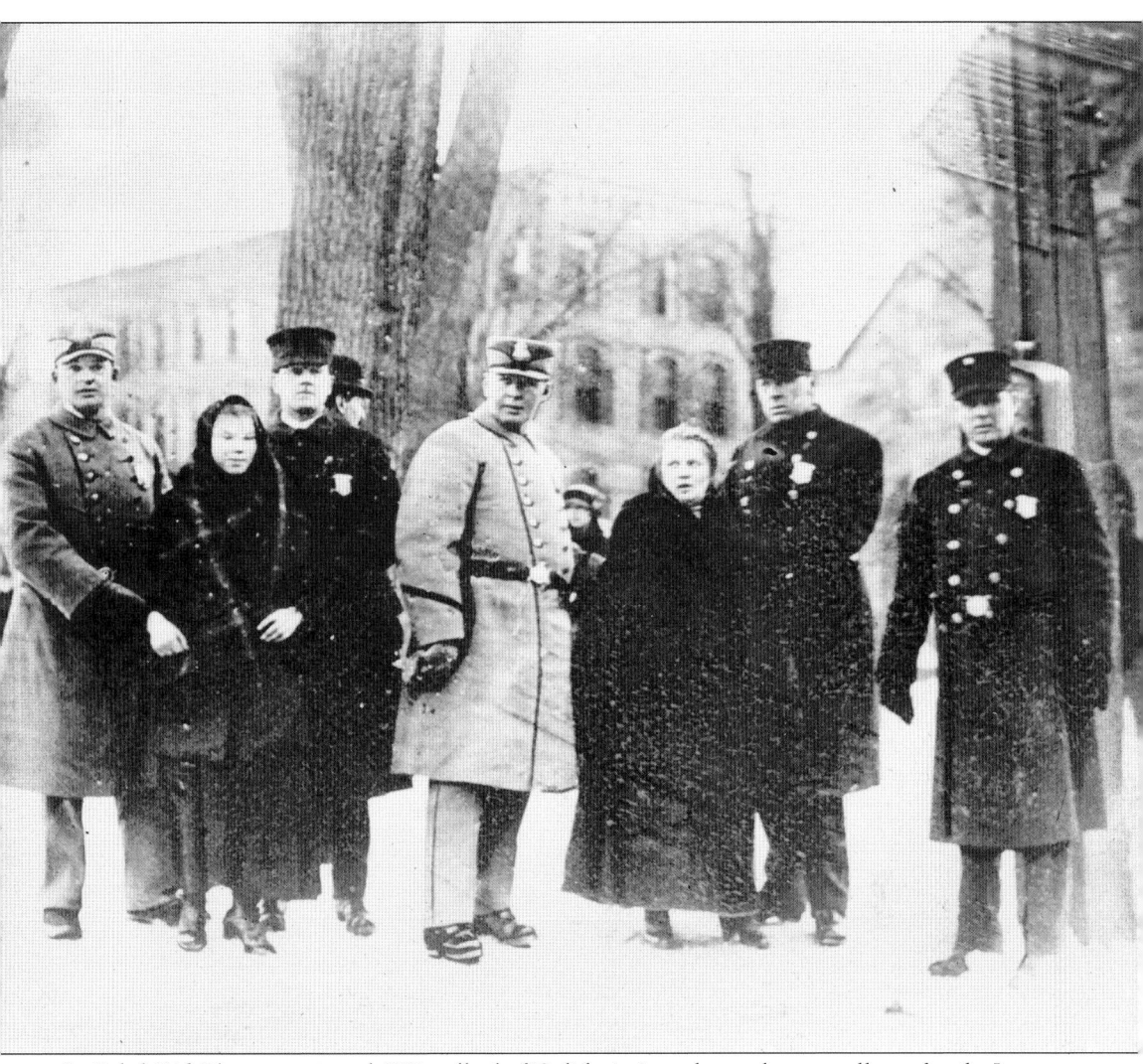

In *Rebel Girl*, Flynn continued: "We talked of 'Solidarity' . . . the workers are all one family. It was internationalism. It was also real Americanism—the first they had heard. 'One nation indivisible, with liberty and justice for all.' They hadn't found it here, but they were willingly fighting to create it . . . As the terrible New England winter dragged along the terror and violence increased. On February 19, 200 policemen with drawn clubs routed 100 women picketers. A Boston newspaper described the scene: 'A woman would be seen to shout from the crowd and run into a side street. Instantly two or three police would be after her. Usually a night-stick well aimed brought the woman to the ground like a shot and instantly the police would be on her, pulling her in as many ways as there were police.' " This photograph shows two women being arrested by five men from the Lawrence and Metropolitan Park police. (Courtesy of UNH.)

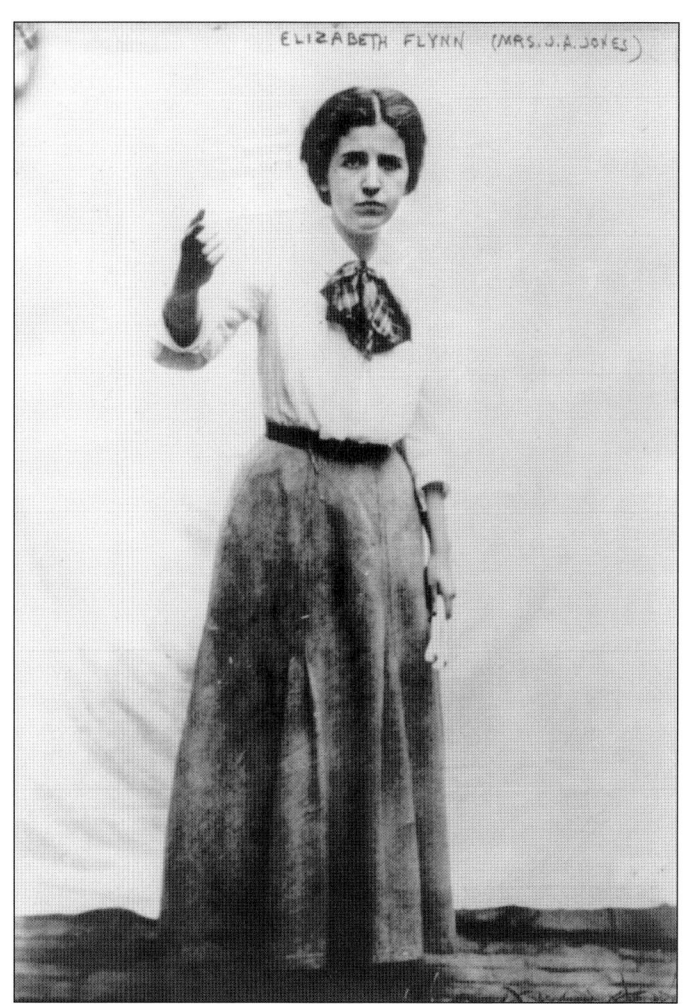

In 1935's *A Footnote to Folly*, journalist Mary Heaton Vorse said the following after observing Elizabeth Gurley Flynn during the strike: "When [Flynn] spoke, the excitement of the crowd became a visible thing. She stood there, young, with her Irish blue eyes, her face magnolia white and her cloud of black hair, the picture of a youthful revolutionary girl leader. She stirred them up, lifted them up in her appeal for solidarity. Then at the end of the meeting they sang. It was though a spurt of flame had gone through this audience, something stirring and powerful, a feeling which has made the liberation of people possible; something beautiful and strong had swept through the people and welded them together, singing." Flynn died in Russia in 1964; however, she is buried in German Waldheim Cemetery in Forest Park, Illinois.

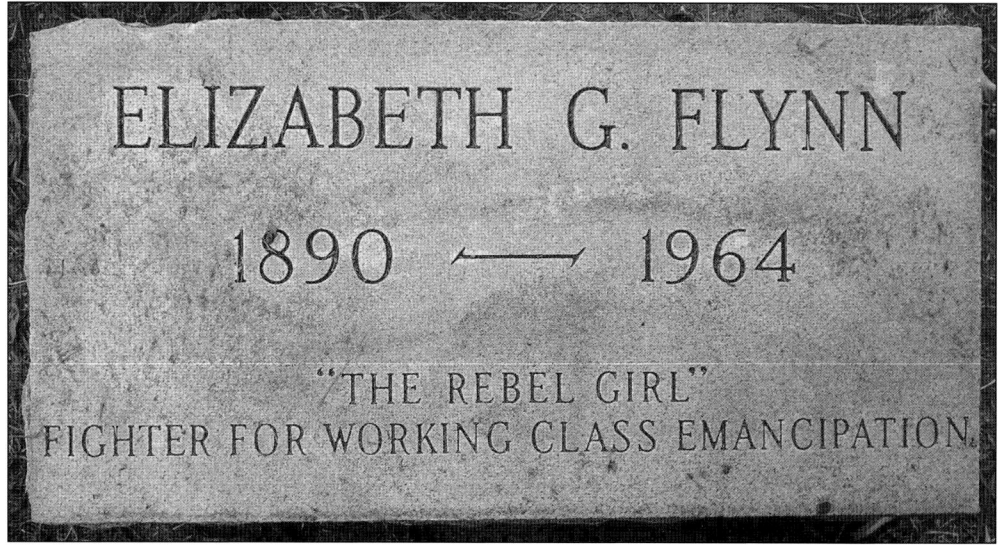

Four
CHILDREN ARE SENT AWAY

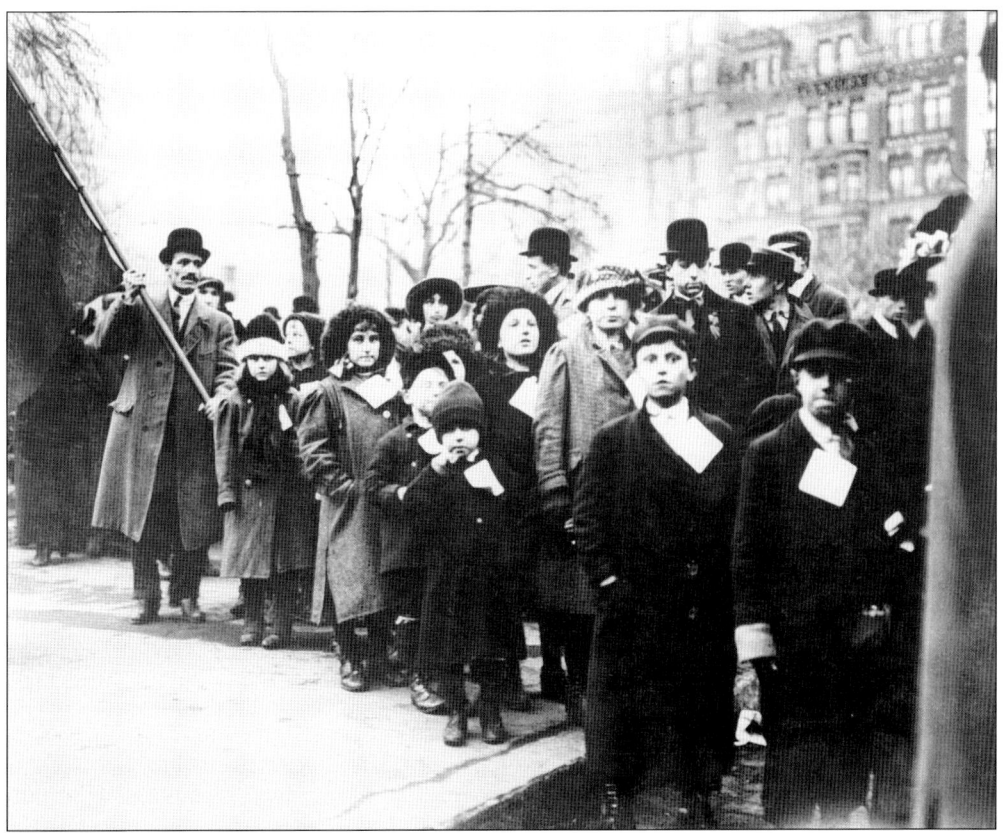

On February 10, the children's exodus began. Employing a strategy conceived in Europe, hundreds of strikers' children were sent to sympathetic families in places such as New York, Philadelphia, and Barre, Vermont. This tactic had helped European workers win strikes in their home countries, and it was time to try the tactic in the new world. (Courtesy of LOC.)

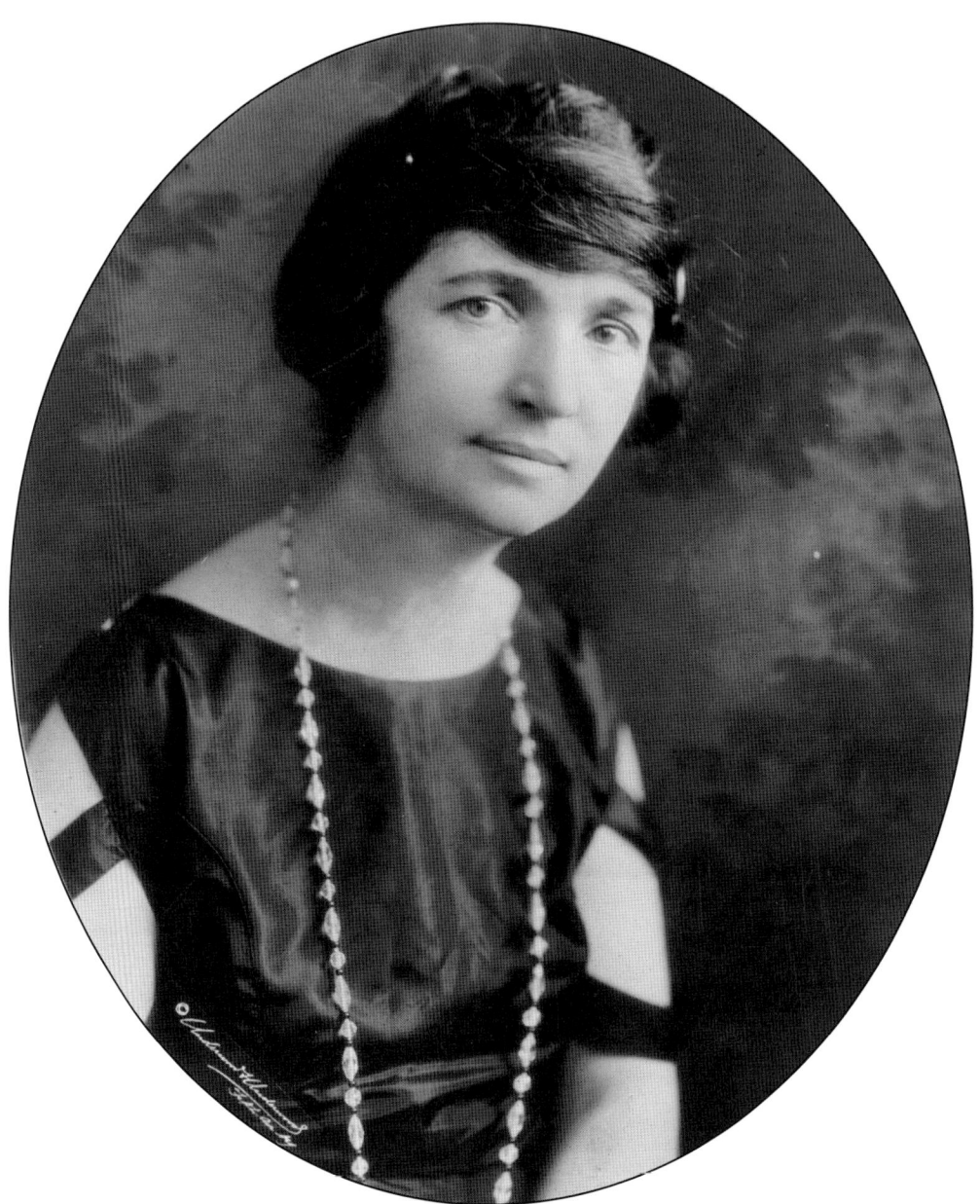

On February 9, Margaret Higgins Sanger (1879–1966), the famous birth control activist, sex educator, and nurse, arrived in Lawrence to assist with the children's exodus. In an article for the *New York Call* entitled "The Fangs of the Monster at Lawrence," Sanger wrote, "As soon as you board the train for Lawrence at Boston, you are aware that war is going on about you somewhere not far off. Dozens of soldiers in uniform, relieved for a few hours of such laborious work as waiting for trouble are seen strutting in and out of the railway trains, pompous and important as defenders of the bosses and private property. When you get to Lawrence, on every corner are soldiers with guns bayoneted, ready at a moment's notice to plunge this deadly instrument into the living flesh of the working men or women who have rebelled against these degrading conditions of wage slavery which has reduced them and their families to human machines used only to pile up enormous profits for the bosses of the mills." (Courtesy of LOC.)

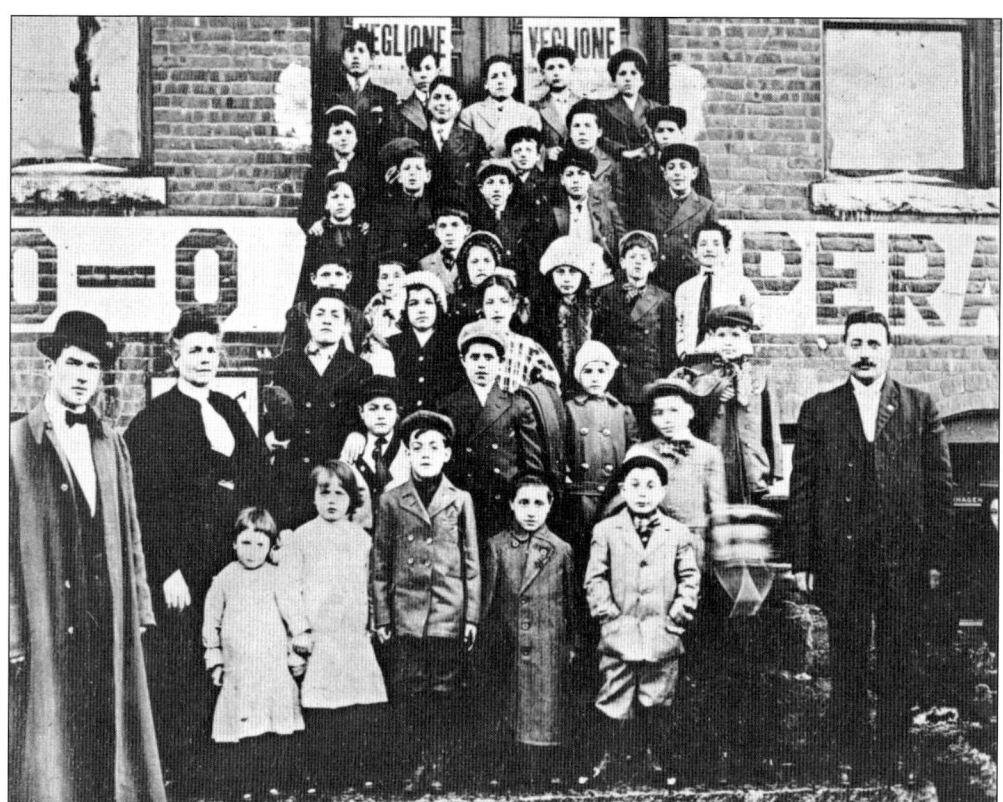

On February 10, Margaret Sanger and associates of hers examined 119 children before sending them to New York City. A few had active cases of chicken pox and diphtheria and had to be isolated from other children. When called to testify before Congress in March, Sanger noted that the children "were very much emaciated; every child there showed the effects of malnutrition, and all of them, or almost all of them, according to the doctor's certificate that night had adenoids and enlarged tonsils." Later in February, 35 more children were sent to Barre, Vermont, where they were welcomed into the homes of Italian granite workers. The children are seen above in front of Old Labor Hall in Barre (see page 123). The poem at right appeared in the *New York Call* on February 15, 1912. (Above, courtesy of Aldrich Public Library, Barre, Vermont.)

The Coming of the Children

By Jane Roulston

Was it an army's martial tread
That beat through the traffic's sullen roar?
And was it the shouting of warriors' dread
That the icy blasts of North wind bore?
Nay, 'twas but the patter of little feet
And children's voices clear and sweet
Loud rang their call o'er the city's din
"We are the strikers, and we shall win!"

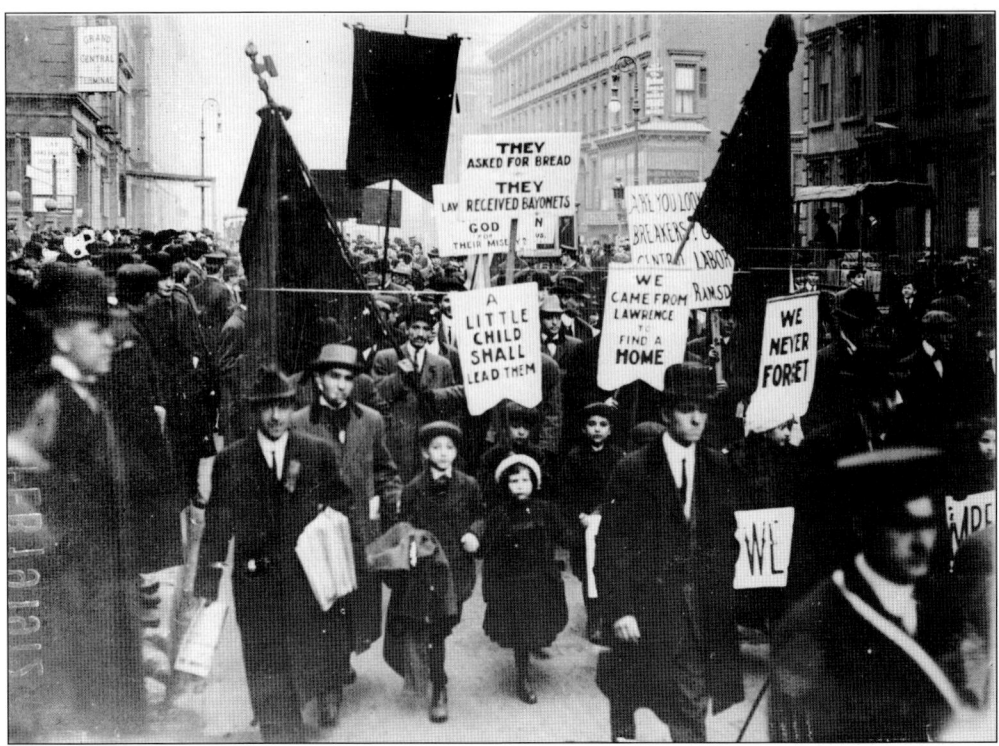

Mary Heaton Vorse met strikers' children sent to New York City for safekeeping. In her 1935 memoir *A Footnote to Folly*, she wrote about a dinner prepared by the Hotel and Restaurant Workers Union. "The air was full of the noises of a hundred young voices," she wrote. "Black-eyed Italian children, French Canadian children, Syrian children, blond-haired children from the Baltic States. How they chattered. How they ate. Meanwhile their friends crowded around, workers helping other workers. A sudden flame of sympathy had brought unity to different groups." At left is one of the identification cards that were fixed to the coats of all children leaving Lawrence. Public officials required that children have signed permission from their guardians. The Strike Committee created the cards for that reason. Despite this, mill owners and their supporters still charged that children were being kidnapped by strike leaders. (Above, courtesy of LOC.)

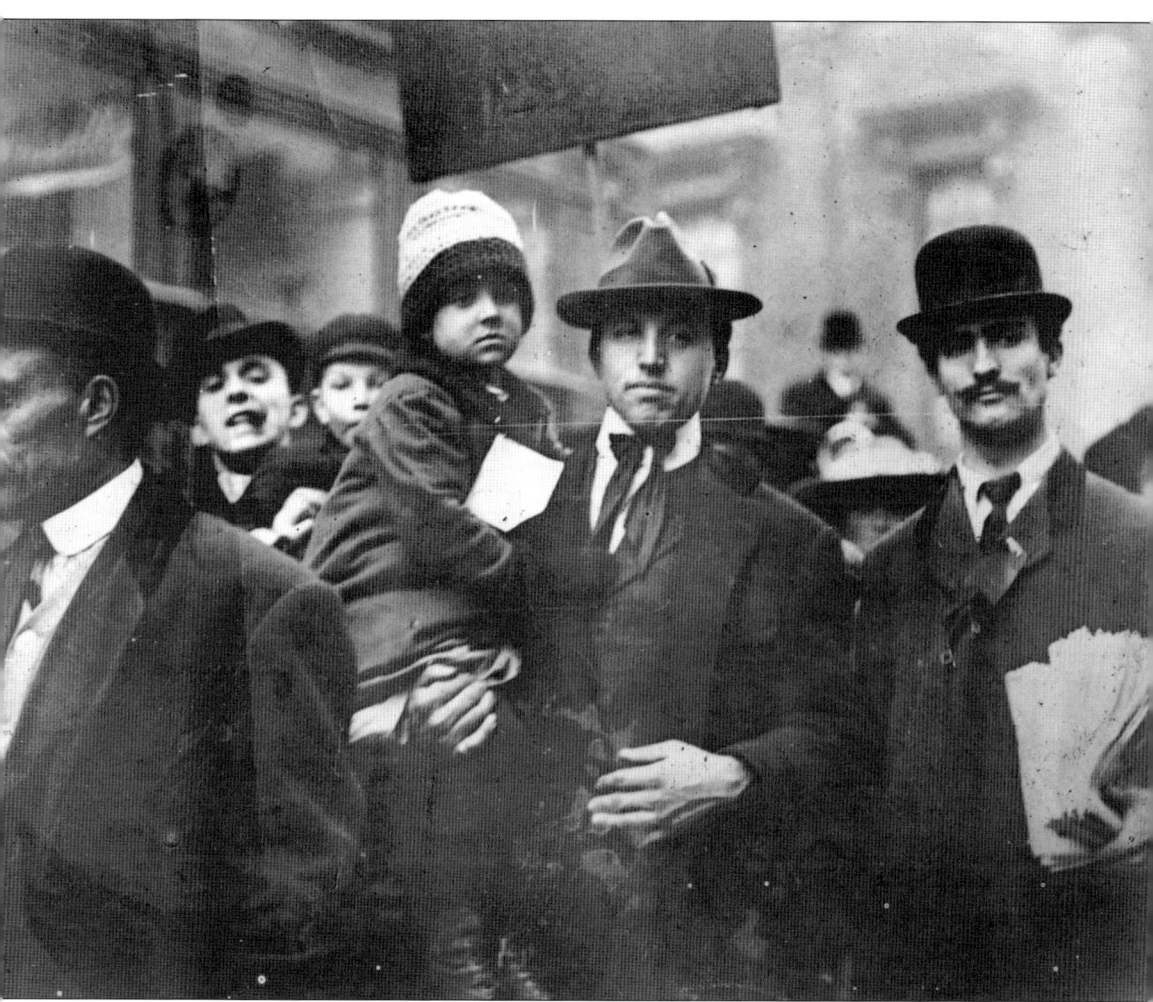

A strike supporter in New York is seen here taking home one of the evacuees. Margaret Sanger described the arrival of the children at Grand Central Station thusly in *The Fighting Women of Lawrence*: "Thousands of men and women stood waiting for the little ones to come . . . their enthusiasm knew no bounds. Tearing off their own coats they wrapped them around the cold and ragged little bodies. Everywhere were men with tears streaming down their faces, tears of joy and gladness at this wonderful demonstration of working class solidarity; at this great fact that no matter what our nationality or creed, no matter what our methods of gaining our goal, the working class will take care of its own. Italian men carried Polish children, German men carried Italian children; Scotch, English, Polish, Italians and French, were one and all carried upon the shoulders of class-conscious men, who felt only that every child was a workingman's offspring, and as such has to be tended and cherished." (Courtesy of UNH.)

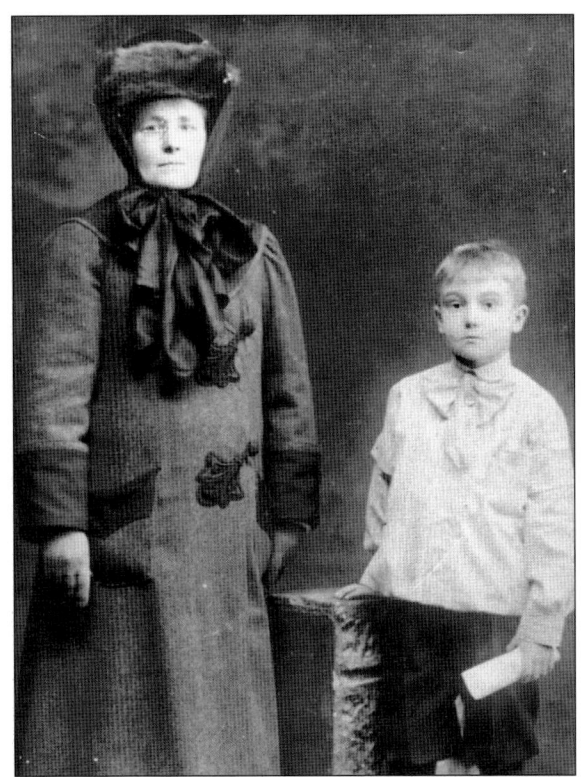

Charles Peter Averka (at left) was born in 1904 in Maynard, Massachusetts, to parents who had came separately from Lithuania to the United States. His family then moved to Lawrence, and he was sent to New York City during the 1912 strike. He is seen here with his host mother in a studio on Madison Avenue. It was noted on the back of the photograph that he was the oldest child, and, according to an unnamed sister, he never talked about his trip to New York. All he ever said was, "I used to cry and say that I want my mommy." When he came back to Lawrence, he worked in the Arlington Mills. Below are two French-Canadian girls identified simply as Adrienne and Marie. In a letter to them, their parents told them that they were pleased they were being treated so well by their hosts. (Below, courtesy of UNH.)

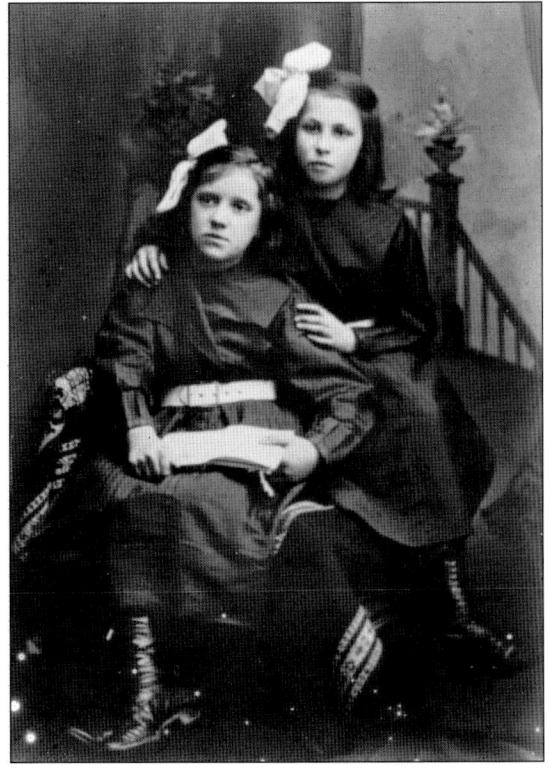

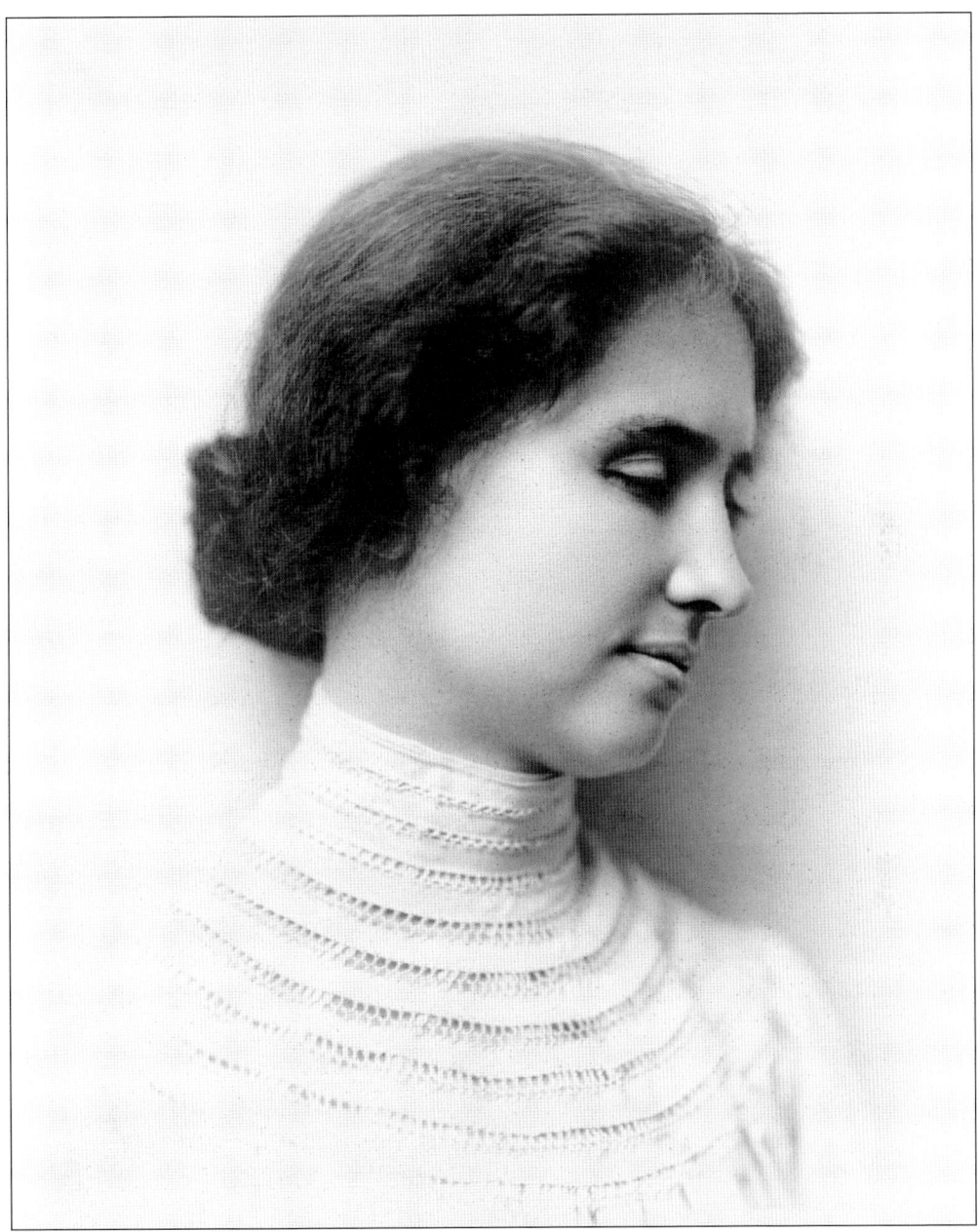

Helen Keller, a part of numerous social movements in the 1900s, was so much more than the brilliant deaf and blind woman children learn about in school. A socialist, she once said, "I owed my success partly to the advantages of my birth and environment. I have learned that the power to rise is not within the reach of everyone." Keller, who was 32 at the time of the Lawrence strike, was a major force to be reckoned with throughout. She raised money to feed strikers, participated in the children's exodus by helping to find safe homes for children for the duration of the strike, and was an active member of the New York City Ettor-Giovannitti-Caruso defense committee. Speaking prominently in their defense, she said, "The crime with which [Giovannitti] was charged was, of course, a legal fiction devised by the mill owners and their agents. Giovannitti's real crime was helping the strikers in their assault on the pocketbooks of the owners." (Courtesy of LOC.)

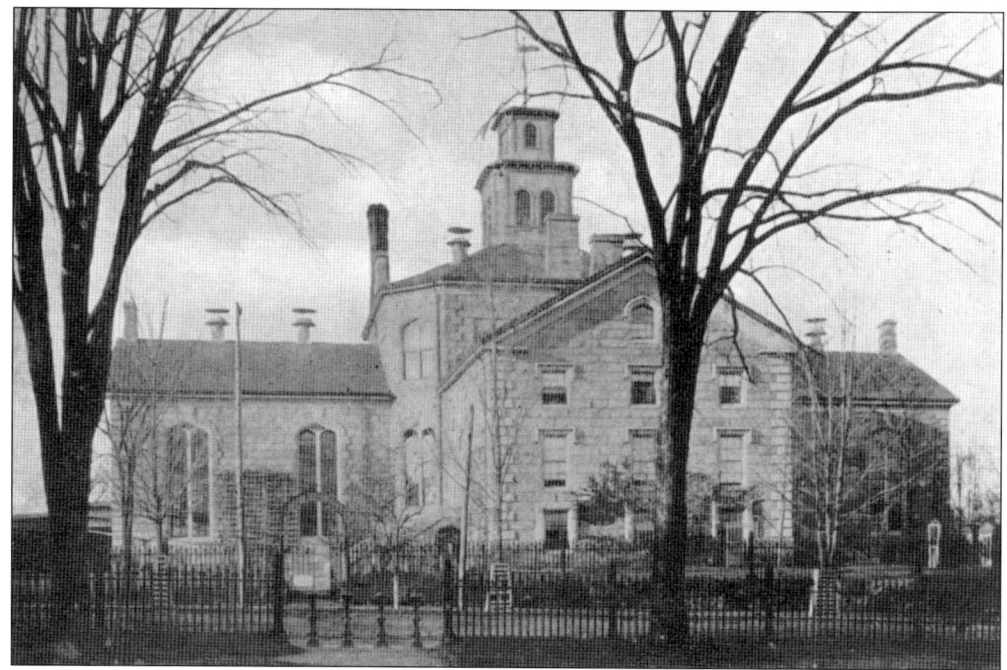

On February 24, police and the militia tried to prevent 46 children from going to Philadelphia at the train station. When the children, parents, and Philadelphia chaperones insisted on getting on the train, the police clubbed and dragged children and mothers off to the Essex County Jail in Lawrence. Those unable to escape were herded into military convoy trucks and shuttled to the Lawrence Police Station. Not one child made it to the railcar. At the police court, most of them refused to pay the fines levied, opting instead for a jail cell, some with babies in their arms. Newspaper headlines read, "Arrest Children in Textile Strike," "Police Prevent Children's Exile," "Children and Mothers Taken by Police," and "Police Clubs Keep Waifs In." The five children below were strikers' children who were sent to the Lawrence City Farm after police stopped them from leaving town. (Below, courtesy of UNH.)

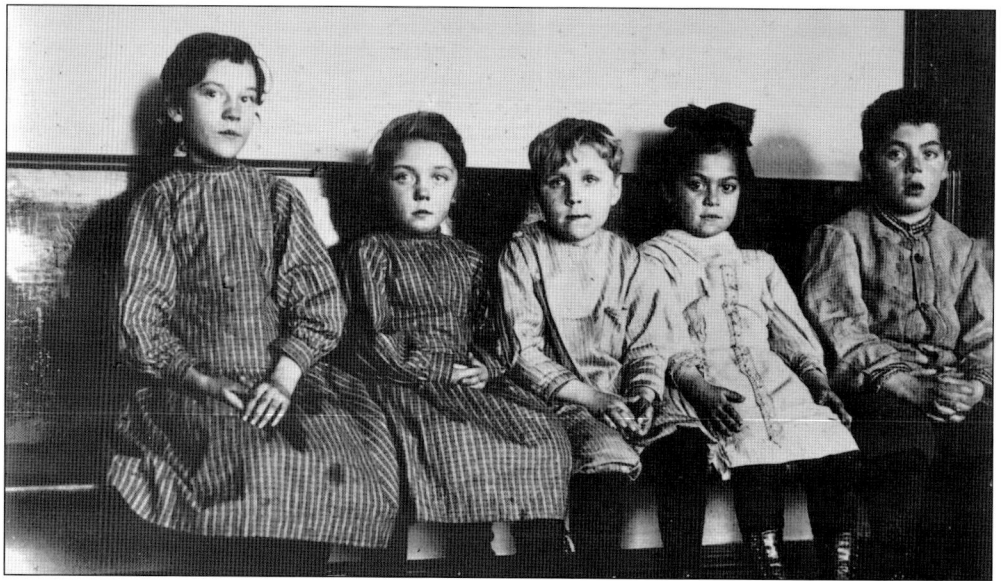

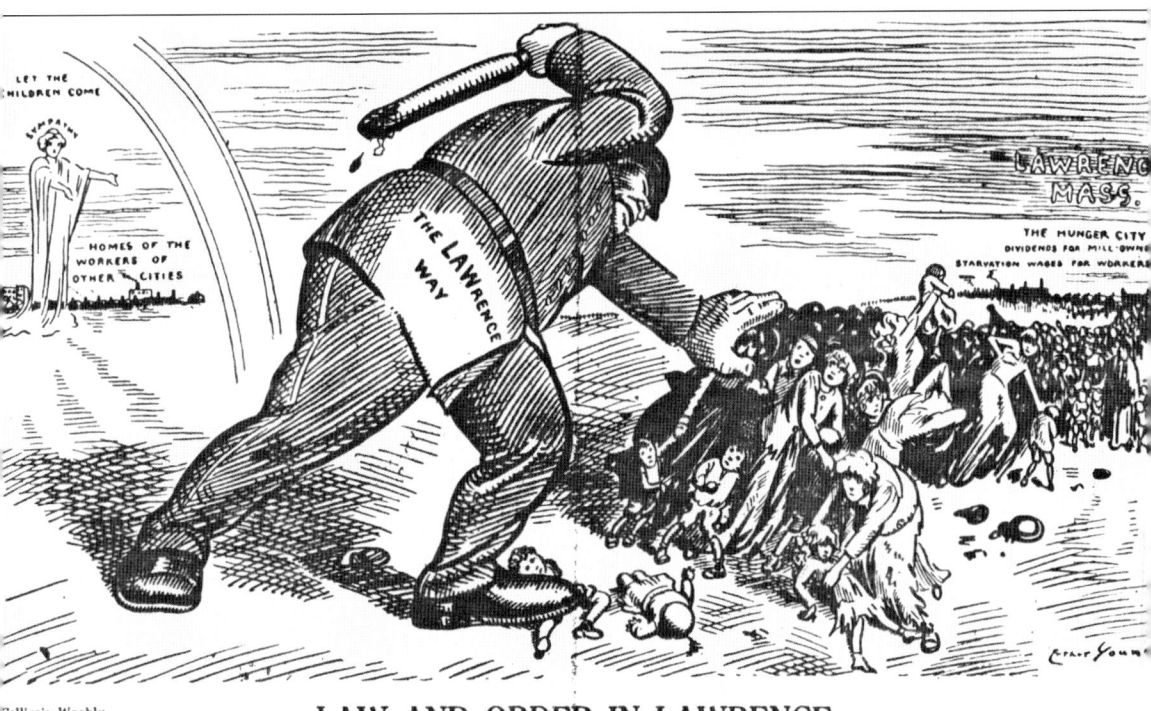

LAW AND ORDER IN LAWRENCE

The police action against mothers and children gained national attention. The *Boston Globe* reported, "The women shrieked and clung to their children"; the *Philadelphia Inquirer* wrote, "No discrimination was shown as [the] women were beaten"; and the *New York Times* stated, "To discourage any attempt on the part of the strikers to rescue the children, four companies of infantry and a squad of cavalry surrounded the railway station." This illustration by Art Young, entitled "Law and Order in Lawrence," appeared in *Collier's* on March 9, 1912. In it, a giant police officer labeled "The Lawrence Way" crushes women and children under his feet as he swings his bloody club at them. On one side of the illustration, Lawrence is labeled "The hunger city. Dividends for mill owners—starvation wages for workers." On the opposite side, a woman labeled "Sympathy" says, "Let the children come" as she stands over a place labeled "Homes of the workers of other cities." (Courtesy of WSU.)

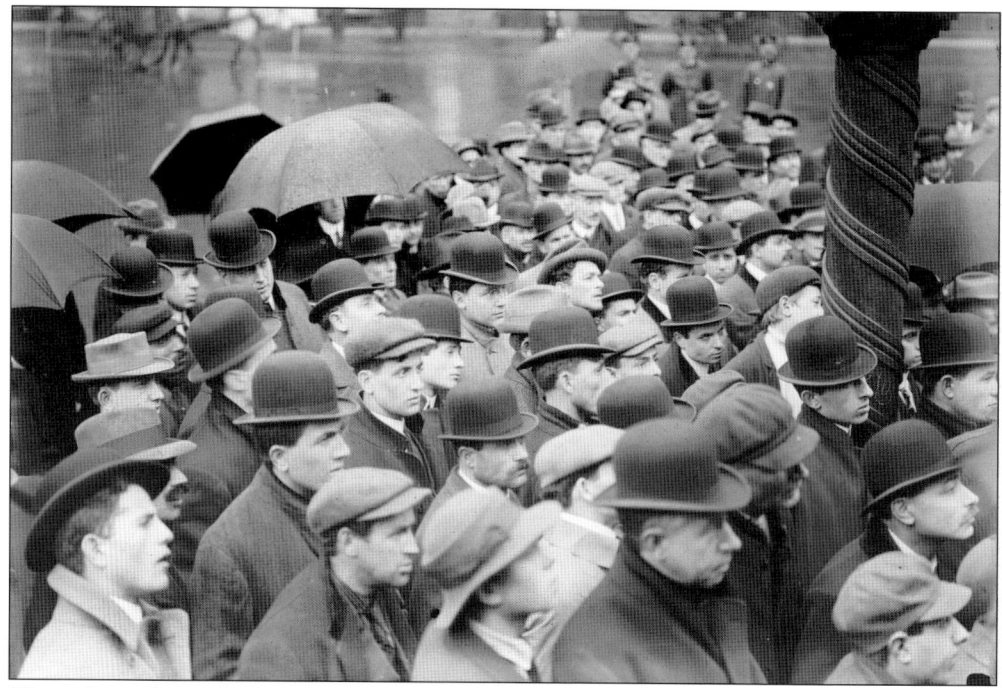

Throughout the strike, sympathetic actions were held across the nation—a testament to the groundbreaking nature of the mill walkout. Soon, people across the world traveled to Lawrence to march with strikers. They also rallied in support in their own cities, like these workers seen at a meeting in New York City. (Courtesy of the LOC.)

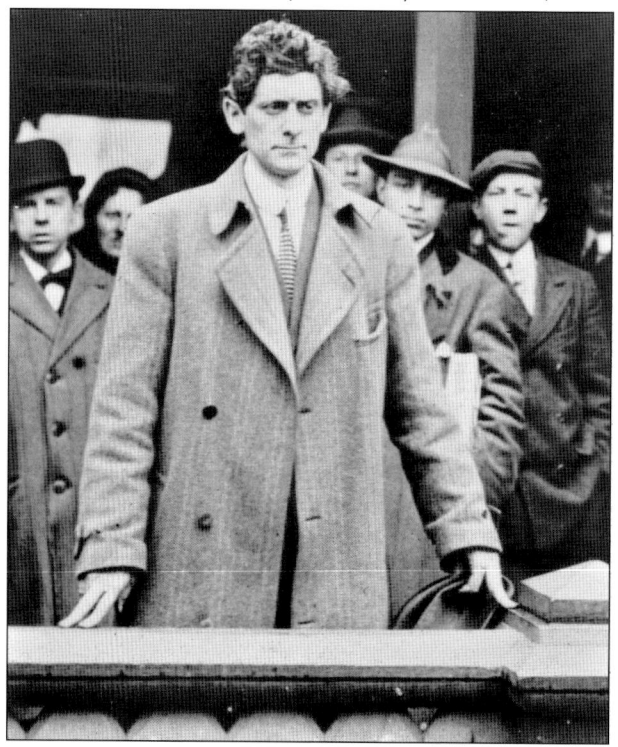

William Sanger (1873–1961) was an architect and artist and the first husband of Margaret Sanger. They were married 1902 and divorced in 1921. He is seen here addressing the crowd at a mass meeting about the Lawrence strike on a rainy day in New York City's Union Square. He was the chairman of the meeting. (Courtesy of UNH.)

Five
CONGRESSIONAL HEARINGS BEGIN

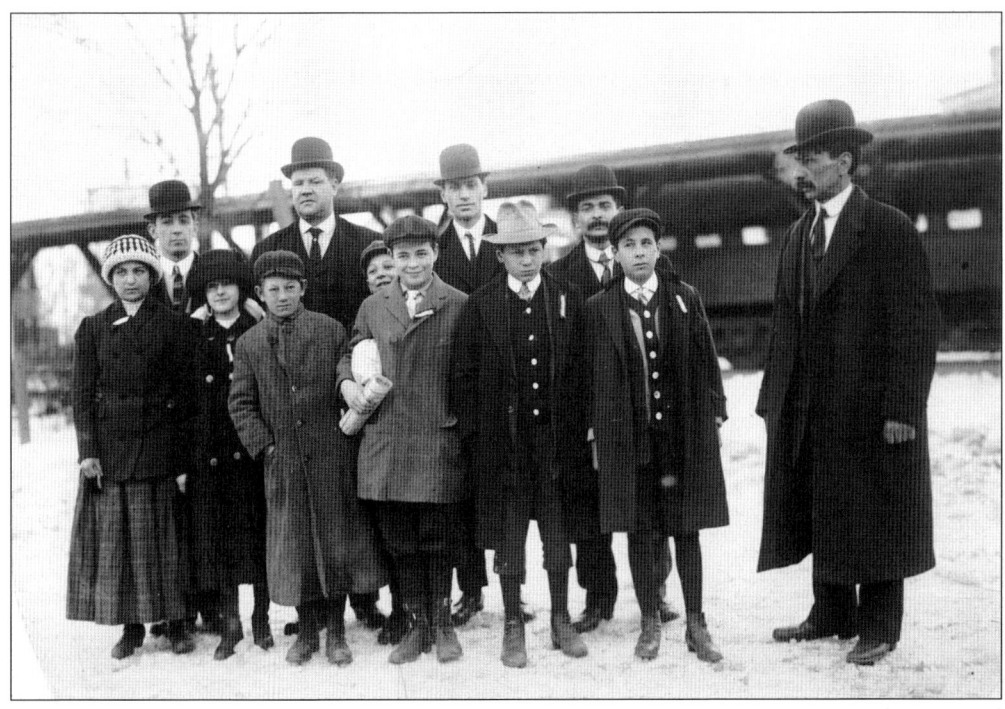

On March 2, Congress began investigative hearings on the strike. The children who testified to them were mill workers. These seven children waiting for the train were among 13 who were sent by the Lawrence textile mill strikers to tell their side of the story to Congress. The tall man second from the left is the IWW's William Haywood. (Courtesy of WSU.)

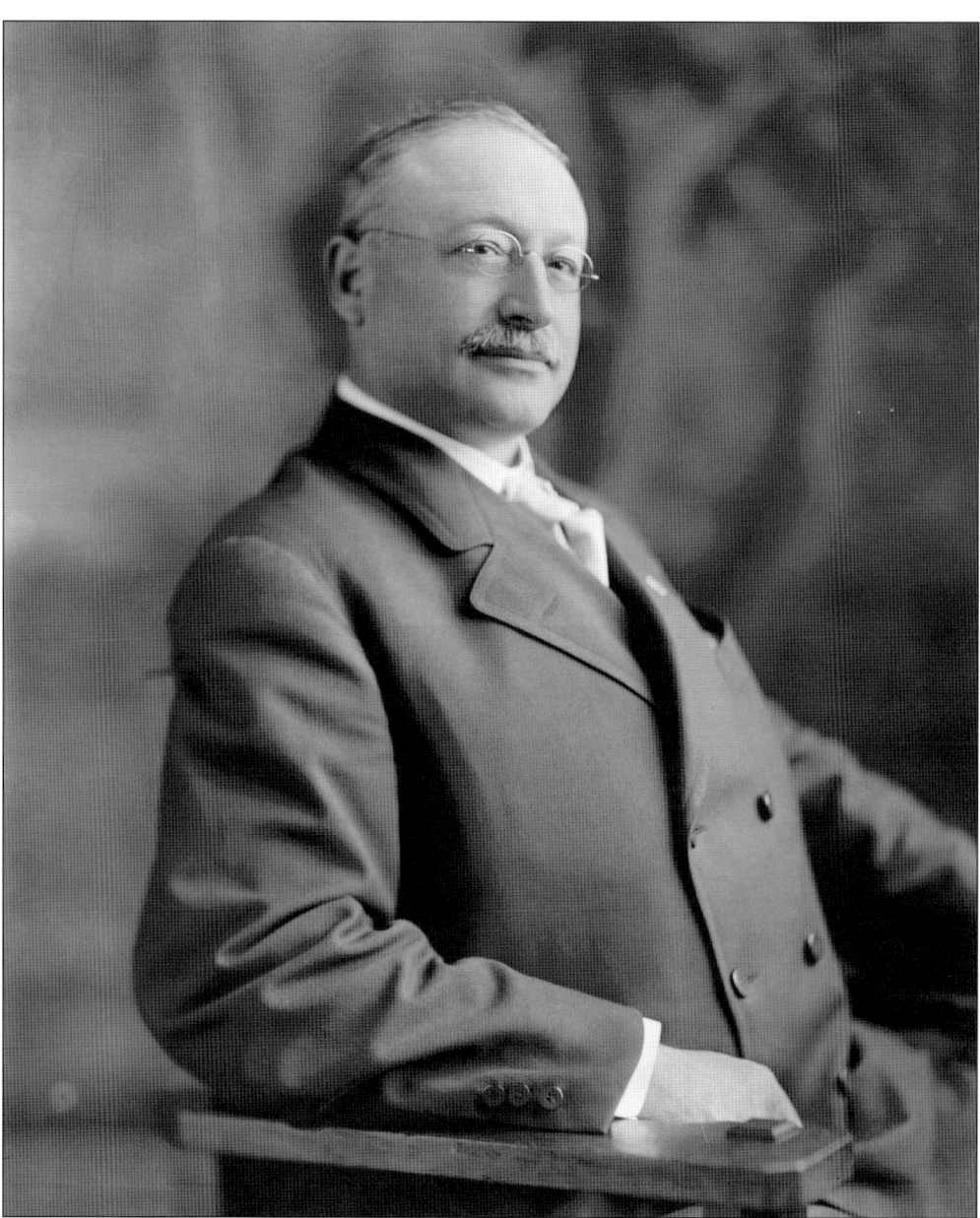

Milwaukee socialist and congressman Victor Berger introduced House Resolution 409 to conduct hearings into the Lawrence strike. Berger, born in Austria-Hungary in 1860, came to the United States in 1879. Hearings commenced on March 2 with Berger's opening remarks on his resolution: "The American Woolen Company has for years been recipient of a Government subsidy in the forms of a high tariff. The claim has been made that this high tariff is levied in order to protect labor. Yet in spite of this claim it is generally conceded that these operatives are among the lowest paid of any industry in America." He had this to say about the train station incident: "I want to call attention to one of the most outrageous invasion of Constitutional rights that has ever occurred in this country. I refer to the brutal manhandling and clubbing of women and children in Lawrence by the official and unofficial agents of the state." (Courtesy of LOC.)

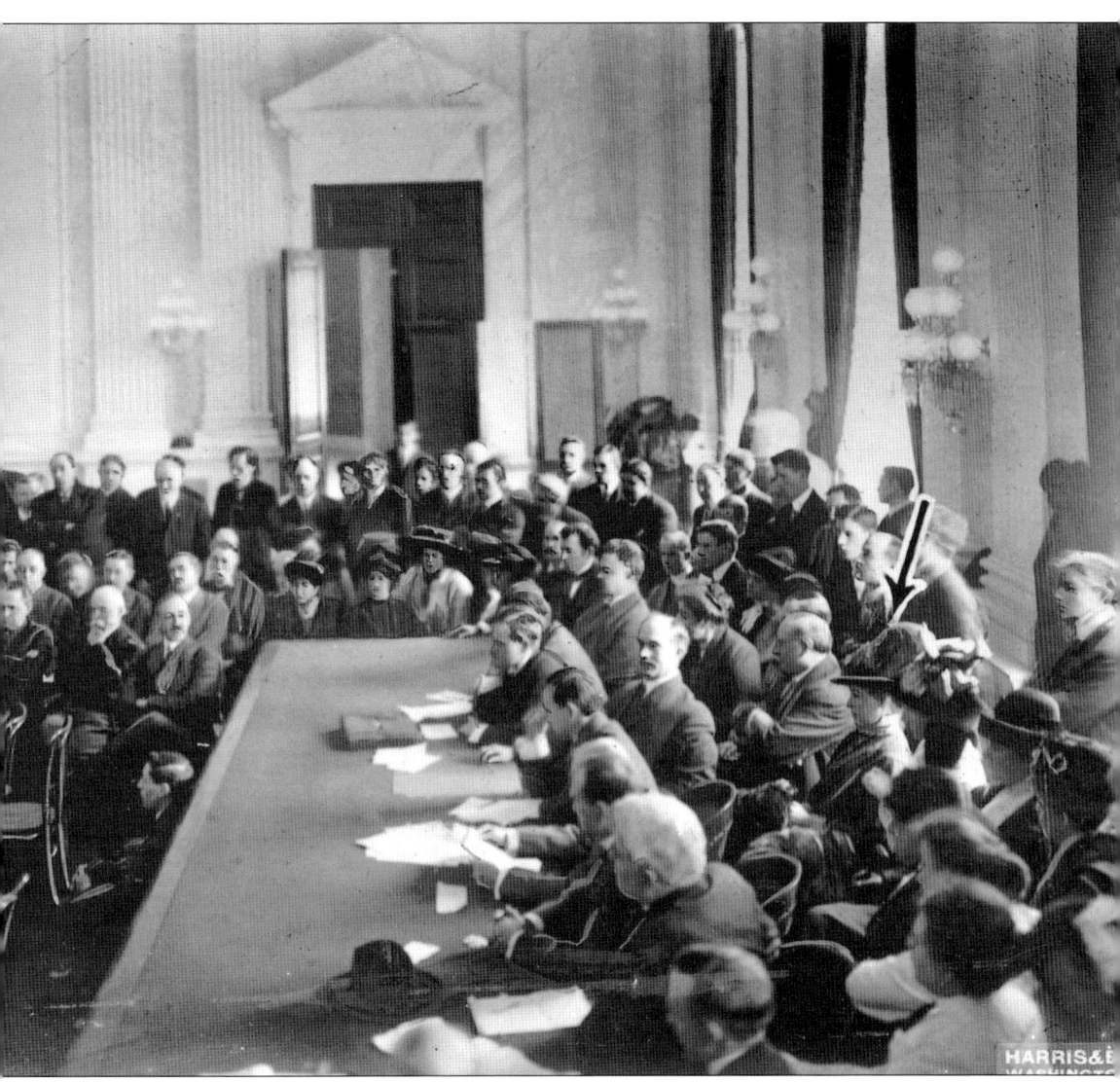

As Congress opened its hearings, the Strike Committee issued an impassioned plea for the ranks to remain solid: "The textile manufacturers are yielding!," they wrote. "The strike is nearly won; it will be won! . . . The world is with us. We will, we must win! . . . the echo of the struggle for more bread has aroused the citizens of the United States, and all the workers of the world . . . Congress, aroused by the fiendish, savage treatment of pregnant women, of innocent babes, responds to the thunderous voice of an aroused Nation. They are investigating; they are acting, and the sores and wounds of our suffering and brutalized wives and children has laid bare the outrages of capitalist tyranny run mad and amuck! . . . Nobody goes back to work until all go back together! Win! Win! Win!" This photograph shows Congressional testimony on Tuesday, March 5, 1912. The arrow on the right points to the first lady, Helen Herron Taft. (Courtesy of UNH.)

| 62D CONGRESS
2d Session | HOUSE OF REPRESENTATIVES | DOCUMENT
No. 671 |

THE STRIKE AT LAWRENCE, MASS.

HEARINGS

BEFORE

THE COMMITTEE ON RULES

OF THE

HOUSE OF REPRESENTATIVES

ON

HOUSE RESOLUTIONS 409 AND 433

MARCH 2–7, 1912

APRIL 4, 1912.—Ordered to be printed

WASHINGTON
GOVERNMENT PRINTING OFFICE
1912

On Friday, March 1, a total of 1,000 people showed up at the city's train station to see off 5 adults and 13 youngsters who would be testifying before Congress. Big news in Lawrence, the Congressional investigation exposed the plight of the strikers to the world and pressured the city's textile interests to settle up with their workers. The scale of public interest could be seen by the fact that, according to Bruce Watson, "an overflow audience crammed into the hearing room of the House office Building." Congressman Victor Berger noted, "I have here from Lawrence some of the workers employed by this company [American Woolen] and I propose to let them tell their own story." First Lady Helen Taft's attendance at the hearings, the words of notables like Margaret Sanger who had been to Lawrence, and the desperate stories of the teenagers likely proved too much for William Wood and other mill owners to continue to resist. The fact that some members of the House of Representatives threatened to further investigate American Woolen's labor practices surely inched Wood closer to the bargaining table.

Mr. BERGER. Why did you go on a strike?

Mr. LIPSON. I went out on strike because I was unable to make a living for my family.

Mr. BERGER. How much wages were you receiving?

Mr. LIPSON. My average wage, or the average wage of my trade, is from $9 to $10 a week.

Mr. BERGER. What kind of work do you do?

Mr. LIPSON. I am a weaver.

Mr. BERGER. You are a skilled workman?

Mr. LIPSON. Yes, sir; for years.

Mr. BERGER. You have been a skilled workman for years and your wages average from $9 to $10 per week?

Mr. LIPSON. Yes, sir; that was the average.

Mr. BERGER. How many children do you have?

Mr. LIPSON. I have four children and a wife.

Mr. BERGER. You support a wife and four children from a weekly wage averaging from $9 to $10 per week and you are a skilled workman. Did you have steady work?

Mr. LIPSON. Usually the work was steady, but there was times when I used to make from $3 to $4 and $5 per week. We have had to live on $3 per week. We lived on bread and water.

Mr. BERGER. What is the price of meat in Lawrence?

Mr. LIPSON. I tell you we do not eat meat there every day. You must consider that we usually have it twice or three times a week, and when we have it it is a sort of holiday. When we eat meat it seems like a holiday, especially for the children.

Mr. BERGER. What is the price of eggs in Lawrence, Mass.?

Mr. LIPSON. Eggs are about 35 cents a dozen; the price is from 30 to 35 cents per dozen.

Mr. BERGER. What is the price of butter there?

Mr. LIPSON. It is 43 cents per pound.

Mr. BERGER. You did not give me the price of meat in Lawrence.

Mr. LIPSON. Meat is 18 cents per pound—that is, the cheap kind. We do not buy the high-priced meat, because we can not afford it.

Mr. BERGER. How much rent do you pay?

Mr. LIPSON. I pay $2.50.

Mr. BERGER. Per week?

Mr. LIPSON. Yes, sir.

Mr. BERGER. You pay $2.50 per week for rent out of $10 weekly wages?

Mr. LIPSON. Yes, sir. You asked me whether I supported my family out of $10 per week. Of course we do not use butter at the present time; we use a kind of molasses; we are trying to fool our stomachs with it.

Mr. BERGER. It is a bad thing to fool your stomach.

Mr. LIPSON. We know that, but we can not help it. When we go to the store without any money, the storekeeper tells us that he can not sell us anything without the money.

Mr. BERGER. How much were you reduced by reason of the recent cut in the wages?

Mr. LIPSON. From 50 to 65 to 75 cents per week.

Mr. BERGER. How much does a loaf of bread cost in Lawrence?

Mr. LIPSON. Twelve cents; that is what I pay.

First to testify March 4 was Samuel Lipson, a 29-years-old employee of American Woolen. He said, "The laws in the mills are made by the bosses, you know, and we never see any inspector there to see to it, and they do what they want to do. If we dare to say a word, they show us the door; they call a watchman and drag us out. We do not dare to say a word." More of Lipson's testimony is above. Peter Studies, age 14, testified: "They make us go quicker and quicker all the time. As soon as I come home I have to go to sleep. I am so tired that I can no longer help out with the family chores. I know my family is counting on me to make some money to help out but I feel like all I do is work."

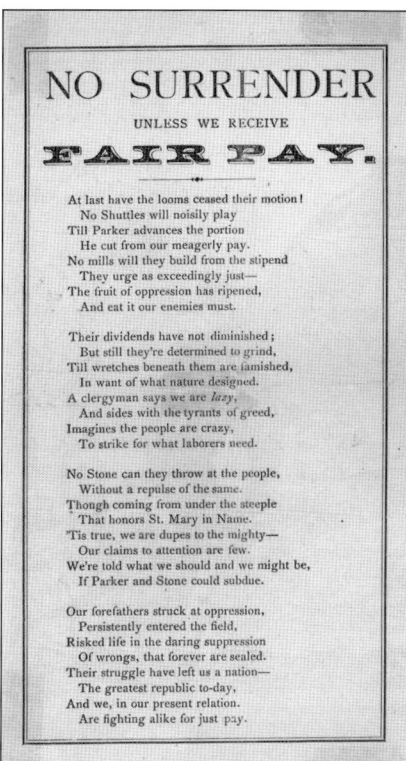
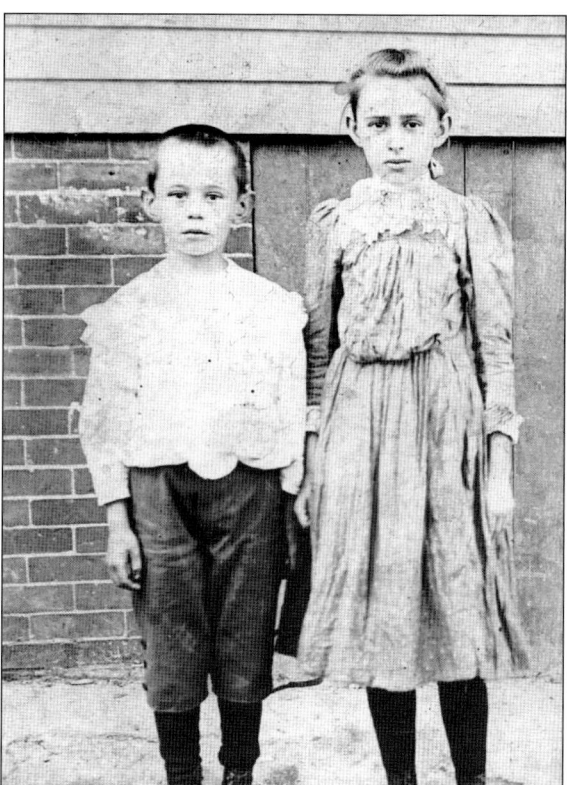

On March 4 and 5, the pay records of several children who testified were admitted into the Congressional record, including the following:

Tony Bruno, age 14, lived at 14 Common Street, worked at the Wood Mill:
February 12, 1910   56hrs $4.92
February 19, 1910   56hrs $5.10

Peter Strodas, age 14, lived at 45 Allen Street, worked at the Wood Mill:
September 30, 1911   56hrs $5.10
November 25, 1911   56hrs $5.10

Victoria Winiarczyk, age 14, lived at 20 Allen Street, worked at the Wood Mill:
December 16, 1911   56 hrs. $5.23
January 6, 1912   54 hrs. $6.22

Lawrence families often survived on bread, molasses, and beans before the 1912 strike. One worker testified during the Congressional investigation that "when we eat meat it seems like a holiday, especially for the children."

WARNING !
Do not drink this canal water — it will make you sick.

AVIS !
Il est défendu de faire usage de l'eau du canal pour boire — elle pourrait vous rendre malade.

OSTRZEŻENIE!
Nie pijaj wody z kanalu tego, bo zachorujesz.

ACAUTELEM-SE!
Nao bebam a agua do Canal. Fas-te doente.

ΠΡΟΣΟΧΗ
ΜΗ ΠΙΝΕΤΕ ΝΕΡΟ ΑΠΟ ΤΟ ΚΑΝΑΛΙ: Θ' ΑΡΡΩΣΤΗΣΕΤΕ.

E. H. WALKER, Agent

Auguste Wante also testified on March 4. When asked if he had to pay for water to drink while in the mill, he replied, "Yes sir, 10 cents a week." And when asked if it was good water, he replied, "Canal water, that is what we get." The multilingual poster seen above warned that canal water would make one sick. When asked about work speed, he said, "I don't know, they make you go quicker and quicker all the time." He was asked, "And you have to go just as quick as the machine goes?" He responded, "Yes, sir." Graphic testimony heard from 14-year-old millworker Camella Teoli helped galvanize international support for strikers. In *Bread and Roses*, Bruce Watson writes, "At 5:30 p.m., Teoli had broken a mill rule by letting her hair down before the machines stopped. When a friend called to her, she tossed her hair over her head. Instantly the draft gear of a spinning frame wrenched it. Teoli was rushed to the hospital with two pieces of scalp wrapped in newspaper." (Courtesy of ATHM.)

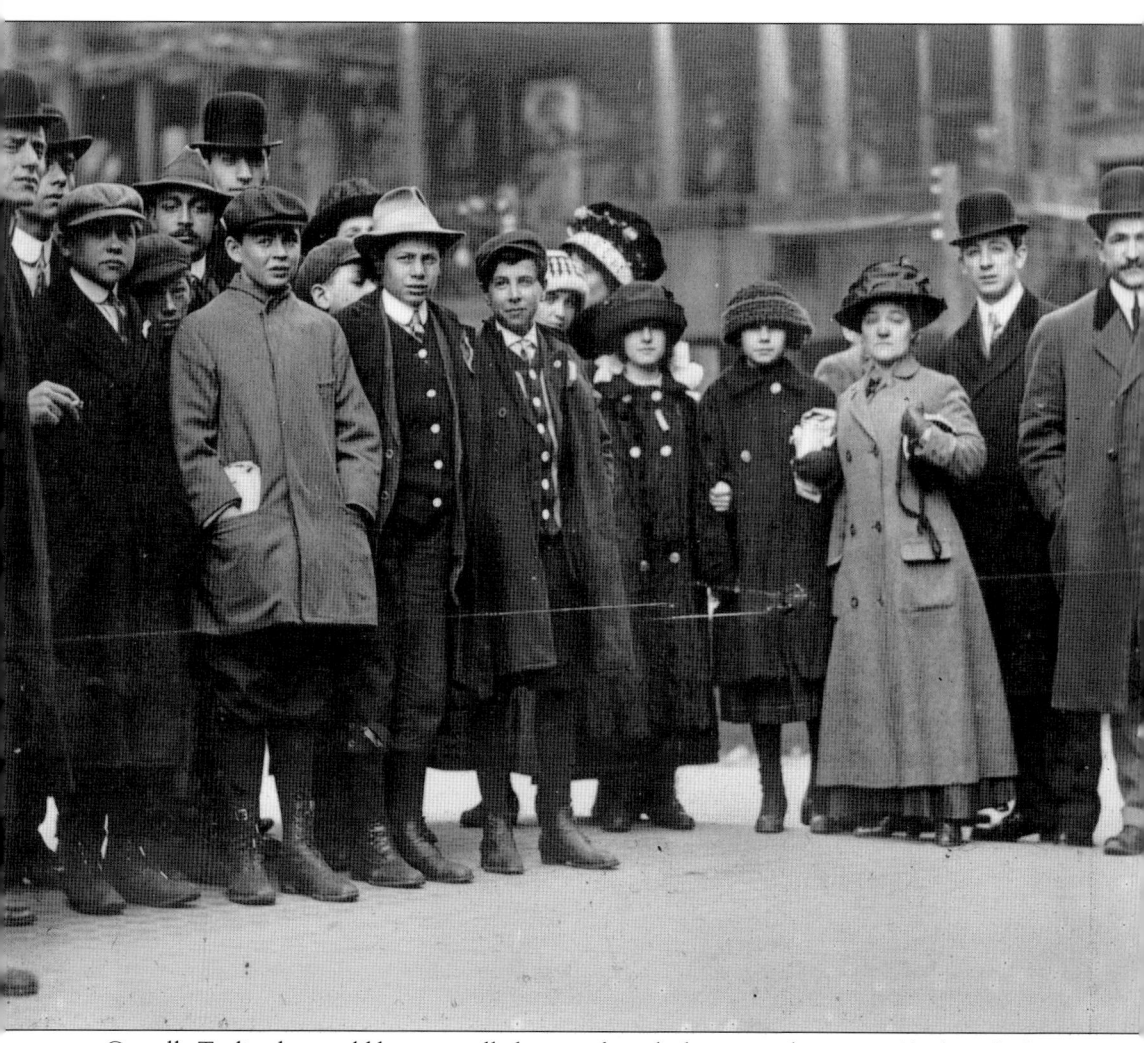

Camella Teoli, who would have travelled to testify with the group above, was 13 when she began working in the Washington Mill. She testified: "Well, I used to go to school, and then a man came to my house and asked my father why I didn't go to work, so my father says I don't know whether she is 13 or 14 years old. So, the man say you give me $4 and I will make the papers come from the old country saying you are 14. So my father gave him the $4 . . . I went to work and about two weeks got hurt in my head." Teoli testified that the machine pulled her scalp off. She was in the hospital for seven months, after which she returned to work in the mills. Joseph Cardella, a child during the strike of 1912, remembered her in his oral history in the Lawrence History Center collection: "Yes, that girl, I know her parents, the one who got caught in the belt," he said. "Ripped part of her scalp off. Safety wasn't the by-word there. Everything was production." (Courtesy of UNH.)

Six

VICTORY

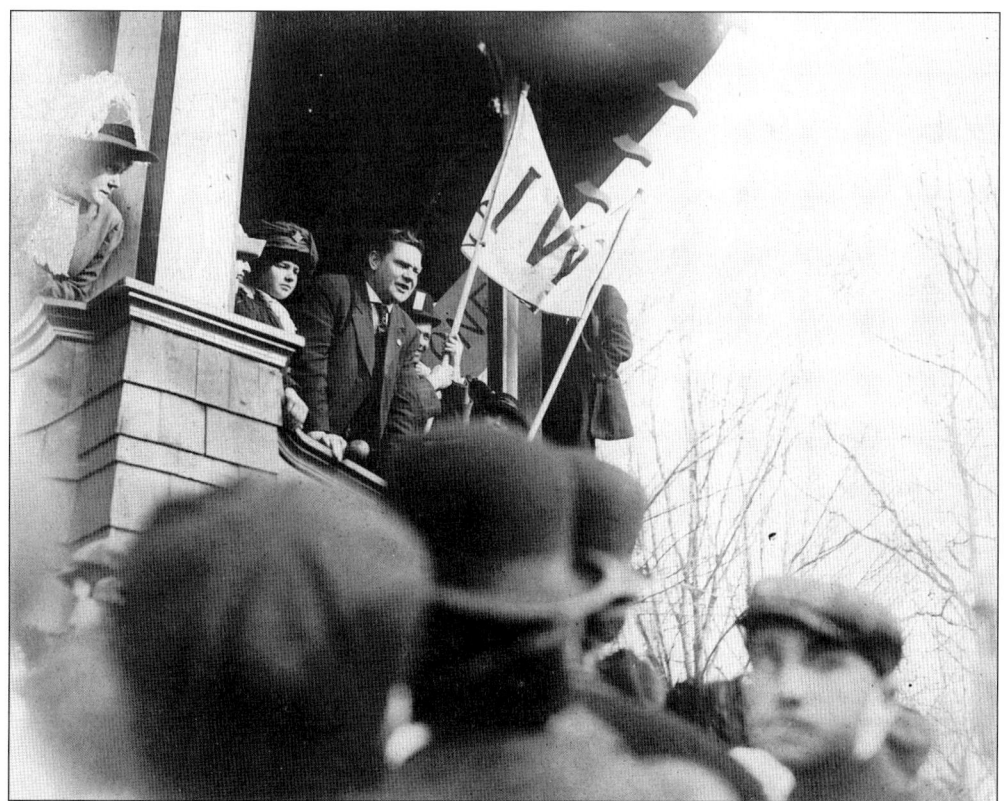

A tentative strike settlement was reached on March 12 in Boston with William Wood. On March 13, a meeting of 300 strikers reviewed the settlement. On Thursday, March 14, at a final mass meeting on the Lawrence Common, 15,000 workers voted to end the walkout. IWW leader William Haywood is seen here speaking to a crowd. (Courtesy of ATHM.)

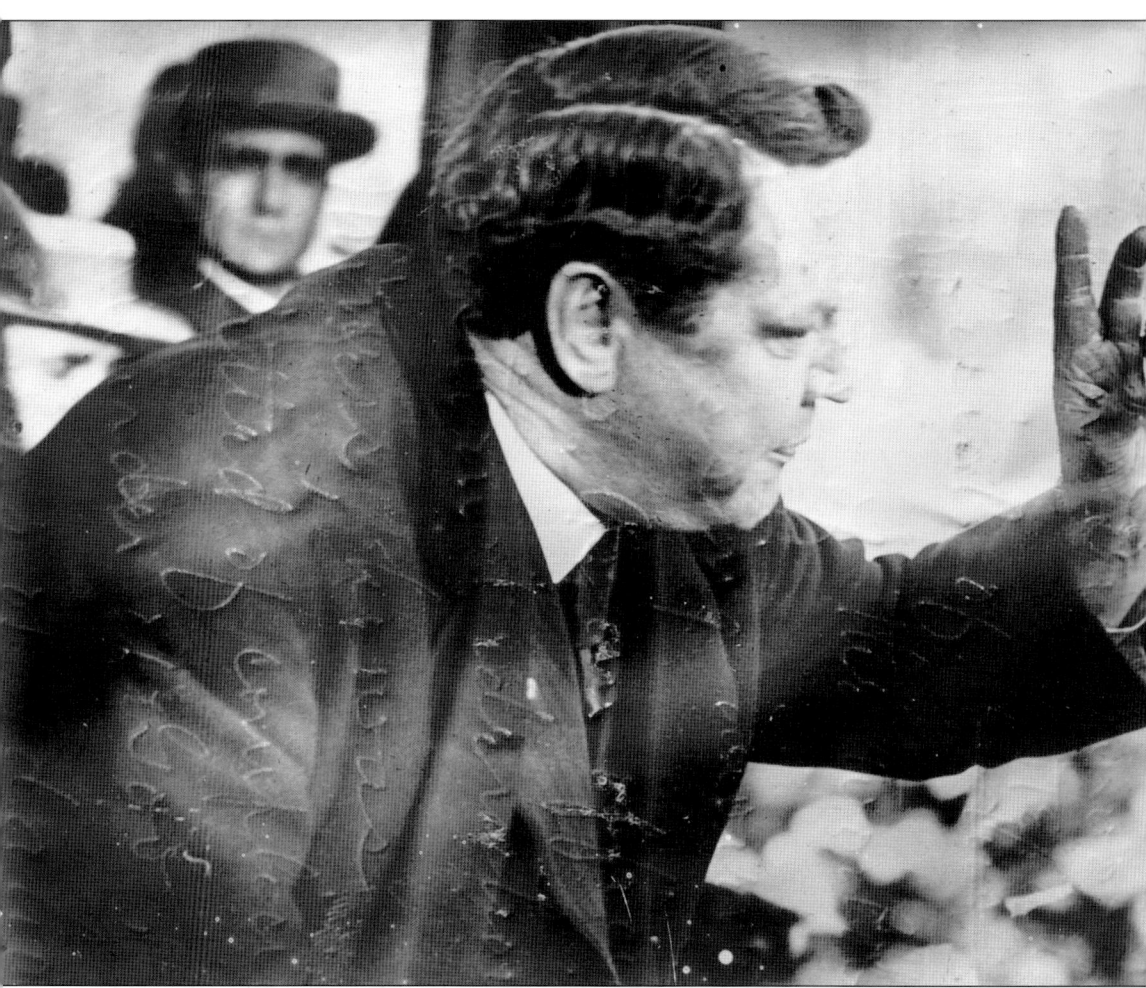

At the end of the strike on March 14, William Haywood told the strikers on the Lawrence Common the following: "You are the heart and soul of the working class. Single-handed you are helpless but united you can win everything. You have won over the opposed power of the city, state, and national administrations, against the opposition of the combined forces of capitalism, in face of the armed forces. You have won by your solidarity and brains and muscle . . . I want to say that this is the first time in the history of the American labor movement that a strike has been conducted as this one has. You, the strikers of Lawrence, have won the most signal victory of any organized body of working men in the world. You have demonstrated that there is a common interest in the working class that can bring all its members together." (Courtesy of UNH.)

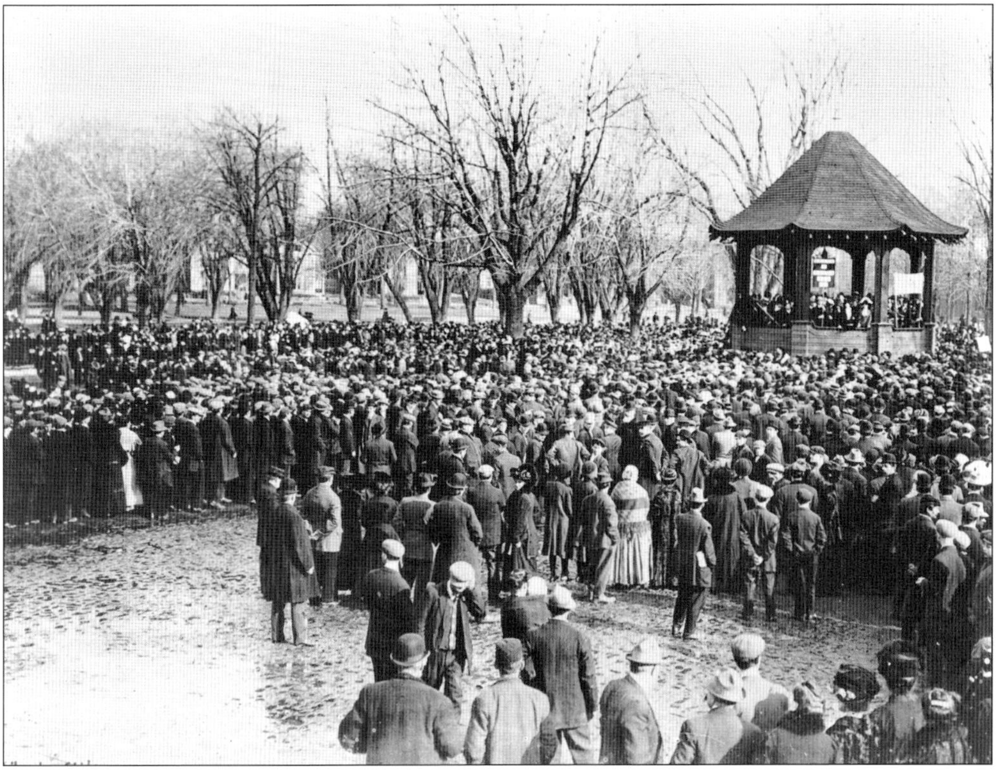

Before the historic vote was taken, everything was translated into several languages. Bruce Watson described the ratification meeting using contemporary newspaper accounts: "Bill Haywood and others made sure language by language the terms of the settlement were explained in Arabic, Italian, German, Polish, Armenian. The translations continued in Latvian, Greek, French, and finally Yiddish." According to local newspapers, banners around the Lawrence Common proclaimed: "In Struggle You Gain Your Rights" and "Release Our Prisoners Ettor and Giovannitti." At right, strikers raise their hands and vote to accept the settlement, which included, on average, a 15-percent pay increase, overtime pay, adjustments to the premium system to ease pressure on the workers, and lastly that mill owners would not discriminate against those who had participated in the strike. (Both, courtesy of UNH.)

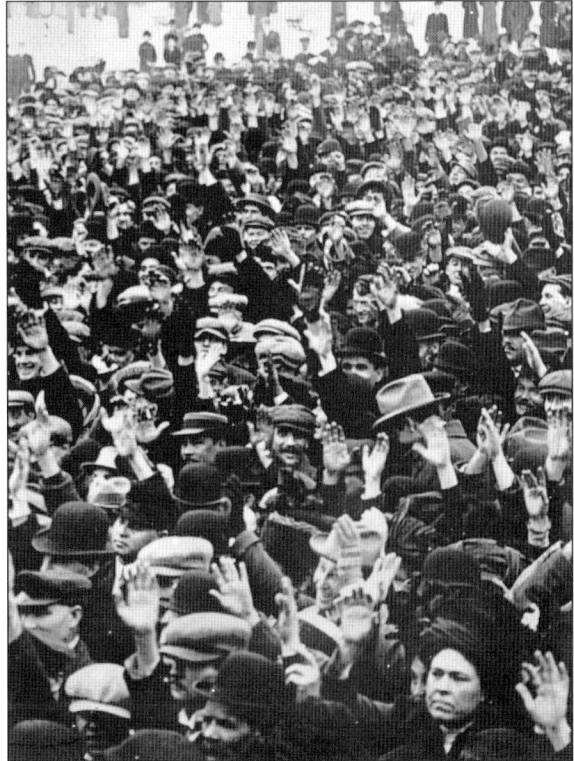

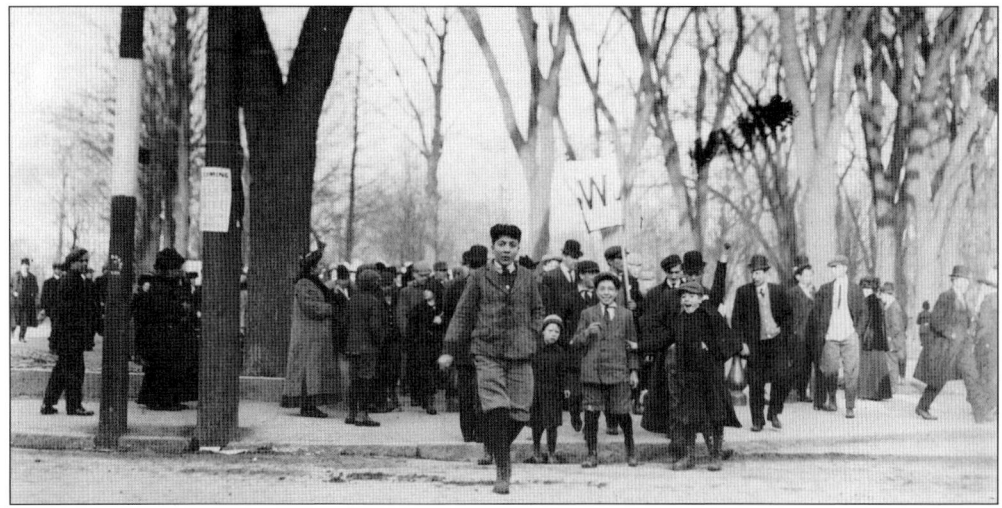

Above, exuberant strikers, young and old, leave victoriously from the mass meeting on the Lawrence Common on March 14. Eugene Debs, the founder of the American Railway Union and four-time presidential candidate on the Socialist Party ticket, said this about Lawrence strike: "The victory at Lawrence, one of the most decisive and far-reaching ever won by organized workers, demonstrated the power and invincibility of industrial unity backed by political solidarity." Below, a parade runs through the streets after the strikers' victory. The participants are smiling and waving up at the photographer. (Above, courtesy of ATHM; below, courtesy of UNH.)

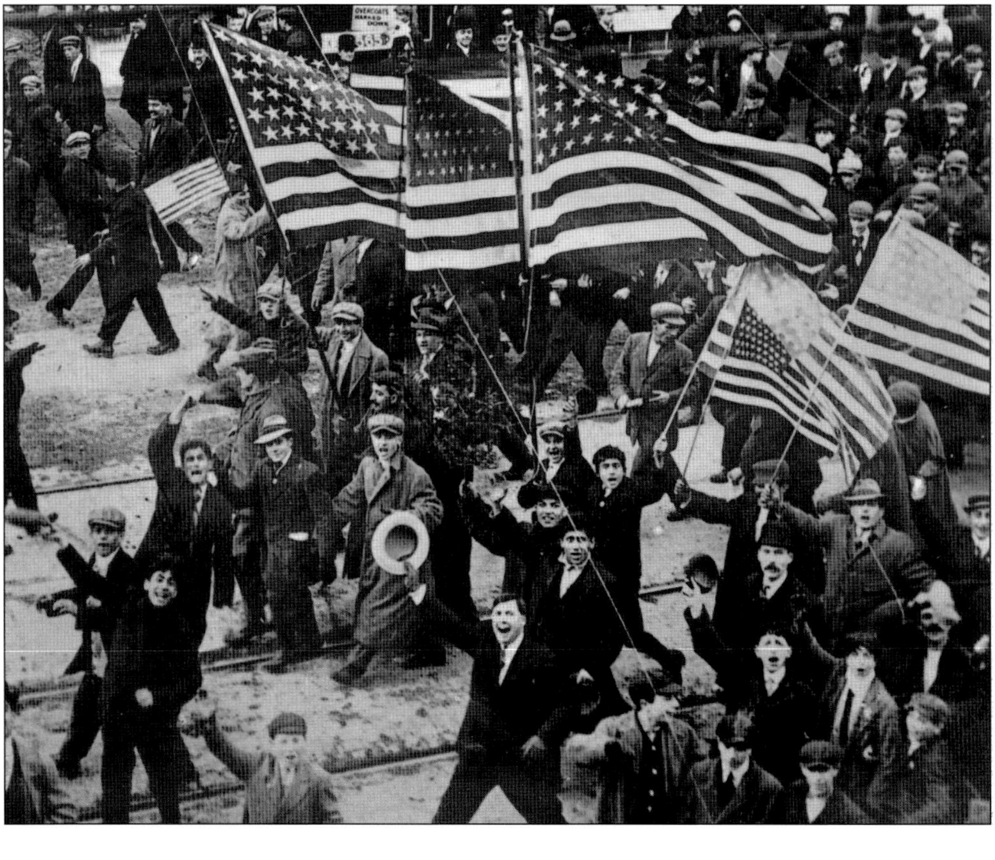

According to the IWW's William Haywood, "The women won the strike." In *Radicals of the Worst Sort*, Ardis Cameron wrote the following about the role women played: "While almost 24 nationalities were represented in the strike, the vast majority of female activists came from 'new' immigrant groups, especially Lithuania, Poland, Russia, Italy, and Syria. Most worked in the mills, yet each national group contained small proportions of unpaid housewives who battled alongside working neighbors, their offspring frequently in tow . . . Alliances between generations of women, formed in the performance of customary tasks, were activated and made visible throughout the strike . . . By marching together older women and young girls called attention to issues not specifically defined as wage related." (Right, courtesy of UNH.)

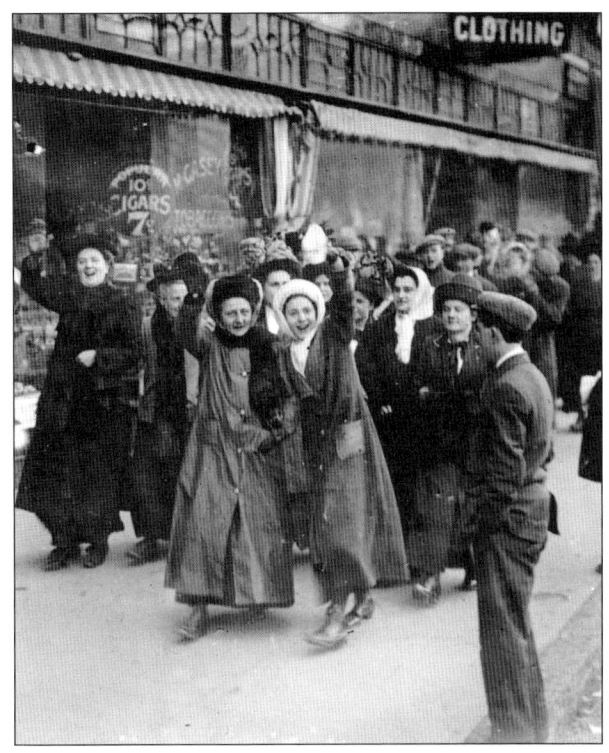

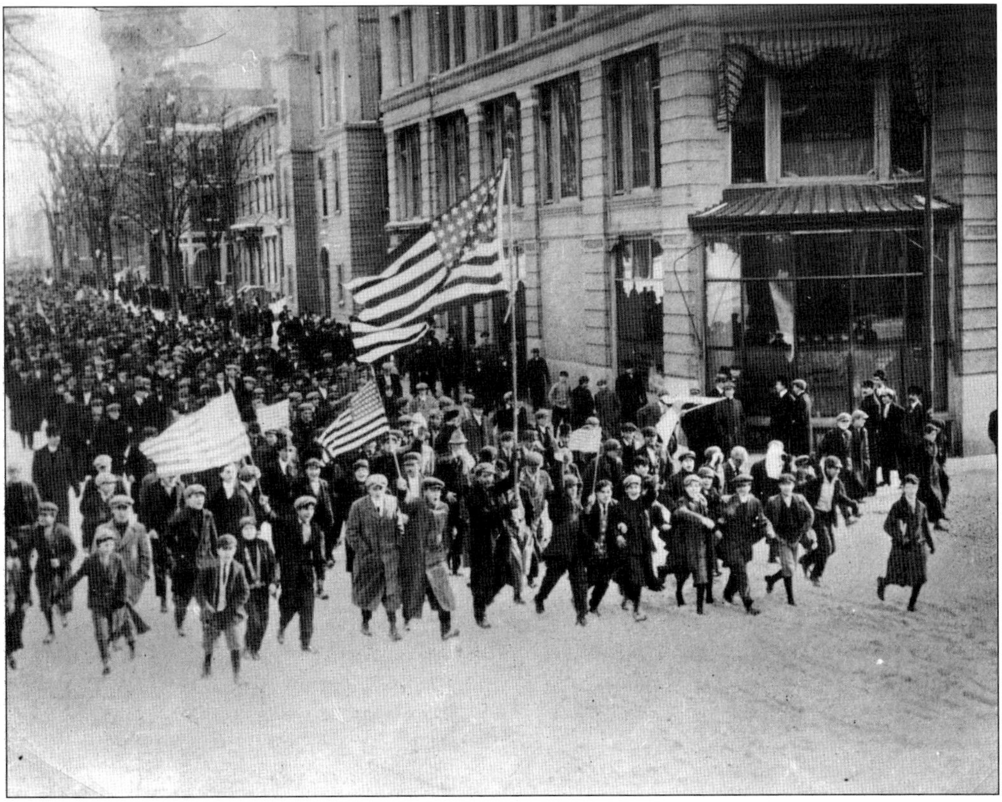

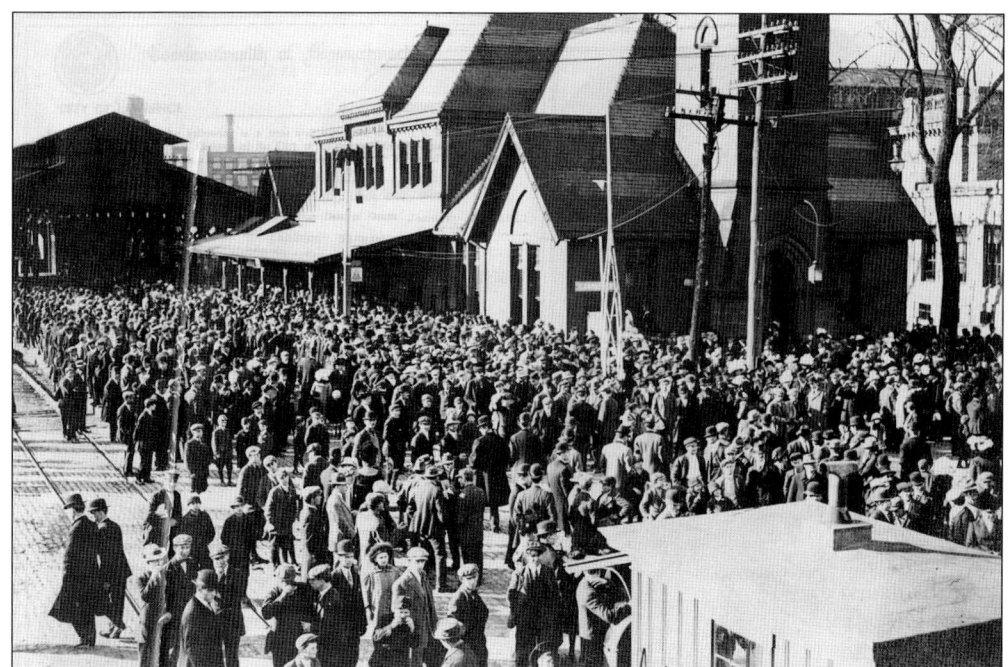

On March 30, after singing "The Star-Spangled Banner," more than 200 Lawrence children waded through the morning commuters of Grand Central Station and boarded the 8:00 a.m. train to Boston. According to a March 31 story in the *Lawrence Eagle Tribune*, "with happy and contented faces scrubbed to a picturesquely healthy glow," the Lawrence exiles were home. The strikers' children, who had been sent to supporters in Barre, Vermont; New York City; Philadelphia; Manchester, New Hampshire; and elsewhere, returned home to a rousing parade at the same downtown train station where women and children had been assaulted by the police and the militia on February 24. These two photographs show crowds of onlookers, several horse-drawn wagons containing children, and a band. The caption, "When 'kiddies' came home," is written on the back of the photograph below. (Both, courtesy of ATHM.)

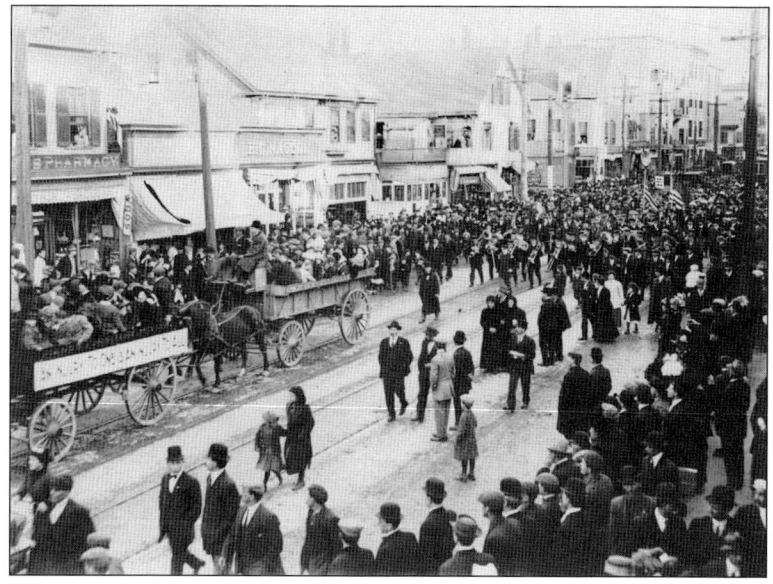

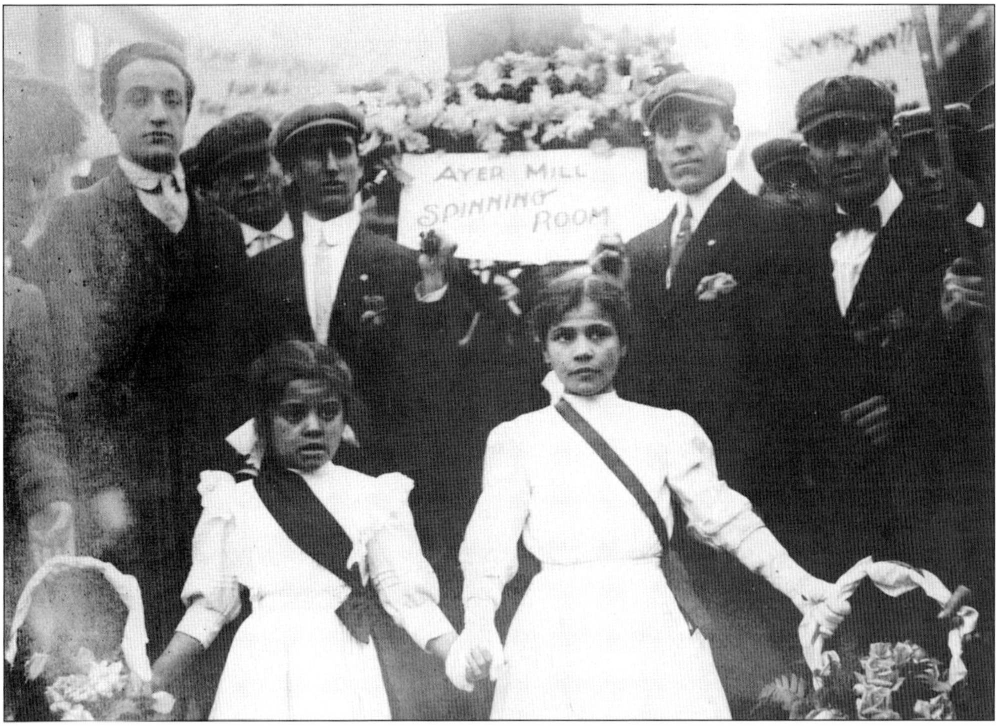

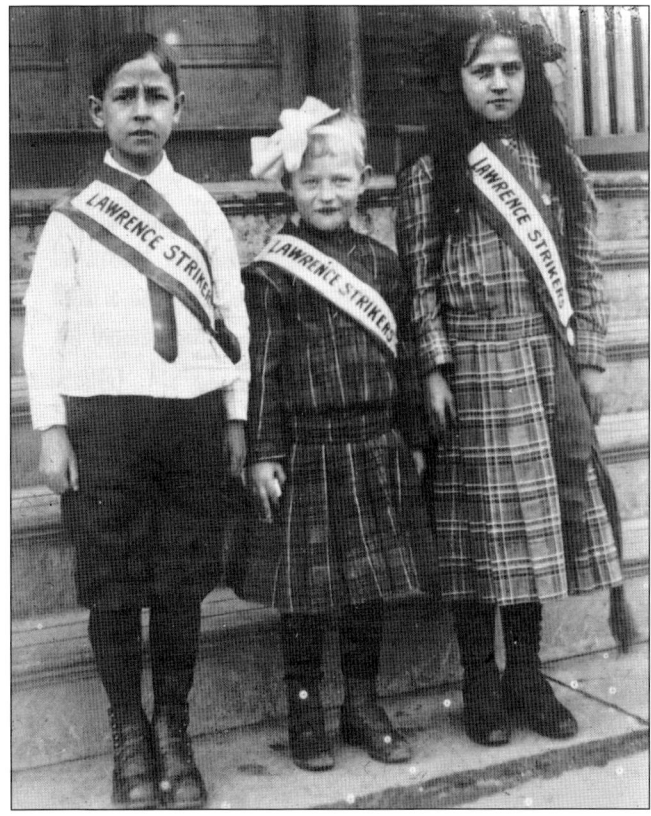

Above, two little girls holding flower baskets lead a group of Ayer Mill spinning room workers in the parade celebrating the return of the children of strikers who had been sent from Lawrence during the strike. At right, three evacuees at Grand Central Station in New York City await their return trip to Lawrence. Their host families dressed them in sashes to identify them as Lawrence strikers' children. (Above, courtesy of ATHM; right, courtesy of UNH.)

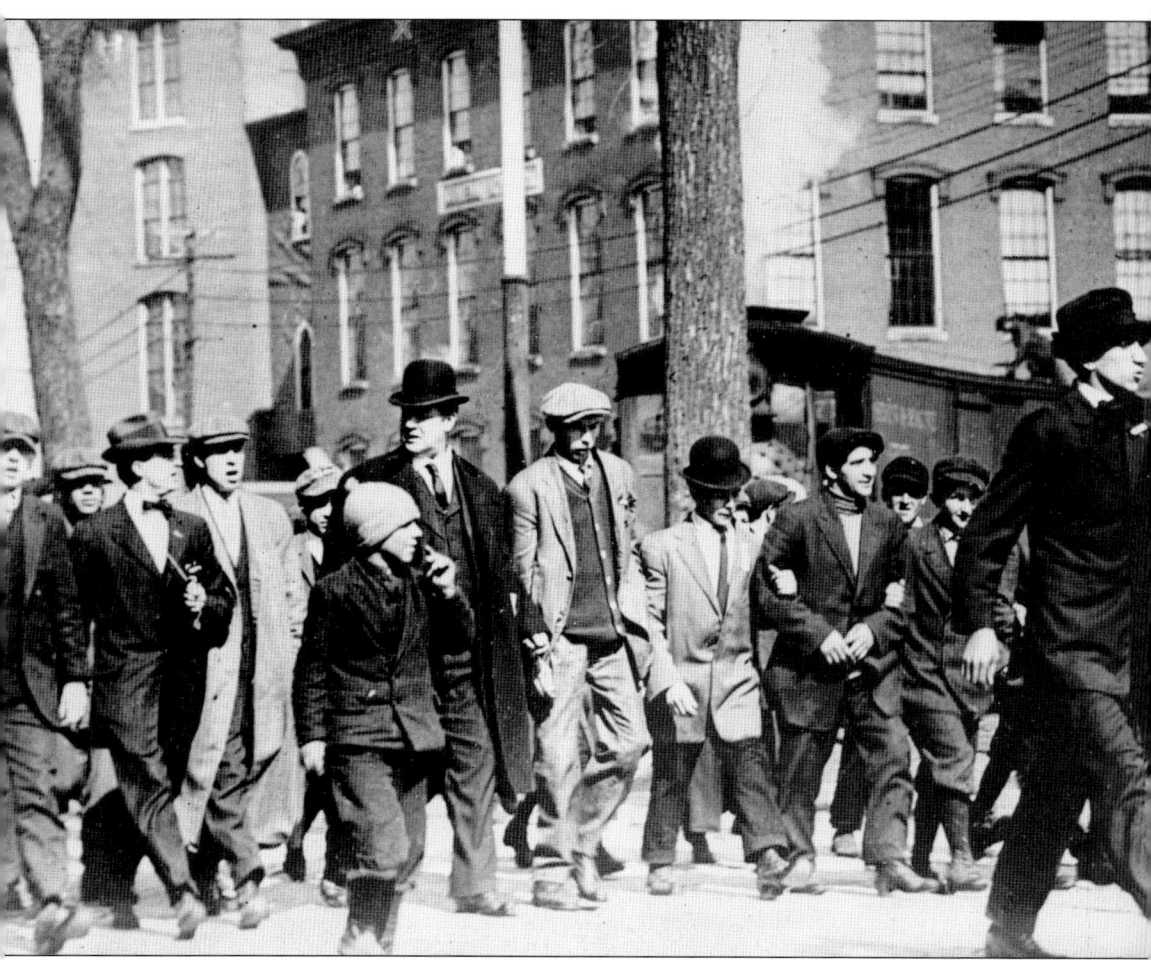

Lawrence's struggle became the nation's struggle. Emboldened by the success in Lawrence, workers across New England struck their own blows for a decent life. Here, the IWW's William Haywood (center, in dark hat and overcoat) marches with strikers on Merrimack Street in Lowell. Mill owners' worst fears were realized when workers flexed their collective muscles and voices. When the Lawrence textile strike ended in mid-March, walkouts broke out across New England, with other mill workers demanding significant wage increases. On March 25, Lowell mill workers struck and daily two-hour strike marches took place. Newspapers reported that marchers carried large American flags, big red Industrial Workers of the World banners, emblems of their national groups, and signs demanding 15-percent wage increases. Marching bands frequently led the processions, and workers loudly banged on pots and pans. (Courtesy of LOC.)

Seven

IN DEFENSE OF CARUSO, ETTOR, AND GIOVANNITTI

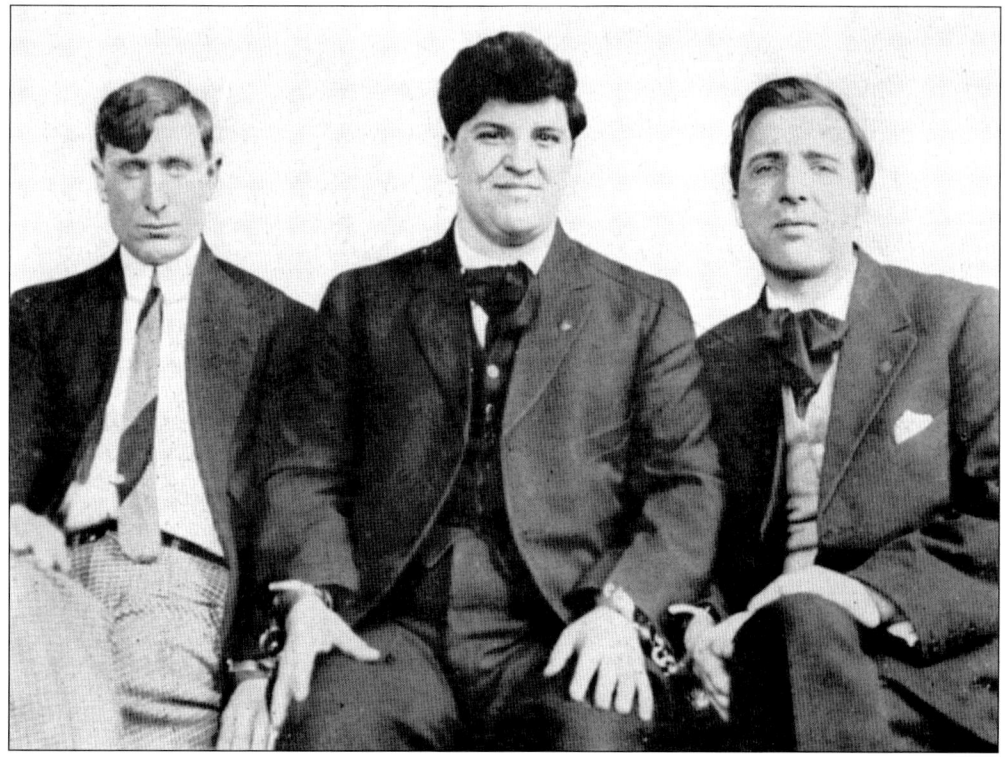

The January 29, 1912, the arrests of Joseph Ettor and Arturo Giovannitti for their alleged role in the shooting death of striker Anna LoPizzo were made to break the mill strike. Connecting the two men to LoPizzo's death, the thinking went, would cause the growing legions of strikers to dissipate. Instead, the week after their arrests saw the largest number of street demonstrators of the entire strike. Striker Joseph Caruso, left, was arrest later in April and charged with murder.

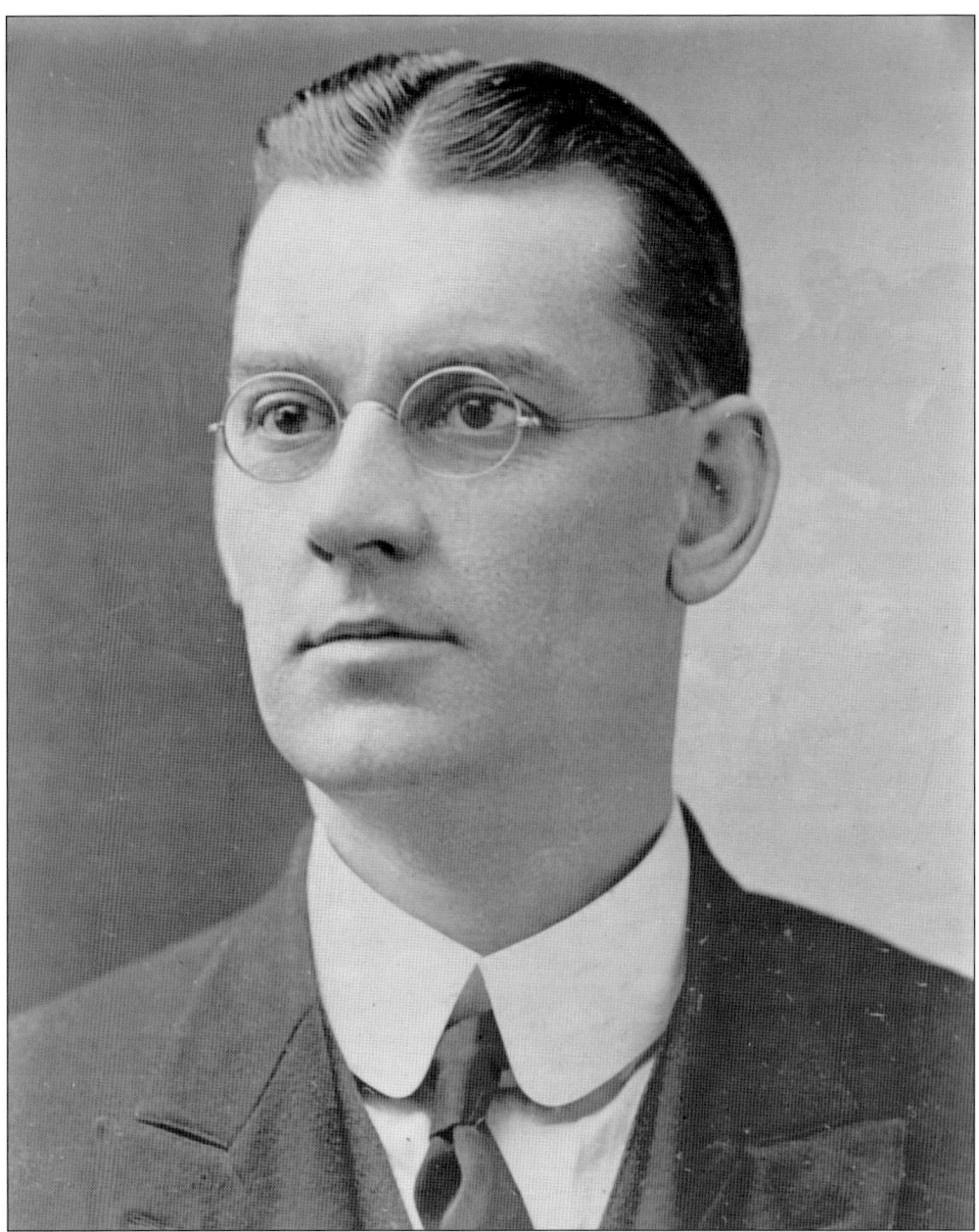

Taking an active interest in the defense of Joseph Caruso, Joseph Ettor, and Arturo Giovannitti was Rev. Roland D. Sawyer, a Protestant minister and eventual Massachusetts state legislator. The son of a shoemaker and a teacher, Sawyer dropped out of school at 16 to learn the craft of shoemaking from his dad. After four years, his attention turned toward religion, and he entered the Revere Lay College (later Gordon College) in Revere, Massachusetts, in 1895. Sawyer graduated in 1898 and took a position as the pastor of Hope Chapel in Brockton, Massachusetts. In the early 1900s, Sawyer embraced Christian Socialism and affiliated himself with the Socialist Party. He ran for governor of Massachusetts on the Socialist ticket in 1912 and lost. He eventually changed his affiliation to the Democratic Party and was elected to the legislature, where he served from 1913 to 1941. (Courtesy of UNH.)

Sawyer went on an extended speaking tour to raise money for the defense and to tell his audiences of the connections between the upcoming trial and the wintertime strike. In the summer and fall of 1912, he delivered slide lectures on the strike as part of a campaign to defend Ettor and Giovannitti, whom authorities were trying to frame as accessories to murder. A third defendant was Joseph Caruso, a striker charged as an accomplice. All three men faced the death penalty. Sawyer made the point that the men were really on trial for helping to raise the pay of textile workers across New England. Many of the 60 or so slides grace the pages of this book.

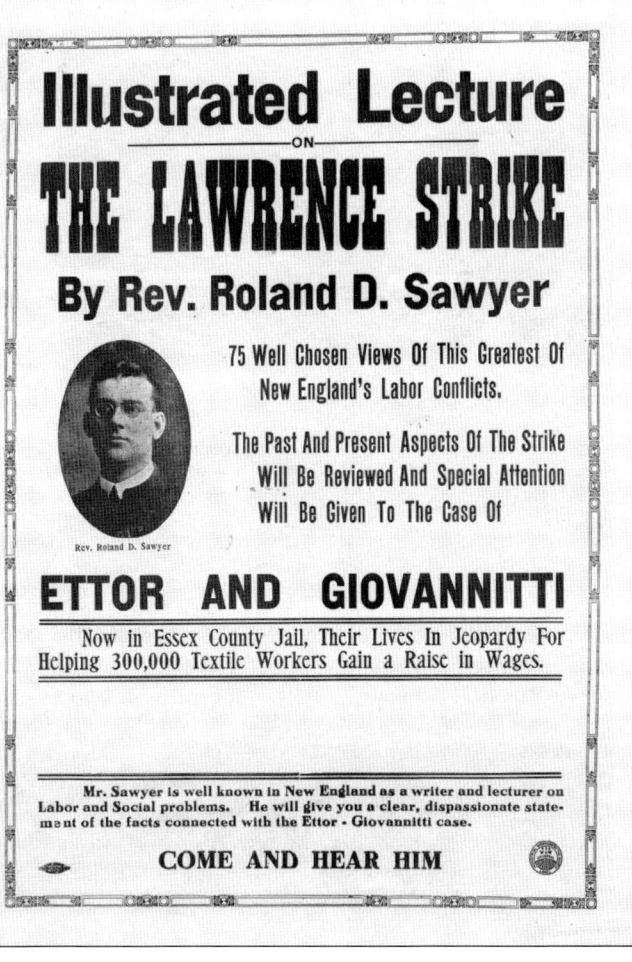

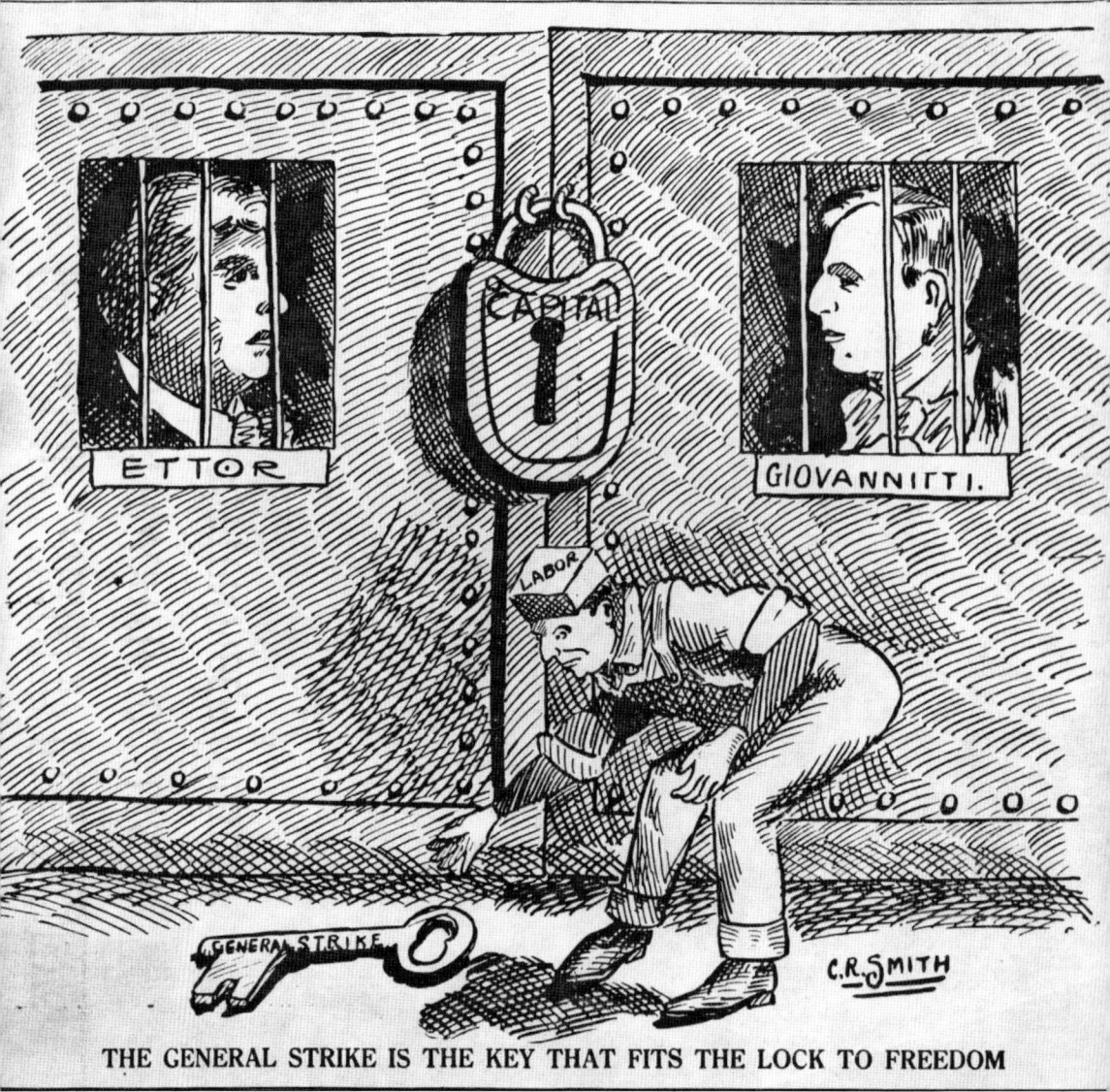

This illustration by artist C.R. Smith urges a general strike by workers to show support for Ettor and Giovannitti. At an Ettor-Giovannitti-Caruso protest meeting at Cooper Union in New York City on May 21, 1912, William Haywood said, "You realize that the men who are in jail at Lawrence, are in jail because they are fighting your battles. I felt that when I was in jail in Boise. And I know that without the united action of the workingmen and women of New York City, of the state of New York, of the United States of America and of the world, instead of appealing to you here tonight on behalf of Ettor and Giovannitti, my comrades and I would have been judicially murdered by the authorities of the State of Idaho. The mine owners of Colorado, like the woolen and cotton kings of Massachusetts and the New England states, had determined to bring about our death, even as these vultures of capitalism intend to make horrible examples of Ettor and Giovannitti." (Courtesy of WSU.)

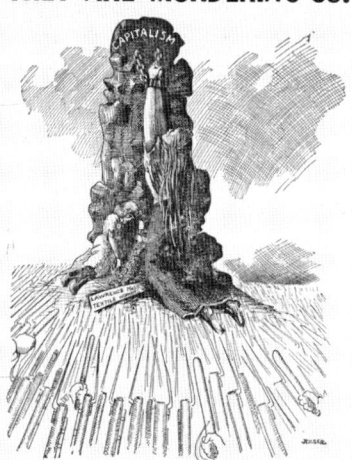
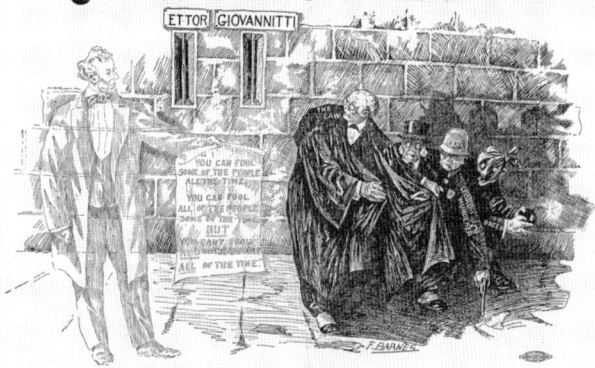
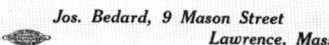

There was support from around the world for the release of Joseph Caruso, Joseph Ettor, and Arturo Giovannitti. Posters such as these were issued by the IWW and the Ettor-Giovannitti defense committee. On September 30, about 15,000 Lawrence workers held a one-day strike to demand that they be released from jail. Swedish and French workers proposed a boycott of woolen goods from the United States and a refusal to load ships going there. Their Italian supporters rallied in front of the United States consulate in Rome. The IWW raised $60,000 for their defense at demonstrations and mass meetings throughout the country. At one public meeting in Boston on September 15, the police arrested William Haywood on a variety of strike-related charges.

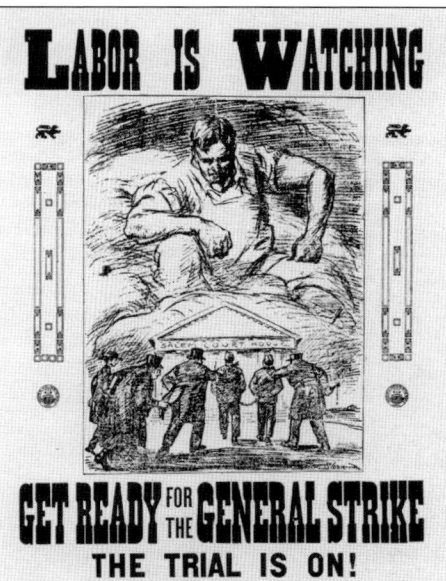

In 1913's *The Trial of a New Society*, Justus Ebert reported, "The work of the defense received much support from the working class in general. This came through the formation of Ettor-Giovannitti Defense Conferences, composed of representatives of Socialist, labor, and progressive organizations." Workers traveled regularly from Lawrence to Salem to show their support. Daily gatherings in front of the courthouse were common, especially when rumors swirled that a verdict was near. When the jury began its deliberations, the *New York Times* reported, "Squads of mill workers walked back and forth in front of the Court House for hours, and as long as they kept moving they were not bothered by the officers. These men kept their eyes in passing the Court House on the windows of an upper room of the building where the jurors deliberated."

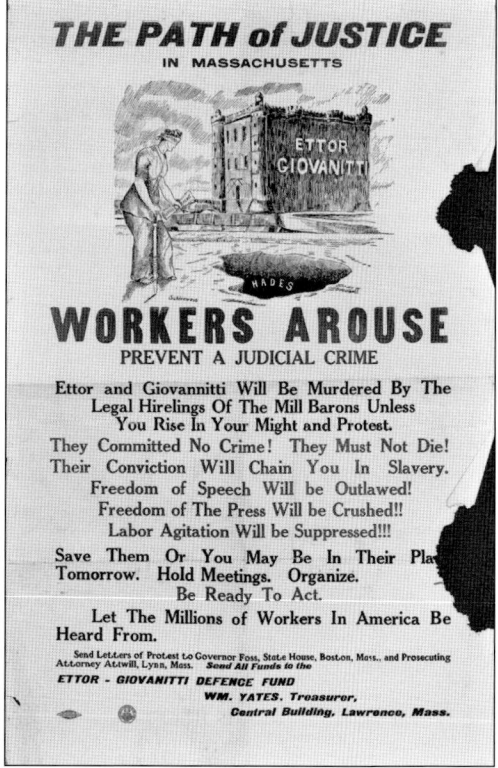

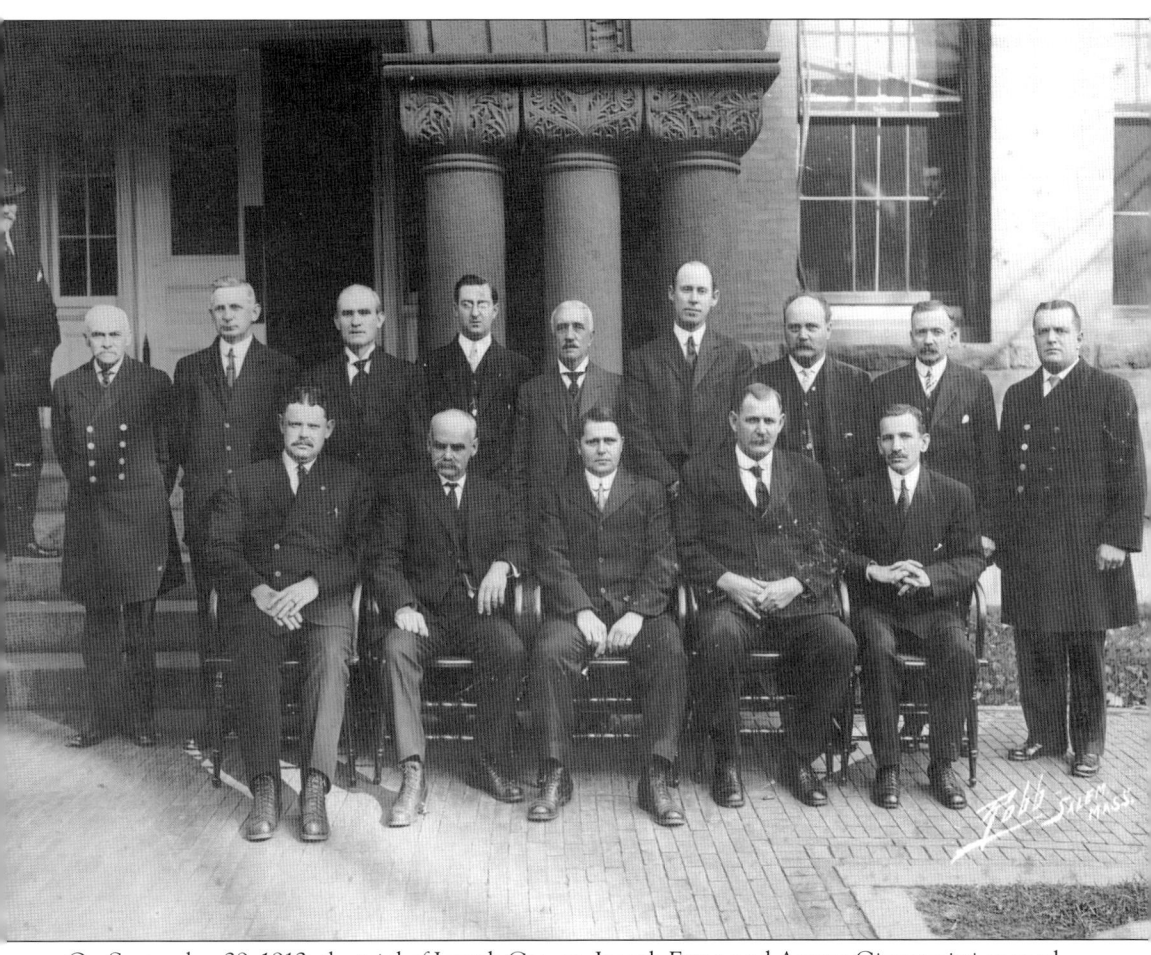

On September 29, 1912, the trial of Joseph Caruso, Joseph Ettor, and Arturo Giovannitti opened in Salem, but it was adjourned for lack of a jury and did not reopen until October 14. Numerous workingmen and unionists were members of the jury, including two who identified themselves as Socialists. The jury was made up of Robert Stillman of Rockport, a member of the carpenters' union; Samuel Bond of Lynn, a stock-fitter and active unionist; George Burgess of Lynn, a member of the cutters' union; John Carter, a teamster from Newburyport; Willis Creadsay of Gloucester, a member of the sailmakers' union; Thomas Doran of Methuen, a carpenter in a union shop; Daniel Duellea, a laborer from Peabody; George Edmonds of Amesbury, a lamp worker and socialist; and Harvey Elliot, a boss carpenter and employer of union labor. The speculation at the time was that several middle- and upper-middle-class people in the jury pool found ways to get out of jury duty because of the demonstrations and loud public outcry to free the three men. Seen here fourth from the right in the second row is Thomas J. Doran. A relative of Doran's donated this photograph to the Lawrence History Center.

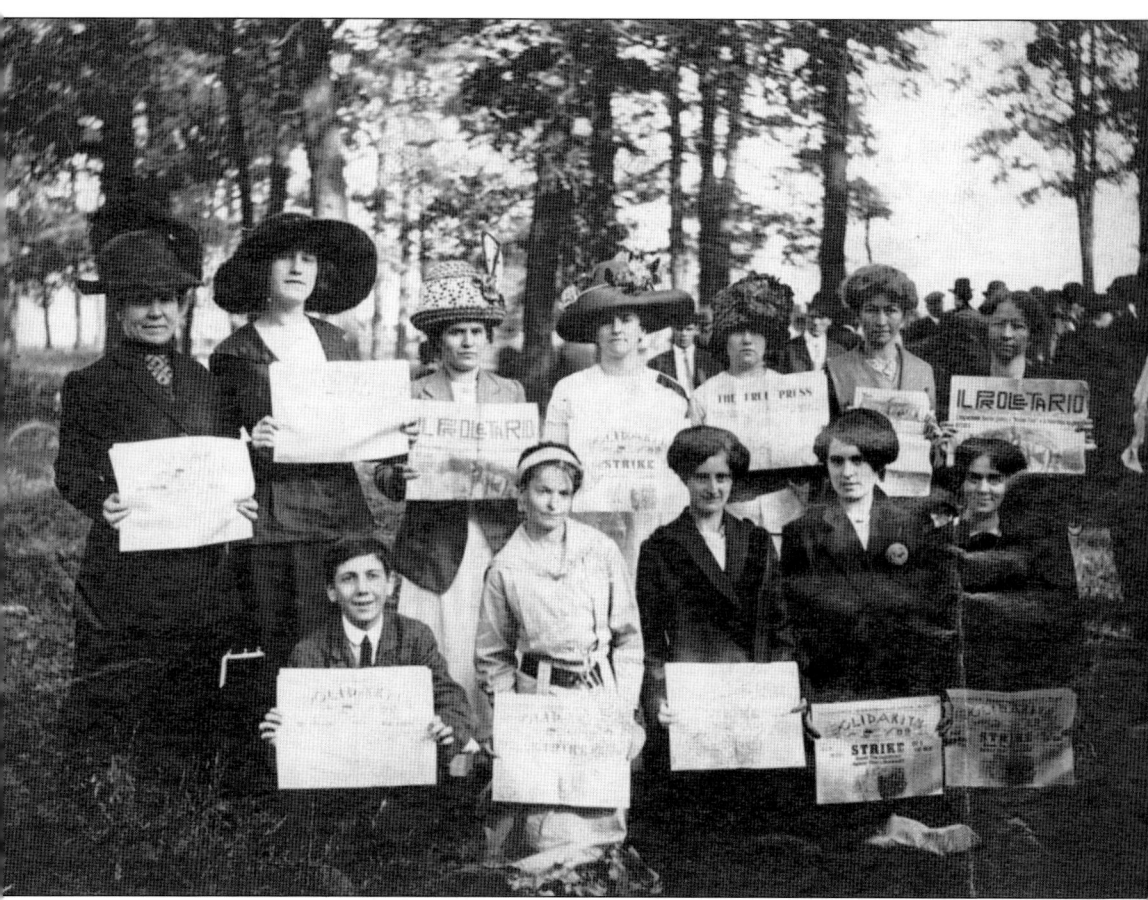

During the fall 1912 trial, large-scale support was received from workers around the world. Here, women demonstrate at the trial, holding aloft newspapers with headlines about the trial, including *Solidarity*, *Il Proletario*, the *Free Press*, and the *National Rip-Saw*. In closing statements to the jury on November 23, Giovannitti said this: "They say you are free in this great and wonderful country. I say that politically you are, and my best compliments and congratulations for it. But I say you cannot be half free and half slave, and economically all the working class in the United States are as much slaves now as Negroes were forty and fifty years ago; because the man that owns the tool wherewith another man works, the man that owns the house where this man lives, the man that owns the factory where this man wants to go to work—that man owns and controls the bread that man eats and therefore owns and controls his mind, his body, his heart, his soul." (Courtesy of WSU.)

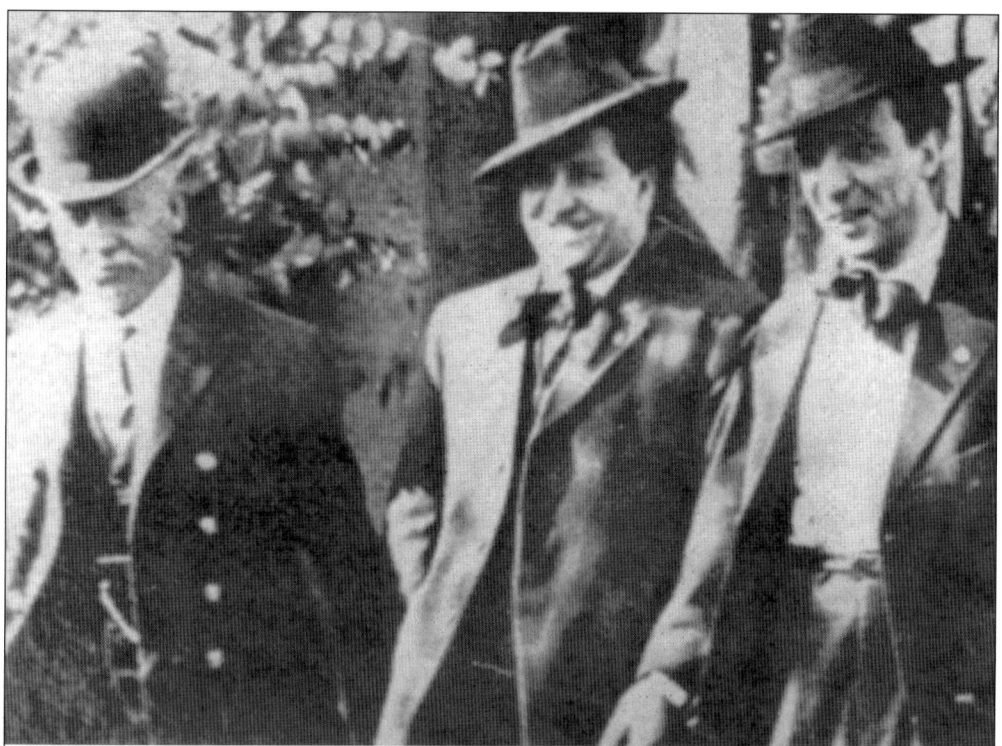

SALEM, Mass., Nov. 26.

ACQUITTED, THEY KISSED.

Ettor, Giovannitti, and Caruso Thanked Judge and Jury.

On November 26, 1912, the *New York Times* headline ran: "Acquitted, They Kissed; Ettor, Giovannitti, Caruso Thanked Judge and Jury." The three men entered the courtroom wearing red carnations in their lapels. When they heard the words freeing them from the murder charge, they embraced and kissed each other in the prisoners' cage. Giovannitti then sprang to his feet. "Gentlemen of the jury," he said, his face beaming with joy, "in the name of justice, truth and civilization, I thank you." "May it please the court," Joe Ettor continued, "I thank you not only for myself, but in the name of my companions. The thanks we offer are not only ours but thanks in the name of the working class." Many contend that their acquittal marked the true end of the strike.

I. W. W.

Thanksgiving day Ettor and Giovannitti will speak on the lots at the corner of Short and Chestnut Sts. at 2.30 p. m.

Giovedì, Thanksgiving day, alle ore 2 pom.

Ettor e Giovannitti

parleranno nei lotti tra Short e Chestnut Sts.

Non mancate, compagni!!

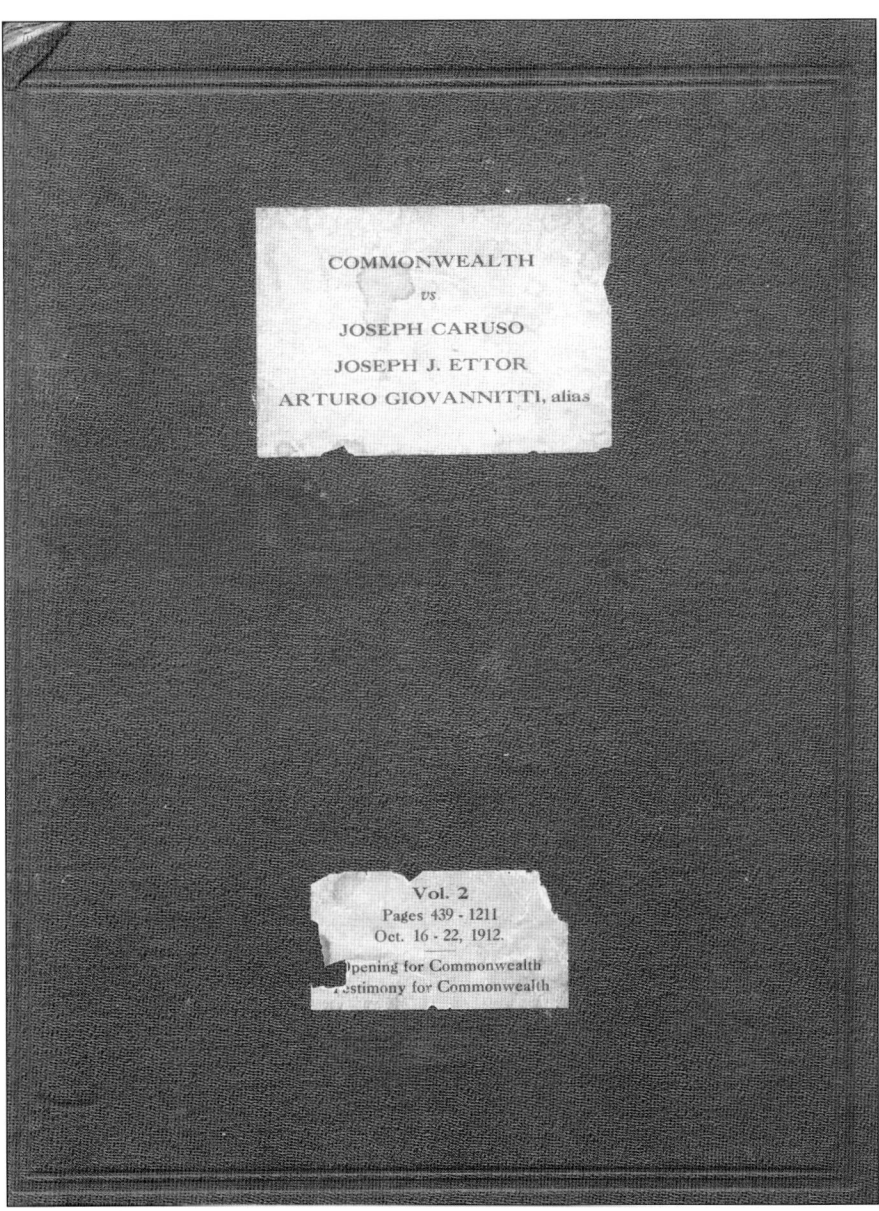

On November 27, the *New York Times* reported that when Caruso was released, "his wife waiting at the rail behind the prisoners' cage, fell into his arms." Giovannitti commented, "I am going to my home in Brooklyn for a day or two." Ettor and Giovannitti were in great demand after their release, as supporters wanted to see the two men and hear about their ordeal. Speaking engagements in Lawrence, Boston, and New York City were quickly arranged. On December 1, the *New York Times* headline ran: "Mob Bears Ettor Down Fifth Avenue; Wildly Cheering Marchers Storm Railroad Station to Welcome Freed Strike Leader." The story read, "To the chorus of the Marseillaise, sung by 3,000 marching followers of the Industrial Workers of the World, Joseph J. Ettor, the Lawrence textile strike leader, recently acquitted of the charge of murder, was borne triumphantly down Fifth Avenue yesterday afternoon upon the shoulders of enthusiastic admirers." Brian Mahoney, the grandson of Ettor's defense attorney, John P.S. Mahoney, donated the original trial transcripts to the Lawrence History Center, where they are available to researchers today.

Eight
"God & Country"

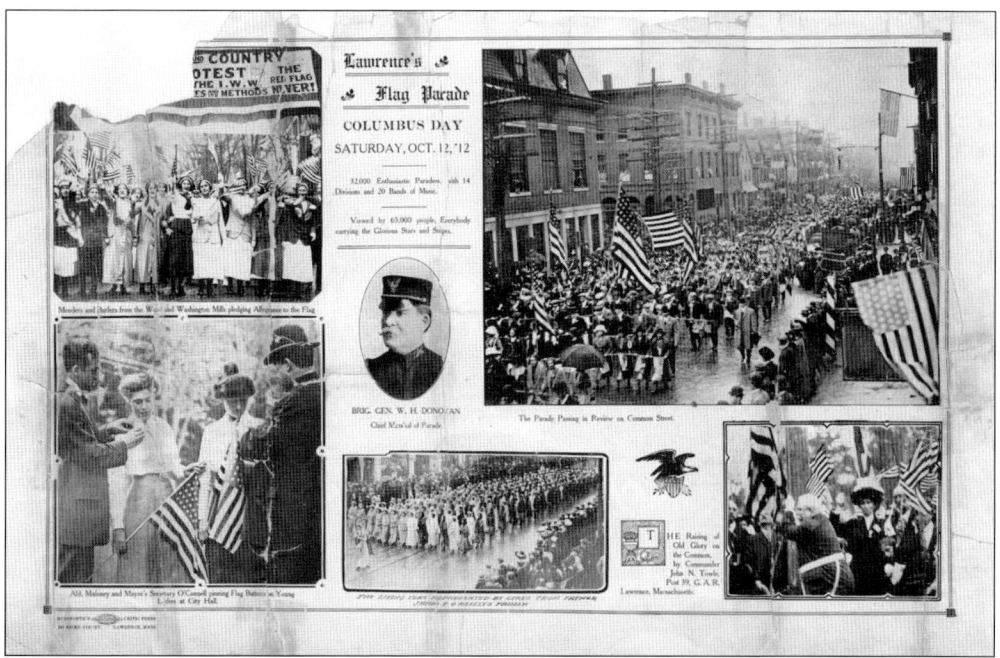

Local opponents of the strike, upset over the influence of the IWW in Lawrence, organized a massive demonstration in the fall in an effort to eradicate its favorable reputation among thousands of the city's mill workers. The city's commercial district was draped in red, white, and blue on Columbus Day, October 12, 1912, and an estimated 30,000 people participated in the parade. (Courtesy of LPL.)

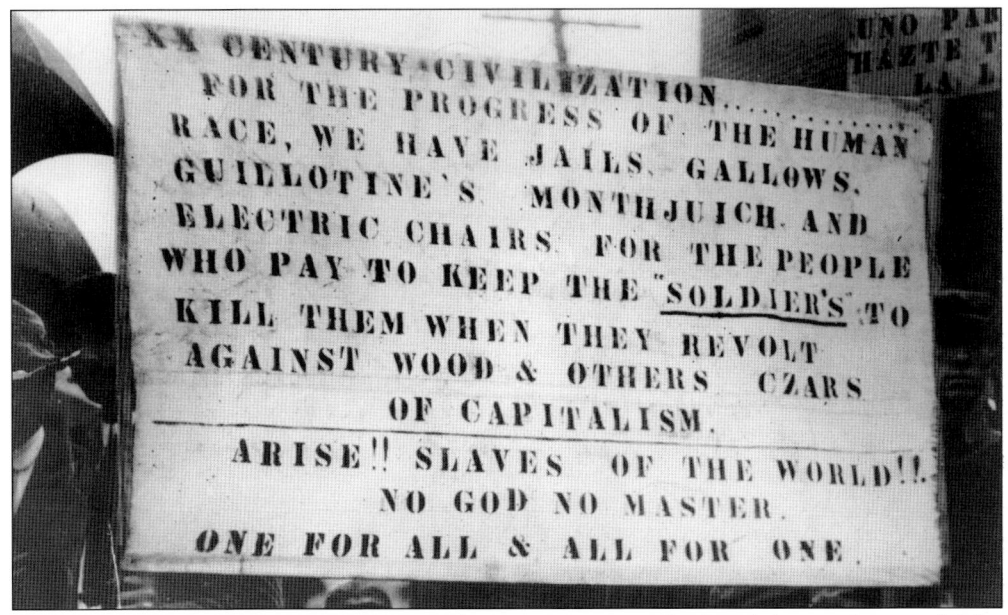

The placard above, in support of Ettor and Giovannitti, was displayed during their trial. The saying, "No God, No Master," in particular, angered many. By fall 1912, the business and religious communities in Lawrence had escalated their verbal attacks on what they repeatedly called the "godless, communist, and immigrant-led" IWW. Lawrence mayor Michael Scanlon and a highly influential Catholic pastor, Fr. James T. O'Reilly (below), organized a "God & Country" parade on Columbus Day 1912. In this anti-IWW climate, members, known as "wobblies," were fined for distributing leaflets downtown and had their buttons torn from their coats, prompting a series of street fights. (Above, courtesy of WSU; below, courtesy of Jack Lahey.)

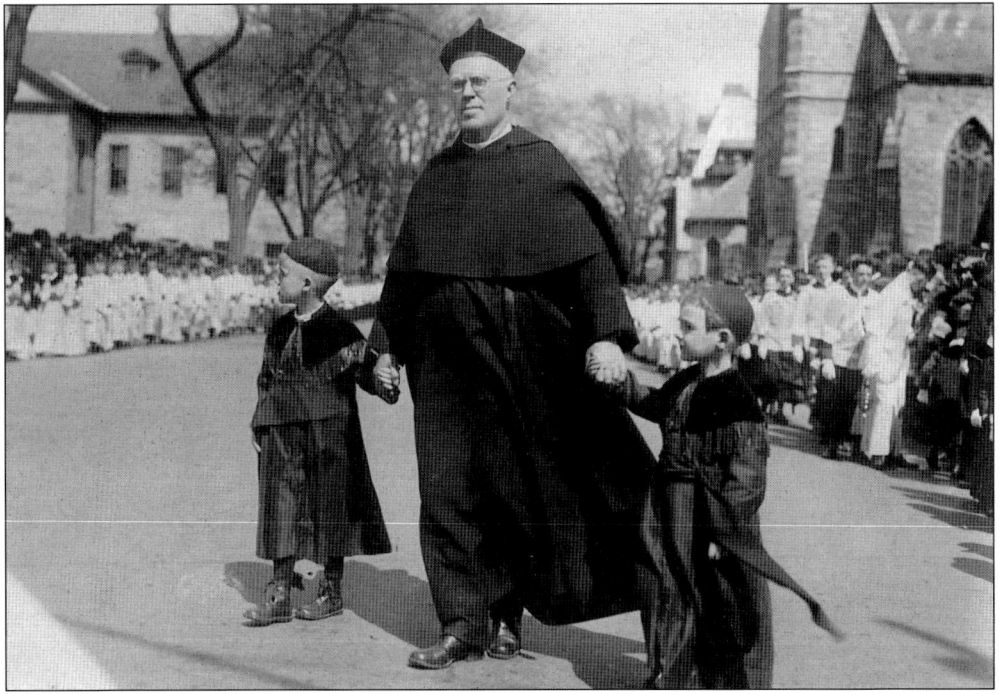

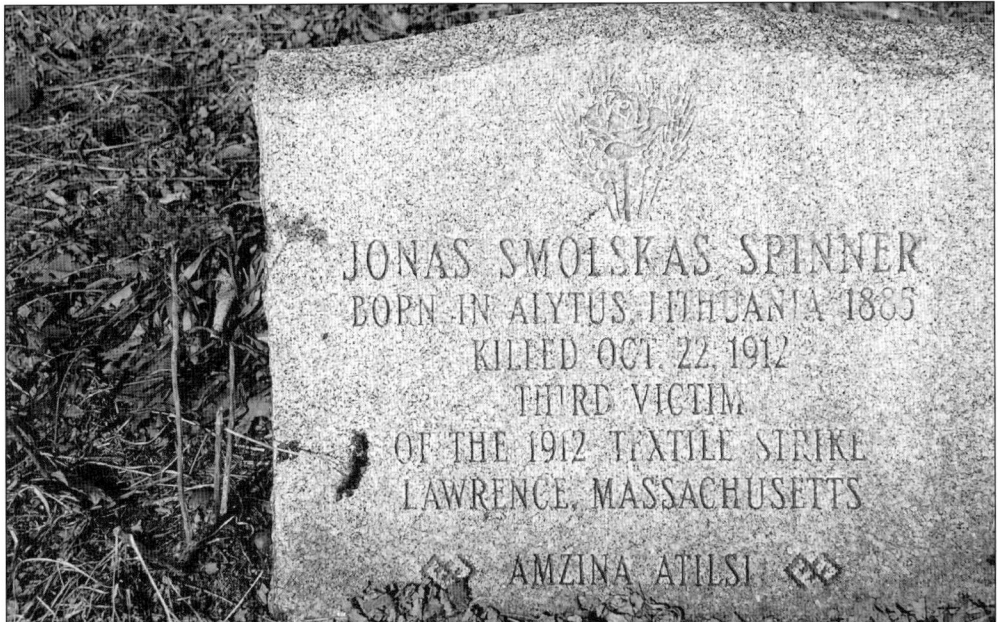

Less than one week after the God & Country parade, on October 19, Jonas Smolskas was assaulted for wearing an IWW button on his work jacket rather than an American-flag pin. He died three days later as a result of his injuries. Smolskas was a spinner in the Arlington Mill, a member of the IWW, and the third victim of the strike. He was buried in Immaculate Conception Cemetery in Lawrence along with Anna LoPizzo and John Ramey (see page 121). (Above, courtesy of Kathleen Flynn.)

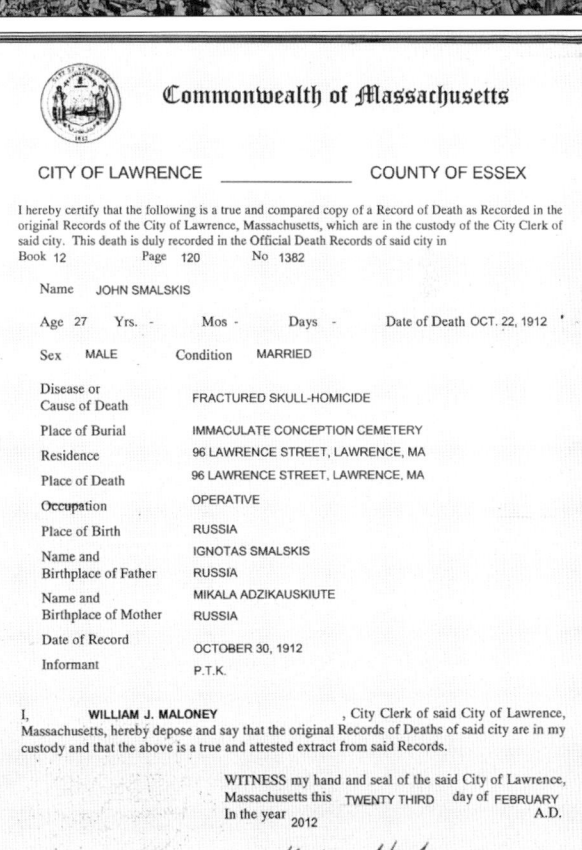

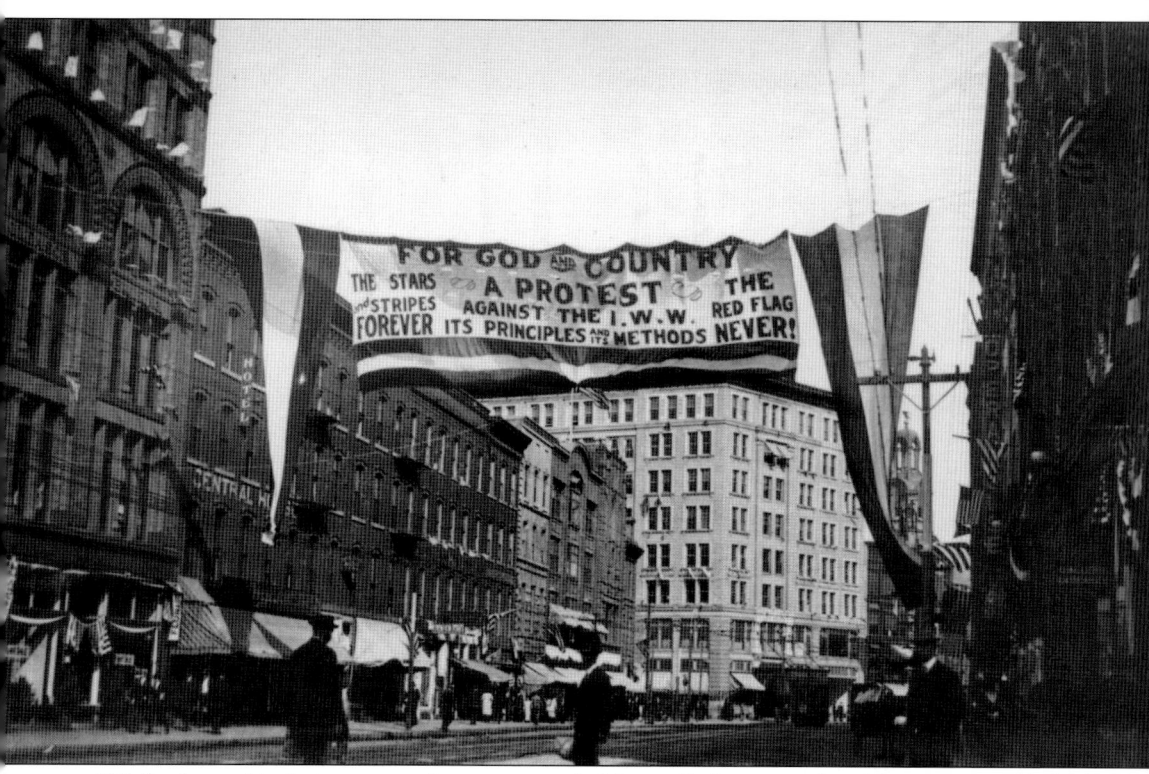

While the multiethnic cooperation was remarkable to all observers, the older, more established immigrant groups were less supportive of the strike. The Irish in particular, having been in Lawrence for three generations and been influenced by conservative Catholic priests, were eager to be accepted as Americans and were well represented in city government and the police department. They often opposed the strike for its perceived radicalism and lawlessness. The Lawrence City Council resolution on the God & Country parade, released on October 2, 1912, read, "If all good citizens unite on this matter we could have a parade thousands strong. It would have a demonstrative effect to eclipse all demonstrations seen here for years. It would be a glorious and inspiring sight going down Common Street around Union Street and up Essex Street with thousands of the most beautiful and best loved emblems of nationhood, the American flag, floating in the breeze. Patriotic songs could be sung. The American flag carried in such numbers through those streets would also cleanse the air there recently befouled with anarchistic rags and sacrilegious banners."

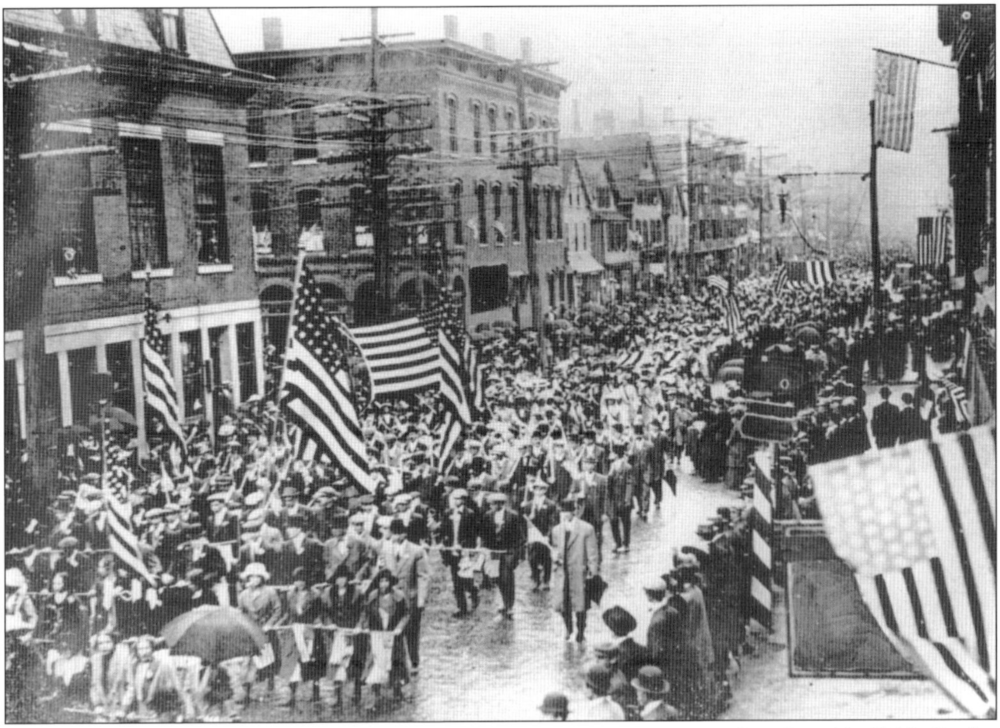

The God & Country parade proceeded down Common Street on October 12, 1912. Strike opponents organized the massive demonstration to try to drive the IWW out of Lawrence. Led by Fr. James T. O'Reilly, the parade received support from local businesses, churches, and mill owners. For decades to come, the collective local memory of 1912 was dominated by the God & Country version of events: that the IWW were outside agitators and "godless communists" who had duped the immigrant mill workers and that participation in the strike was shameful. The image below shows 13 workers from the Lower Pacific Mills offices in the parade in October 1912. (Below, courtesy of ATHM.)

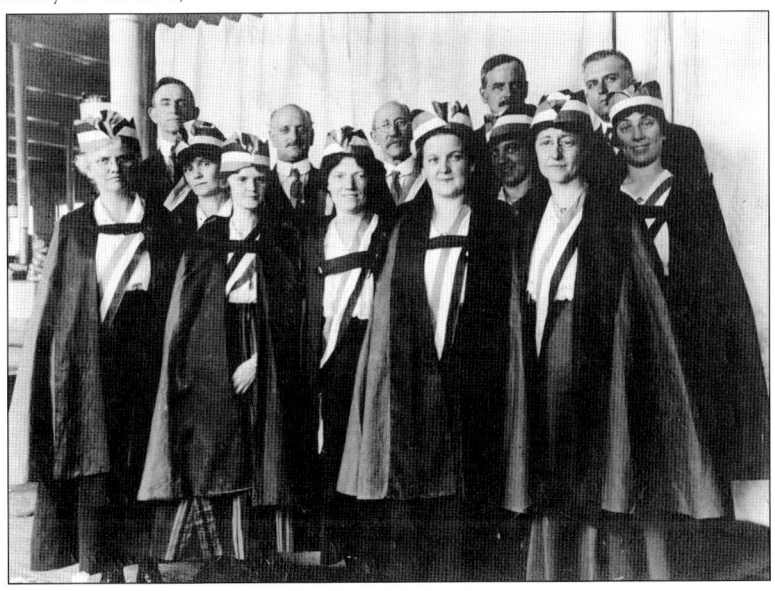

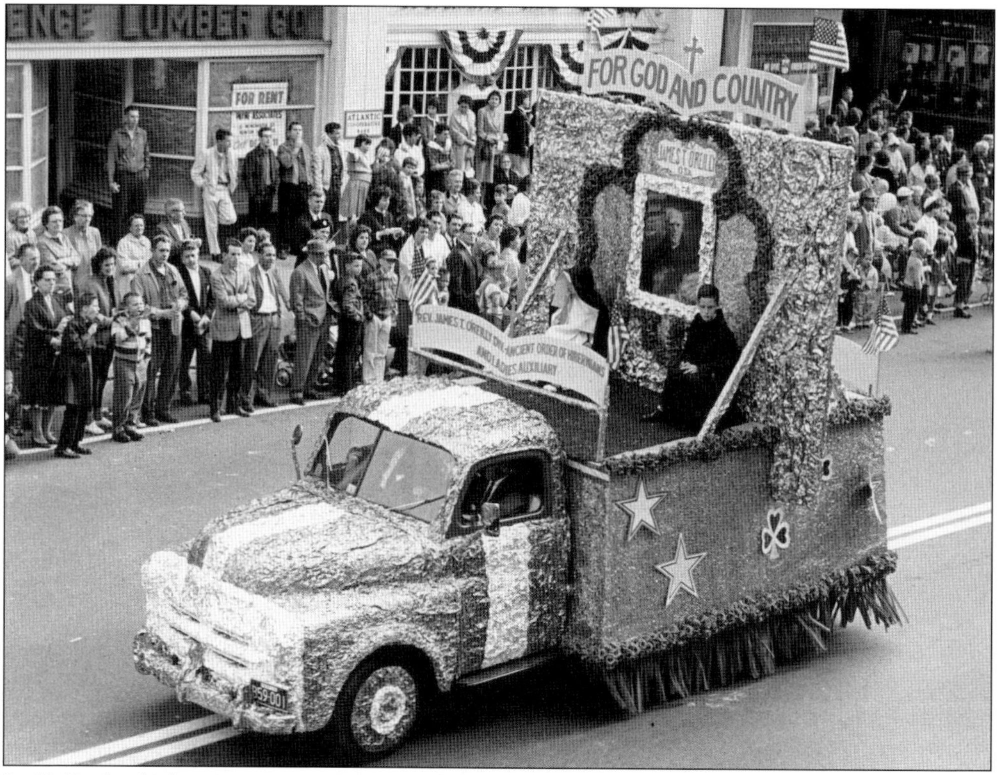

In 1962, the 50th anniversary of the 1912 strike, a reenactment of the God & Country parade was held on Essex Street, with little mention of the events of the strike and its importance. In a letter to the students and staff of the Lawrence Public Schools preparing for the reenactment of the parade in 1962, Lawrence superintendent James F. Hennessey wrote, "Their [IWW] methods and thinking were forerunners of many tactics used by modern Communism. They inflamed our working people; there were riots, bloodshed, and even deaths in our streets. The news of this violence in Lawrence gave our city a black name all over the world." In the 1970s, local historians, aided by artist Ralph Fasanella and New York City journalist Paul Cowan, took a fresh look at the strike. The strike's history has been a source of local pride since the 1980s.

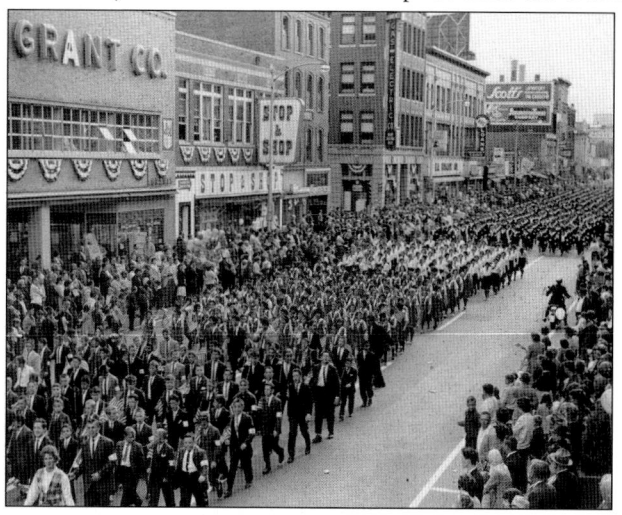

Nine

How Do We Remember?

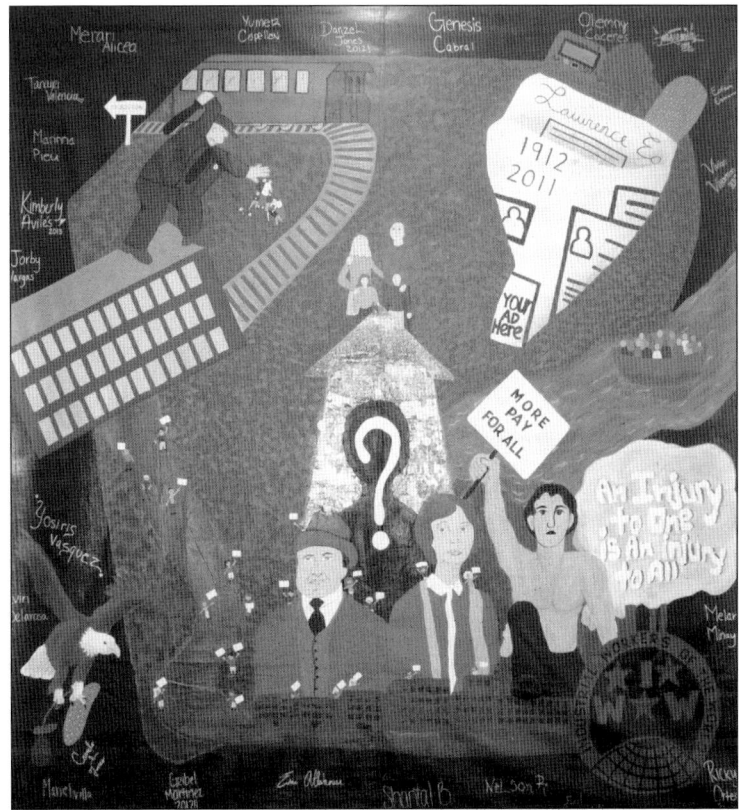

After 1912, local memory was dominated by the God & Country version of history for decades. Since then, people in Lawrence and around the world have debated, suppressed, celebrated, and reexamined the strike's multiple legacies. To commemorate the centennial of the strike, students at the Lawrence Humanities and Leadership Development High School painted this mural called "United We Stand" for the Lawrence History Center's strike exhibit (see page 122).

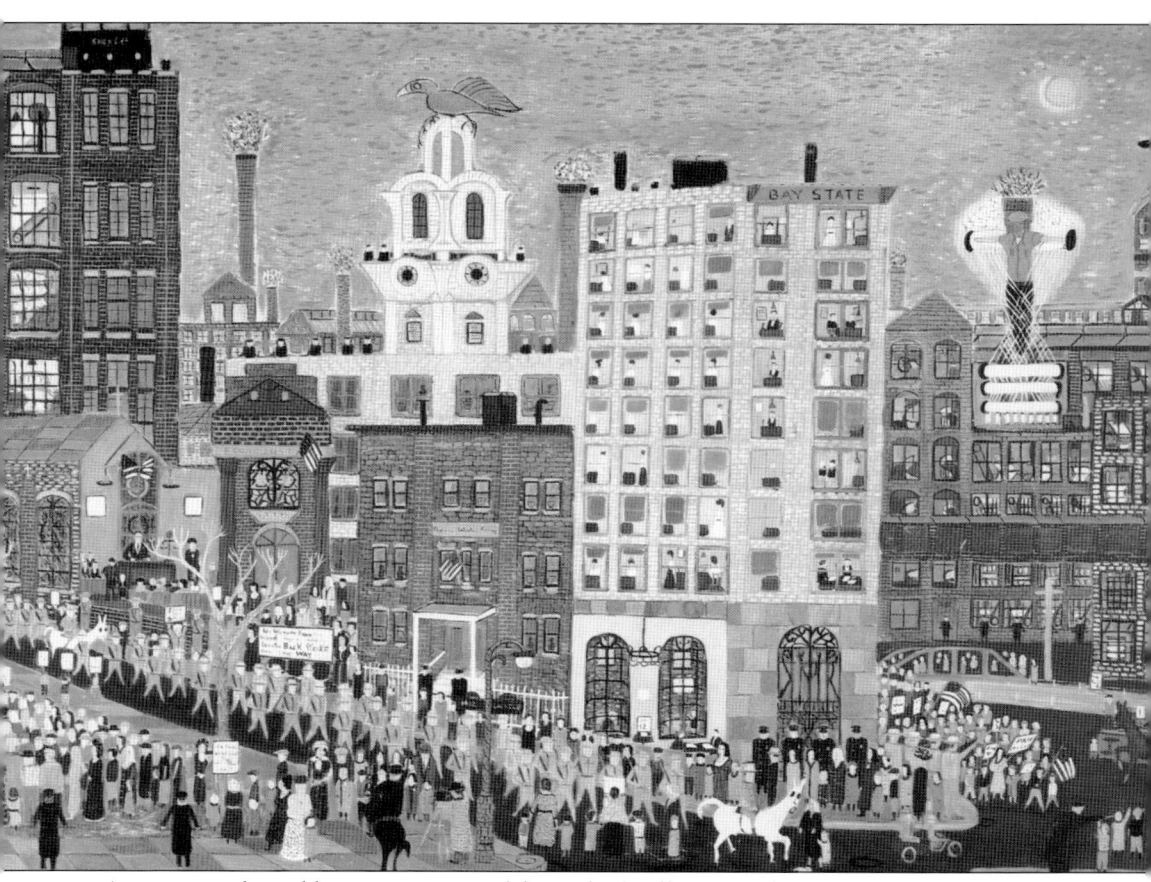

A new, more favorable interpretation of the strike finally emerged in Lawrence in the late 1970s. Instrumental figures included three New Yorkers, folk artist Ralph Fasanella, journalist Paul Cowan, and labor leader and historian Moe Foner; some local Lawrence historians, including attorney Ignatius Piscitello, Lawrence History Center founder Eartha Dengler, and Lawrence mayor Lawrence Lefebre; and some academic practitioners of the "new social history," including James Green and Ardis Cameron. Most of these people were present for Bread and Roses Day, held on the Lawrence Common on April 27, 1980. It was the first officially sanctioned pro-strike public commemoration in Lawrence. A portion of the painting entitled *Lawrence 1912: The Bread and Roses Strike* is shown above. The original 45-inch-by-90-inch Ralph Fasanella work is on permanent display at the Lawrence Heritage State Park. Fasanella was famous for his colorful images of the American working class. His interest in the history of the labor movement attracted him to Lawrence. For several years, he painted the people, places, and events of the area. The poem "Bread and Roses" was first published in 1911 by James Oppenheim, one of many sympathetic observers who visited Lawrence during the strike (see poem on page 10). He later claimed inspiration from seeing female strikers in Lawrence carrying a banner proclaiming "We Want Bread and Roses, Too!" No other evidence of such a banner exists, yet the phrase is inextricably associated with the 1912 strike. First set to music by Caroline Kohlsaat, and then by Mimi Farina, it became a standard for the labor movement and the women's rights movement.

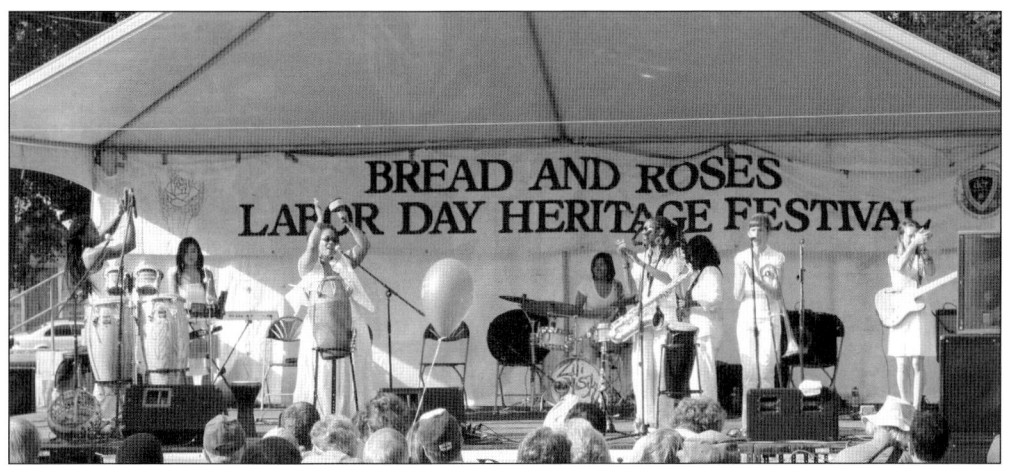

The Bread and Roses Labor Day Festival has been held in celebration of the ethnic diversity and labor history of Lawrence every year since 1985. Organized by the Bread and Roses Heritage Committee, music and dance, poetry and drama, ethnic food, historical demonstrations, and walking and trolley tours all occur. The festival also makes explicit links to contemporary struggles for social justice. The festival's welcome to attendees of the September 2012 event read in part, "Today we gather on the very Common that witnessed and fostered solidarity among Lawrence's workers. In this spirit, we have created a program that honors Lawrence's many cultures, both past and present. In addition to performances, we extend our support to unions and other community organizations for social justice in their fight to secure and improve the lives of all." Below, *Bread and Puppet Theater* performs for a crowd. Lawrence City Hall is pictured on the right. (Both, courtesy of Daniel Solomon Koff.)

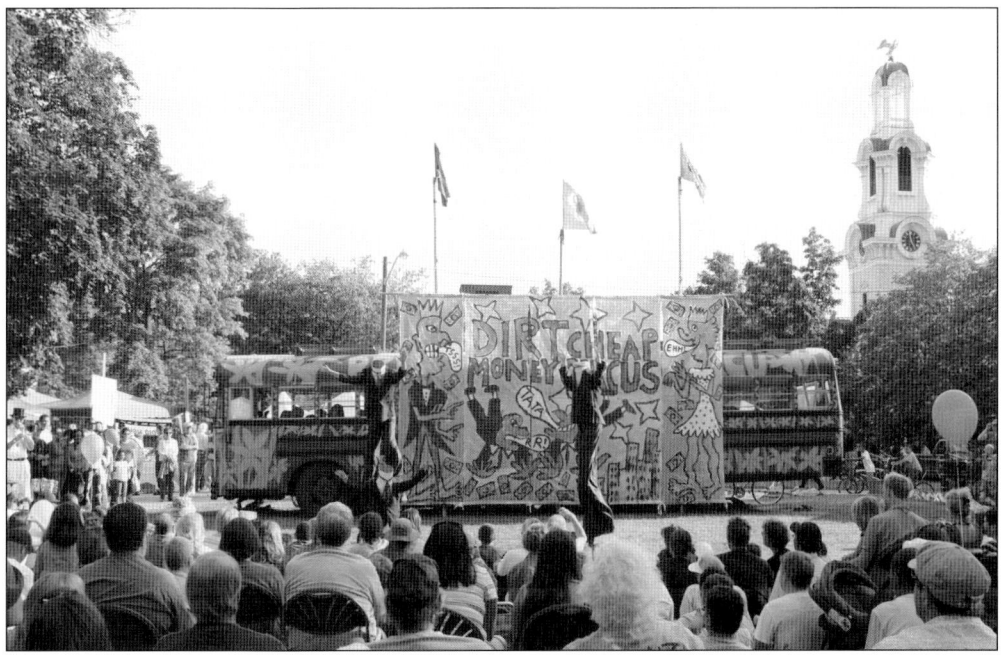

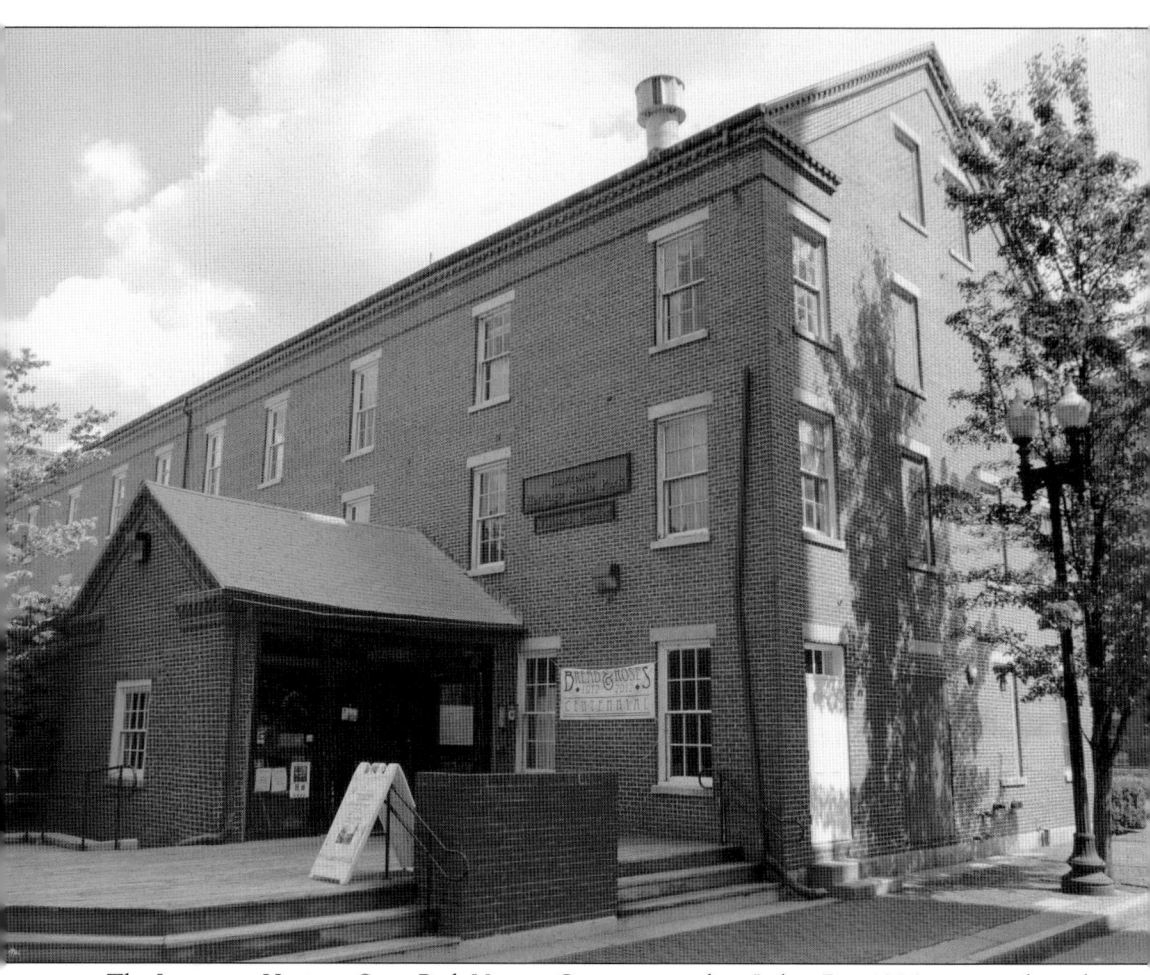

The Lawrence Heritage State Park Visitors Center opened on Labor Day 1986 to coincide with the second, much larger Bread & Roses Labor Day Festival. The park was created through the convergence of two related movements in the 1970s: increased local interest in Lawrence's history and the Bread and Roses strike in particular and the Massachusetts Heritage State Park system, under Massachusetts governor Michael Dukakis, which sought to employ local history and culture as a means of revitalizing some of Massachusetts's older, declining industrial cities. The Lawrence Heritage State Park Visitors Center is housed in one of two remaining original mill-worker boardinghouses and contains a permanent exhibit on the history of Lawrence. The exhibit describes the strike with a—then new—favorable interpretation, while avoiding any reference to the still controversial God & Country version of the events of 1912. It also hosts temporary exhibits, tours, and events.

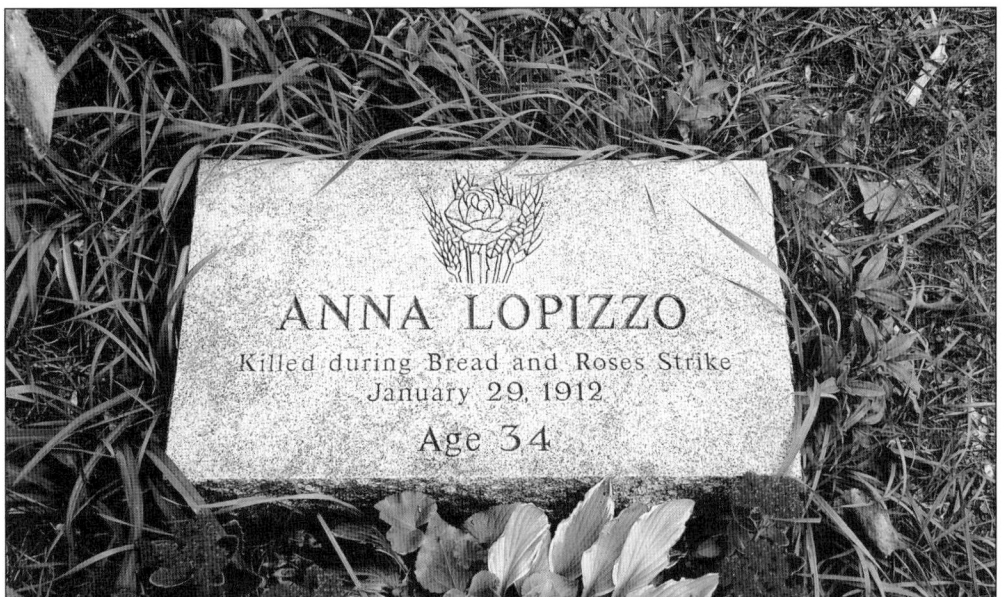

Above is a memorial to Anna LoPizzo in Immaculate Conception Cemetery. LoPizzo was one of the three victims of the 1912 strike who are now memorialized. The others were John Ramey (below) and Jonas Smolskas (page 113). Anna LoPizzo's death was significant to both sides in the struggle. In *Bread and Roses*, Bruce Watson wrote, "If America had a Tomb of the Unknown Immigrant paying tribute to the millions of immigrants known only to god and distant cousins compiling family trees, Anna LoPizzo would be a prime candidate to lie in it." The dedication of the three memorials is part of a recent movement to commemorate the strike as an integral moment in the nation's history and to memorialize the sacrifices of those involved. (Both, courtesy of Kathleen Flynn.)

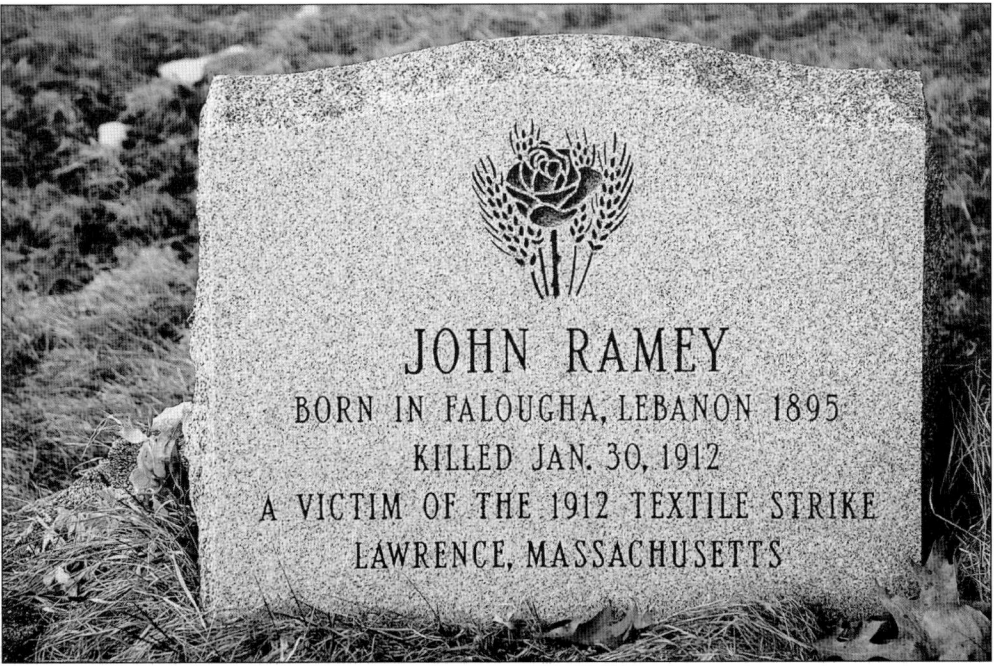

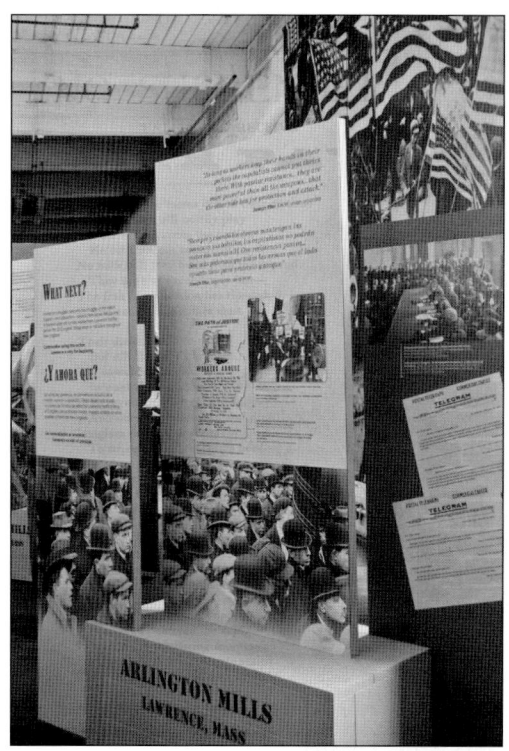

In 2012, to commemorate the centennial of the Bread and Roses Strike, the Lawrence History Center, along with the Bread and Roses Centennial Committee, launched a yearlong series of events in the city. They created a bilingual exhibit, *Short pay! All out! The Great Lawrence Strike of 1912*, which opened on January 12, 2012, on the sixth floor of the Everett Mill. The exhibit showcases the events of the strike and examines the themes of immigration, housing, laborers, labor leaders, working conditions, education, community activism, and community coordination. It is also used as cultural space for lectures, meetings, performances, and community gatherings. The mural below, *Faces of Immigration*, was painted by students at the Lawrence Humanities and Leadership Development High School and was an important part of the strike exhibit. (Left, courtesy of Gabriella Thurman.)

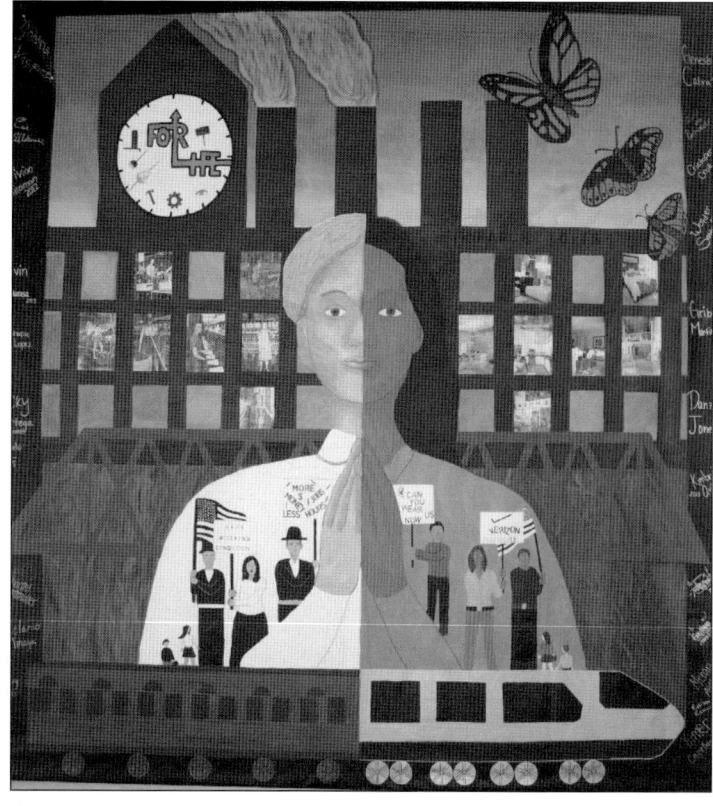

BREAD & ROSES
1912 ◆ 2012
CENTENNIAL

At the age of 104, Salvatore Savinelli provided a powerful living link to the 1912 strike when he attended the grand opening of the Lawrence History Center's strike exhibit on the 100th anniversary of the strike. In 1912, his father, Angelo, was charged with bringing children to Barre, Vermont, as part of the children's exodus. Salvatore went along. In the photograph at right, he is holding up the month of February in a centennial calendar prepared by the Lawrence Public Library. The image on the calendar, also on page 77 of this book, shows Lawrence children in front of Old Labor Hall in Barre. Angelo Savinelli is on the far right and the blurred image of a child to his right is a young Salvatore. Sadly, on March 29, 2013, Salvatore passed away at the age of 105. The story of the children going to Barre inspired the book *Bread and Roses, Too*, by Katherine Paterson. (Right, courtesy of Gabriella Thurman.)

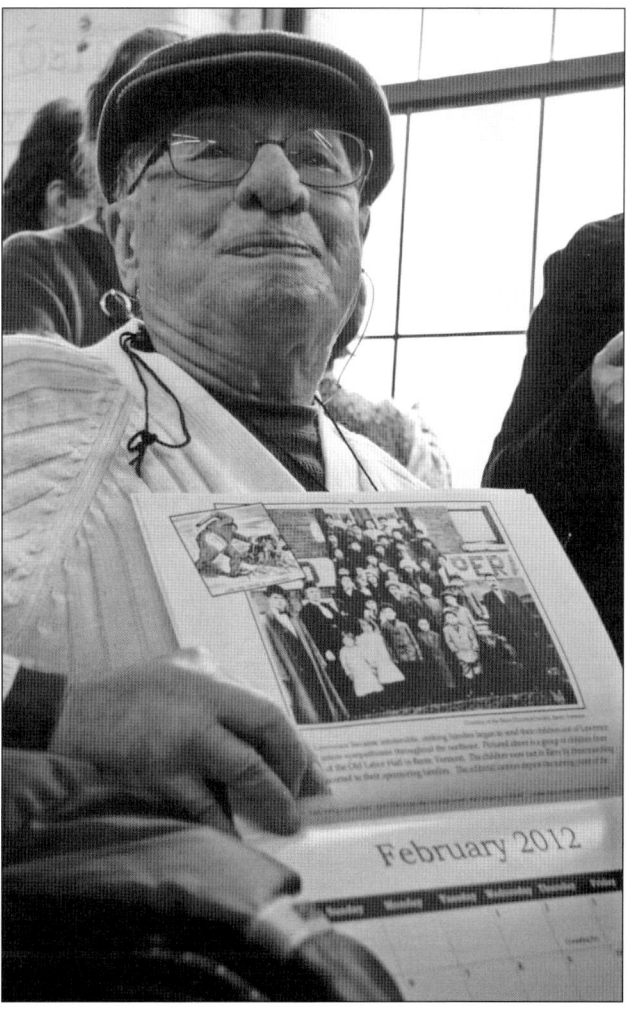

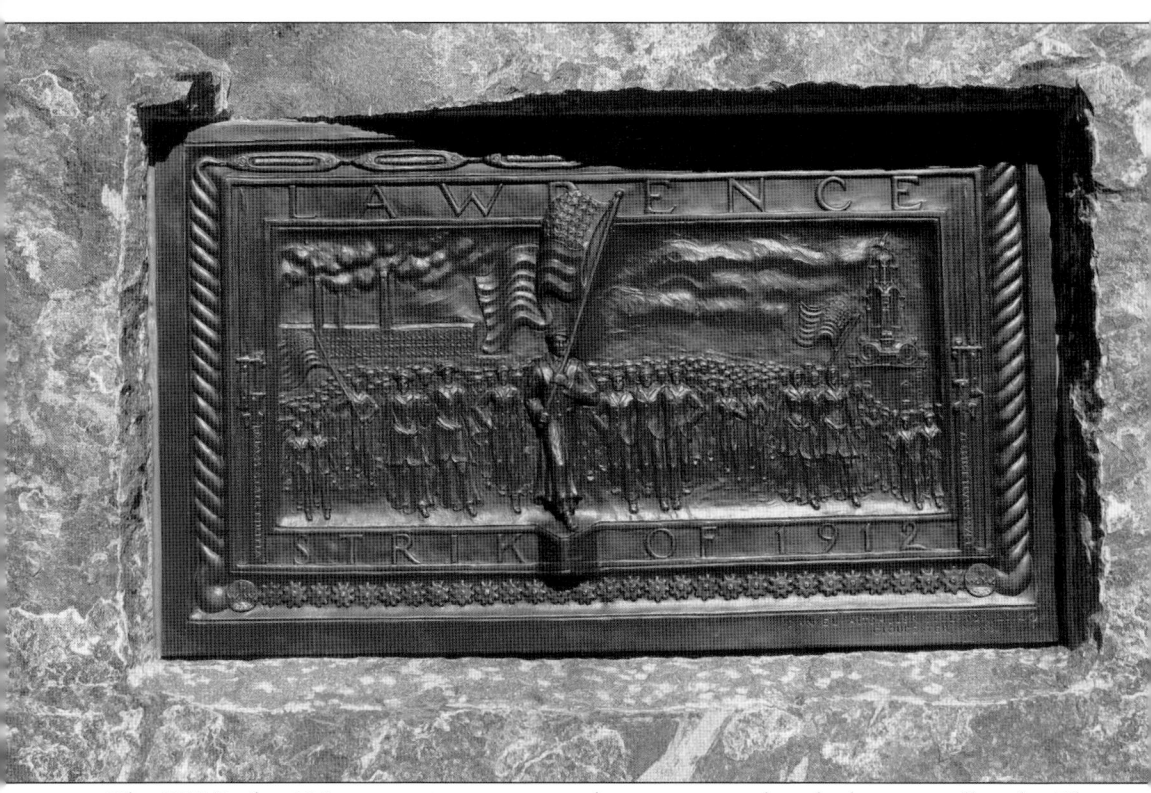

The 1912 Strikers' Monument is a permanent bronze memorial to the historic mill strike. The bronze sculpture was crafted by sculptor Daniel Altschuler of Gloucester and is mounted on a 15-ton basalt granite boulder on the Lawrence Common, across from city hall. The central image depicts hundreds of marching strikers pouring out of the great textile mills and parading through the streets of Lawrence. The animated central relief is framed by images of shuttles, yarns, and gears to symbolize the textile industrial. Two upright bayonets flank the workers, symbolizing the militia's presence during the strike. The insignia of the IWW is carved into the far left and right gears to acknowledge the significant role they played in organizing tens of thousands of strikers and victoriously settling the strike. Inscribed on the backside of the monument is the following phrase, written by David Meehan and Jonas Stundzia, cochairs of the 1912 Strikers' Monument Committee: "Let the gains of the workers past, be recognized by those who labor today, and preserved for those who toil tomorrow." (Courtesy of Amita Kiley.)

Strike Time Line

January 11, 1912	Everett Mill weavers go on strike to protest cut in pay
January 12	Workers across Lawrence leave their jobs and storm other mills
January 13	IWW organizer Joseph Ettor arrives in the city, speaking at city hall and organizing the Strike Committee
January 15	Strikers clash with police and militia troops across the city
January 17–18	Thousands of strikers parade through city streets
January 20	Police discover dynamite planted in three popular meeting locations to discredit strikers
January 23	Relief stations open to serve strikers
January 29	An angry mob attacks streetcars; Anna LoPizzo is shot and killed in a melee
January 30	John Ramey dies from a bayonet wound; police arrest Ettor and Arturo Giovannitti, charging them with murder and inciting a riot; IWW leader William Haywood takes over as the chairman of the Strike Committee
February 10	The children's exodus begins; 119 children leave Lawrence for New York City
February 17	Another 150 children leave for New York and Vermont
February 24	At the train station, police crack down on a third group of children and their parents
March 2	The US House of Representatives begins hearings to investigate the strike
March 4	Children involved in the strike testify before Congress
March 7	William Wood meets with Strike Committee members and is ready to negotiate
March 12	Pacific Mill announces a 15-percent raise in wages; Wood agrees to the strikers' demands
March 14	At the final mass meeting, 15,000 workers vote to end strike
October 12	God & Country parade held in protest against the IWW
October 19	Jonas Smolskas assaulted for wearing an IWW button
October 22	Smolskas dies as a result of his injuries
November 26	Joseph Caruso, Joseph Ettor, and Arturo Giovannitti are acquitted

BIBLIOGRAPHY

Arnold, Dexter. "A Row of Bricks: Worker Activism in the Merrimack Valley Textile Industry, 1912–1922." PhD dissertation, University of Wisconsin-Madison, 1985.

Bourgeoise, Janelle. "Et s'il n'en reste qu'un je serai celui-là: Franco-Belgian Immigrants and the 1912 Strike." unpublished paper, Lawrence History Center, 2013.

Cameron, Ardis. *Radicals of the Worst Sort: Laboring Women in Lawrence, Massachusetts, 1860–1912.* Urbana, IL: University of Illinois, 1995.

Cole, Donald. *Immigrant City: Lawrence, Massachusetts 1845–1921.* Chapel Hill, NC: University of North Carolina Press, 1963.

Flynn, Elizabeth Gurley. *The Rebel Girl: An Autobiography, My First Life (1906–1926).* New York City, NY: International Publishers, 1955.

Goldberg, David. *A Tale of Three Cities: Labor Organization and Protest in Paterson, Passaic, and Lawrence, 1916–1921.* New Brunswick, NJ: Rutgers University Press, 1989.

Hay, Duncan Erroll. "Building 'The New City on the Merrimack': The Essex Company and its Role in the Creation of Lawrence Massachusetts." PhD dissertation, University of Delaware, 1986.

Kornbluh, Joyce, ed. *Rebel Voices: An IWW Anthology.* Chicago, IL: Charles Kerr, 1998.

Neill, Charles P. *Report on Strike of Textile Workers in Lawrence, Massachusetts in 1912.* 62nd Congress, second session, 1912.

Stone, Orra. *History of Massachusetts Industries: Their Inception, Growth, and Success, Vol. 1.* Boston, MA: S.J. Clarke Publishing Company, 1930.

Todd, Robert E., and Frank Sanborn, *The Report of the Lawrence Survey.* Lawrence, MA: Andover Press, 1912.

United States Congress. *The Strike at Lawrence, Mass.: Hearings before the Committee on Rules of the House of Representatives.* 62nd Congress, second session, March 2–7, 1912.

United States Immigration Commission. *Reports of the Immigration Commission: Immigrants in Industries, Vol. 10, Part 4.* William Dillingham, ed. Washington, DC: Washington Government Printing Office, 1911.

Vorse, Mary Heaton. *A Footnote to Folly: Reminiscences of Mary Heaton Vorse.* New York City, NY: Farrar & Rinehart, 1935.

Watson, Bruce. *Bread and Roses: Mills, Migrants, and the Struggle for the American Dream.* New York City, NY: Penguin Books, 2005.

About the Lawrence History Center

Founded in 1978 by German immigrant Eartha Dengler, the Immigrant City Archives, Inc., now called the Lawrence History Center, is a private, nonprofit, 501(c)(3) charitable organization whose mission is to collect, preserve, share, and interpret the history and heritage of Lawrence and its people.

The Lawrence History Center is located at 6 Essex Street, in the former Essex Company complex, a site that has been added to the National Register of Historic Places. The center's largest single collection is the Essex Company business and planning records, which meticulously document the building of the city of Lawrence, starting in 1845. Other collections include noncurrent municipal records, church records, thousands of historic photographs and glass-plate negatives, organizational records from local businesses and agencies, 800 digitized oral histories with eyewitness accounts as far back as 1910, and an array of family and individual records that document the diverse and intellectually challenging nature of Lawrence. The center engages the community by employing these materials through physical and online exhibits, symposia, educational programs, and research services to foster understanding of the interaction of the built community and the lives of ordinary people.

Throughout 2012, the Lawrence History Center led a citywide effort to commemorate the centennial of the Bread and Roses Strike of 1912. The bilingual exhibit, *Short pay! All out! The Great Lawrence Strike of 1912*, opened on January 12, 2012, on the sixth floor of the Everett Mill to a crowd of nearly 500 people, most of whom were students from both public and private middle and high schools in Lawrence. From January through September, the Lawrence History Center hosted 71 meetings, school groups, and events in the exhibit space, including an academic symposium with keynote speaker Richard Trumka, the national president of the AFL-CIO. Through these efforts, 5,000 people from 28 states and several foreign countries became engaged in a robust civic dialogue about the issues that sparked the strike. It is quite clear that many of the same issues still resonate in our lives today.

For more on the Lawrence History Center, please visit www.lawrencehistory.org.

Discover Thousands of Local History Books Featuring Millions of Vintage Images

Arcadia Publishing, the leading local history publisher in the United States, is committed to making history accessible and meaningful through publishing books that celebrate and preserve the heritage of America's people and places.

Find more books like this at
www.arcadiapublishing.com

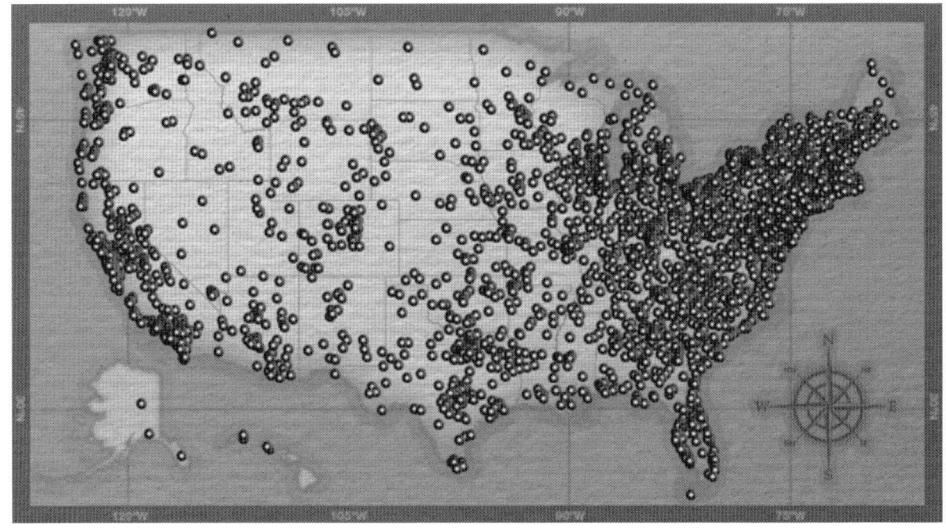

Search for your hometown history, your old stomping grounds, and even your favorite sports team.

Consistent with our mission to preserve history on a local level, this book was printed in South Carolina on American-made paper and manufactured entirely in the United States. Products carrying the accredited Forest Stewardship Council (FSC) label are printed on 100 percent FSC-certified paper.

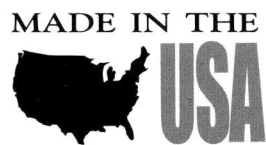